India in a Changing World

India in a Changing World

By

Govind Bhattacharjee

Cambridge Scholars Publishing

India in a Changing World

By Govind Bhattacharjee

This book first published 2019

Cambridge Scholars Publishing

Lady Stephenson Library, Newcastle upon Tyne, NE6 2PA, UK

British Library Cataloguing in Publication Data
A catalogue record for this book is available from the British Library

ISBN (10): 1-5275-3604-1
ISBN (13): 978-1-5275-3604-3

TABLE OF CONTENTS

Section 3: Suboptimal Delivery

Section 4: India and the World

Section 5: The Churning of Society

PREFACE

India made its first tryst with destiny seven decades ago on August 15th 1947, when it freed itself from nearly two centuries of colonial rule and became independent, but the fruits of independence eluded and disillusioned her people for a long time afterwards. For the first 50 years or so after independence, a large number of Indian people remained poor, malnourished and illiterate, deprived of the benefits of health, education and sanitation and a standard of living that could even remotely be called decent. The public delivery system crumbled and became completely dysfunctional and the administrative bureaucracy became completely insensate, close-minded and inward-looking, while the political system remained mired in endemic corruption and cronyism. Guided by the dated socialistic ideas of the first Prime Minister, Jawaharlal Nehru, the party that ruled for the majority of independent India's history, the Congress, followed a disastrous policy of squandering national resources through economically unsustainable welfare programs–basically by distributing dole to the marginalised sections of the electorate to ensure their continuance in power–without creating much capital. The presence of the State became overwhelming, guiding and interfering in every aspect of the life of citizens and businesses. The unlimited creative potential of its people remained shackled under the stifling command and control structure of a corrupt License-Permit Raj regime that was killing all initiative and entrepreneurial spirit. The nation came very close to becoming a failed state, both economically and socially.

However, destiny made another tryst with India in 1991 to rescue the nation from the brink of an impending collapse. The command-control structure was dismantled and India found a new freedom hitherto unknown. As this liberation asserted itself, the new-found energy of the youthful nation soon translated into much higher economic growth with a consequent reduction in poverty. It looked as if the nation had found wings with which to soar, and the sky was the limit. However, this growth story would soon end. The fruits of growth were not recycled into the economy but pilfered away through corruption which became ever more rampant. As scam after scam of ever larger proportions started rocking the government, the economy started failing again, and dole politics was resorted to in a big way to woo the electorate, along with the usual appeals to caste and religion. Hope gave way to pessimism and the country's future again looked uncertain. Another tryst with destiny was badly needed and a new government was elected to power with an overwhelming majority. The new government launched some path-breaking and disruptive reforms, but seems unable to control the social conflicts and tensions engineered by the extremist elements in society who are increasingly becoming more powerful and are trying to create further divisions in an already divided society by raking up the past.

India is currently passing through a period of great churning – socially and economically, as well as politically. It is making a complete break with its past to redefine its priorities and rediscover itself. This churning is something like the primeval *manthan*–the mythological struggle between gods and demons for the eternal nectar that brought the promise of immortality. The nation's future depends on the outcome of this *manthan*, whether it will throw up the nectar of social harmony or increase the polarisation of society; whether it will bring economic prosperity or keep the country permanently trapped in a lower middle-income bracket. Social transformation is a prerequisite for economic prosperity; they usually go together providing positive feedback to each other and altering the nature of socio-economic and political institutions, promoting pluralistic polity and participative decision making and removing the impediments to inclusive growth. Whether the events, initiatives, reforms and ideas of today will usher in such a transformation, only time can tell, but it is up to us to reflect upon the events of today to identify the sign of changing times that can mould and shape our future, and to adjust our strategy and direct our development accordingly. At the same time, we are a part of the larger world and cannot ignore what is taking place outside the country and the ideas that are transforming the future of this fast-changing world.

In this book, I have tried to capture the essence of these remarkably changing times which have the potential to transform the socioeconomic landscape of the country against the backdrop of a globally connected, but changing world, by releasing the energy and creative potential of the billion-plus population of a youthful nation, while drawing attention to the flaws that have seriously bedevilled its development and growth. The book is a collection of 50 essays published in several national newspapers and academic journals on recent events and the landmark reform initiatives undertaken during the last 3-4 years. In that sense, it chronicles the changing times in India so that the reader gets a sense of history, while appreciating the results and shortcomings of these reforms and how they are transforming the nation's economy and society.

The essays are organised in seven sections: (1) Breaking with the Past; (2) Shaping the Future: Disruptive Reforms; (3) Suboptimal Delivery; (4) India and the World; (5) The Churning of Society; (6) Tumult in the States; and (7) The World Around. Each section contains a few essays dealing with its respective topic. Major events that have influenced geo-political developments in our world in recent times and ideas that are shaping its future with consequent impact in India have also been covered here. Each essay is self-contained and narrated in a simple manner to allow the lay reader to understand and appreciate the essence of the topic discussed. There is a short summary at the beginning of each essay to introduce the topic to the reader. With society being dynamic, sometimes new events have overtaken those described in an essay, and wherever this has happened, an endnote has been appended by suitably updating the contents.

The ideas and events described in this book are recent; they have impacted our lives in some way or another, and we have not yet forgotten the excitement, and sometimes also the disappointment, that these have brought to our lives. I wish to re-engage the reader who has lived through these interesting developments and has witnessed the unfolding of these events. These are not events that have happened outside our world or ideas that are alien to us; they are still vibrant and forceful. Being intensely involved with these in a personal way, the reader may immediately relate to and reflect upon them, and contribute to the process of growth by providing useful feedback to the appropriate persons.

I am grateful to the Editor, The Statesman, and editors of all other journals, web portals and blogs where these essays have originally appeared for kindly permitting me to reproduce these essays in this book. I am also deeply grateful to the publication team at Cambridge Scholars Publishing, especially to Mr. Adam Rummens, Ms. Sophie Edminson, Ms. Courtney Blades and Ms. Amanda Millar, for making this book see the light of the day. I am grateful to Dr Shaibal Gupta and Dr P P Ghosh of the Asian Development Research Institute, Patna, and my senior colleagues at the Office of the Comptroller & Auditor General of India, Dr P Mukherjee and Shri Anupam Kulshreshtha, for reviewing the manuscript, besides providing me encouragement and support throughout.

Govind Bhattacharjee
June 21 2019

LIST OF ABBREVIATIONS USED

Most of the abbreviations used in this book have been explained wherever they appear in this book; however, there are still some commonly used abbreviations which have been frequently used. A list of these abbreviations is as follows:

AAP	Aam Admi Party
ASSOCHAM	Associated Chambers of Commerce and Industry in India
CAG	Comptroller and Auditor General of India
CBI	Central Bureau of Investigation
CBSE	Central Board of Secondary Education
CCT	Conditional Cash Transfer
CM	Chief Minister
CSO	Central Statistical Office
DBT	Direct Benefit Transfer
DISCOM	Distribution Company
FRBMA	Fiscal Responsibility and Budget Management Act
GCC	Gulf Cooperation Council
GDP	Gross Domestic Product
GFD	Gross Fiscal Deficit
GSDP	Gross State Domestic Product
GST	Goods and Services Tax
ISIS	Islamic State of Iraq and Syria
JD(U)	Janata Dal (Unity)
LPG	Liquefied Petroleum Gas
MGNREGA	Mahatma Gandhi National Rural Employment Guarantee Act
MODVAT	Modified Value Added Tax
MP	Member of Parliament

MRTP	Monopolies and Restrictive Trade Practices
NATO	North Atlantic Treaty Organisation
NDA	National Democratic Alliance
NGO	Non-Governmental Organisation
NPA	Non- Productive Asset
NREGA	National Rural Employment Guarantee Act
NSG	Nuclear Suppliers Group
OBC	Other Backward Castes
OPEC	Organisation of Petroleum Exporting Countries
PWD	Public Works Department
RBI	Reserve Bank of India
RJD	Rashtriya Janata Dal
RTI	Right To Information
UDAY	Ujjwal DISCOM Assurance Yojana
UPA	United Progressive Alliance
VAT	Value Added Tax

SECTION 1

BREAKING WITH THE PAST

1. Twenty-Five Years of Reform
2. Disband the Planning Commission
3. Choice of Institution
4. Expenditure Reform
5. Will Federalism at Work Let Populism Thrive?
6. Management of Public Debt
7. Taxing Agricultural Income

1. TWENTY-FIVE YEARS OF REFORM[1]

(The economic reforms of 1991 have transformed the country from a poor one to a lower middle-income one. India has already left her dismal past way behind. We now need a second wave of reforms to transform the country into a global powerhouse.)

Three decades are but a speck of time in the history of a nation, yet the last three decades have been truly momentous for India's transformation from a poor underdeveloped country to an economic powerhouse to be reckoned with. The fiscal landscape of India today is unrecognisably different from that of 1986, when V. P. Singh, Finance Minister in the Rajiv Gandhi Government, rose to present his budget on February 28th. The then economic growth rate of 4.5 percent was little better than the Hindu rate of growth, and the fiscal deficit was nearly 12 percent of the country's Gross Domestic Product (GDP).

While attempting "to create a dynamic country that is equal to any other country in the world", Mr Singh reduced the number of income tax brackets from 8 to 4, and the marginal tax rate from 66 to 50 percent. Alongside this, to reduce the cascading effect of taxes on the final price of goods, MODVAT was introduced, allowing duty paid on raw materials to be set-off against the duty on final products. These were probably the first major tax reforms after independence. However, this was still the era of the dictatorship of the Planning Commission, the extra-constitutional, politically-appointed body of so-called 'experts' that decided how resources were to be deployed for development. The License Permit Raj architecture of the command and control economy was in full bloom, and, under its tyranny, the economy was getting throttled by extensive regulations, protectionism and a public sector supposed to dominate the 'commanding heights of the economy', but which was actually defined by cronyism, patronage, pilferage and inefficiency. In such a centralised planned economy, growth and productivity were the ultimate casualties, and the market–the driver of growth in any modern economy–was not allowed to flourish. The result was a forced impoverishment of the nation that earned India the

---

[1] Originally published in *The Statesman as* "Twenty-Five Years After", 3rd August, 2016.

nickname the "Sick Man of Asia". Even though Mr Singh ended by asserting "his faith in [the] new India", that faith would be short-lived. Crisis was already knocking at the door, and would take the nation perilously close to becoming a failed state only five years later when it would have to be brought back from the brink of an impending disaster.

In the history of independent India, July 1991 was perhaps the most eventful month in terms of significance and profundity of impact. While we had attained our political independence in August 1947, it was only in July 1991 that we could finally make an irrevocable break with the past and take active steps to attain our economic independence from the stifling state controls that had stymied the nation's growth for decades. It was in this month that we had finally buried the disastrous legacy of Nehruvian socialism that had restricted the nation to a Hindu rate of growth since independence and kept its people in endemic and abject poverty while flaunting a socialistic pattern of society. We really came back from the brink of disaster, from being perilously close to becoming a failed state.

Since the mid-Eighties, the country had been sinking deeper and deeper into an economic quagmire, primarily because of the continued worsening of its balance of payments position, triggered by an overvalued currency. The Gulf War had exacerbated the crisis by swelling import bills and dwindling our scarce forex reserves. Nehruvian economics of deficit financing had led to escalating fiscal deficits which rose to 8.4 percent of the GDP by 1990-91. Inflation was over 12 percent, and internal debt alone rose to 53 percent of the GDP. India's external debt increased to US$72 billion from only US$20.5 billion in 1980, making India the third largest debtor nation after Brazil and Mexico. By June 1991, foreign exchange reserves fell to only $600 million, or only 2 weeks' equivalent of imports, and the prospect of defaulting on its external balance of payment obligations was looming ominously over the nation.

To escape the humiliating prospect of sovereign default, a desperate government had to secure an emergency loan of $2.2 billion from the IMF by pledging almost its entire stock of 67 tons of gold reserves as collateral. To complete the humiliation, the IMF insisted on the physical transfer of this gold, and the RBI had to airlift 47 tons of gold to mortgage the Bank of England and the remaining 20 tons to the Union Bank of Switzerland. While this gold was being transported to the airport, the carrier-van broke down, creating widespread panic. As a chartered plane ferried the precious cargo to London during the last 10 days of May 1991, an outraged nation and its hapless leaders were jolted out of their deep slumber after 44 years. The

Chandra Shekhar Government that presided over this crisis collapsed shortly afterwards, and on 21st June 1991, Mr P. V. Narasimha Rao took over as Prime Minister, with Dr Manmohan Singh as his Finance Minister. What followed has made the country what it is today. As the *New York Times* reported on June 29th, 1991, "Mr Rao, who was sworn in as Prime Minister last week, has already sent a signal to the nation—as well as the IMF—that India faced no "soft options", and must open the door to foreign investment, reduce red tape that often cripples initiative and streamline industrial policy."

It has been revealed that, irrespective of the government that was to assume power, the reforms would have nevertheless been launched. The then Chief Economic Advisor, Mr Deepak Nayyar, and Mr Singh's predecessor, Mr Yashwant Sinha, both confirmed that any Finance Minister would have read the same budget speech in June 1991. Dr Singh was fortunate to have his name inscribed in golden letters in the annals of India's destiny. In his budget speech that year, he quoted Victor Hugo, "no power on earth can stop an idea whose time has come", asserting that "the emergence of India as a major economic power in the world happens to be one such idea. Let the whole world hear it loud and clear."

In that momentous month of July of 1991, the rupee was devalued by 7 percent and again by 11 percent within the first three days. On 9th July, the Prime Minister addressed the nation, highlighting the need for reforms and promising to remove the cobwebs that had entangled the economy. A New Industrial Policy and a path-breaking Budget defining the course of reforms the country was to embrace were presented together on 24th July. In our universal eulogising of Dr Manmohan Singh as the architect of India's economic reforms and the man who had brought the country from the brink, we often forget that it was actually Prime Minister Rao, also the Industry Minister, who was the real architect of India's economic liberalisation. It was his industrial policy that had finally freed the economy from the suffocating License and Permit Raj architecture of the Nehruvian socioeconomic philosophy and polity, built around a complex labyrinth of licenses, permits and controls that dictated every facet of our production and distribution, setting up entry-barriers at every stage, and which built a strong bias towards state ownership of the means of production. It viewed all private enterprises with extreme suspicion, and believed in the domination of the public sector over every economic activity. It abhorred international trade and erected tariff barriers to prevent India's integration into the global economy, which, in its myopic vision, was capitalist, and hence repugnant. It had infinite trust in the wisdom and ability of its redoubtable bureaucrats and Planning Commission Members to control and direct the market forces towards India's growth.

The defined objectives of the New Industrial Policy were to liberalise industry from all regulatory devices like licenses and controls, enhance support to the small-scale sector, increase competitiveness of industries, ensure the running of public enterprises on business lines, and ensure rapid industrial development in a competitive environment. The cornerstones of this policy were: (1) abolition of all industrial licensing, irrespective of the level of investment, except for certain industries related to security and strategic concerns; (2) de-reservation of industries for the public sector and allowing the private sector in all areas save three–arms and ammunition, atomic energy and rail transport (up until that point, the public sector had exclusive reservation over as many as seventeen sectors); (3) disinvestment of the public sector and its restructuring by giving it more autonomy, closing sick units and reducing the government's stake in it to 26 percent or less; (4) giving free entry to foreign direct investment (FDI) and foreign technology for modernisation, and providing products and services of international standards, through a new FDI policy; and (5) abolition of MRTP[2] clearance for large industries and liberalising industrial location approvals.

There were many other facets of the reform process, each of which contributed to the creation of a competitive industrial climate built around the private, and not the public, sector, by unleashing their immense energy, innovation and entrepreneurship to create wealth and jobs for millions, and by attracting financial capital from across the seven seas. The most pronounced and visible impacts of the economic reforms unleashed in July 1991 have been a drastic fall in our poverty ratio, a dramatic improvement in our growth rates, and a miraculous increase in the inflow of foreign capital, and the consequent build-up of our foreign exchange reserves. India's $356 billion forex reserves in May 2015 were way ahead of the $1.2 billion they had been June 1991, just as the nearly 9 percent growth achieved in 2010-11 was far above the Hindu rate of growth that we had been forced to live with for four decades after independence. But far more impressive is the fact that today the poverty rate by any measure ranges around 20 percent, compared to nearly 50 percent in 1991. That means at least 300 million people have escaped poverty because of the reforms. The India of 2016 is

---

[2] Under the Monopolies and Restrictive Trade Practices (MRTP) Act, 1969, government permission was needed by all firms with assets above a certain value for carrying out business in India. The Act was repealed finally in 2002.

far more integrated in the global economy and indeed is an economic force to be reckoned with in today's world. The stagnation and despair of the 1990s are things of the past; today it is aspiration and growth. We have indeed left our dismal past well behind us, and all political dispensations universally agree that the reform process that began in 1991 is irreversible.

A Tax Reforms Committee (Chelliah Committee) set up soon afterwards submitted its report in January 1993, recommending the radical simplification of the direct tax structure and the rationalisation of indirect taxes. Following its recommendation to widen the tax net, in the 1994-95 budget, a service tax was introduced on only three services, whose number increased to 119 by 2011-12. Today, barring only a few items on the "negative list", all services are taxable and their total contribution today is about 15 percent of the total tax revenue. The 1997 budget of Mr P. Chidambaram further brought the income tax rates down to 10, 20 and finally 30 percent, a level that has not changed since. The reforms boosted revenue, increased demand and accelerated growth. They also corrected the imbalance in the structure of revenue by raising the share of direct taxes in gross tax revenue from 19 percent in 1990-91 to 54 percent in 2015-16.

However, fiscal consolidation is not only about quantity; significant qualitative improvements were affected by the better management of deficits and debt, through the enactment of the Fiscal Responsibility and Budget Management Act (FRBMA) in 2003, imposing limits on government borrowing, debt and deficits, requiring the fiscal deficit to be reduced to 3 percent of the GDP by 2008-09 and forcing greater transparency of the fiscal operations of the government through statutory disclosures. The 12th Finance Commission (2005-10) forced states to enact their own FRBMAs, and reduce their own deficits and debt; all states had enacted these legislations by 2010. This brought the derailed state finances back on the rails and helped them emerge out of the vicious debt traps they were falling into almost irretrievably. Most states were thus able to generate revenue surpluses that financed their capital outlay, boosting significantly the productive capacities of their economies. The higher growth that we see today is a cumulative result of all these measures.

However, many of these gains were frittered away by short-sighted political decisions. The 5-year plans that allocated resources inefficiently were one; another was the unabated proliferation of the centrally sponsored welfare schemes whose number rose to 360 during the 9th plan (1997-2002). All these followed from the faulty Nehruvian economic model, which was perhaps singularly responsible for India's poverty. Fortunately, all these have now been corrected. The spectre of a Planning Commission no longer haunts the Indian economy, and the number of centrally sponsored schemes has also been slashed to only 28.

Reforms so far have penetrated all key economic areas from industry to fiscal and monetary policies, external trade, foreign investment, finance, and capital markets. However, there is still a whole lot of unfinished issues in education, health, labour, employment, land and agriculture. Agriculture employs 55 percent of our population, but generates only 16 percent of GDP; and nearly 660 million people are thus living on an average per capita income of about ₹30000–a meagre ₹2500 per month, far below the national average. Our Human Development Index is among the lowest in the world, as are our educational standards and health indicators. Delivery of public services remains abysmal in terms of quality and outreach. We need to address these areas now on a war footing, to take advantage of the demographic dividend to avoid a demographic disaster. We can no longer afford gradualism and incrementalism. With the prospects for growth accelerating, enacting a unified Goods and Service Tax (GST) to transform India into a single unified common market will indicate that we are keen on having another tryst with destiny, but the GST will be only the beginning of the second wave of reforms that will truly transform India into a global economic powerhouse.

As the 19th century philosopher, Pierre Joseph Proudhon, said, "The life of man is a battle, that of society a perpetual reformation." We have to continue to reform with ever-greater commitment.

(Afterword: A Goods and Service Tax (GST) was launched throughout India on 1st July 2017, replacing 17 indirect taxes and 13 cesses to which businesses were hitherto subjected. It is a landmark reform expected to transform the economic landscape of India in the next 3-5 years.)

2. DISBAND THE PLANNING COMMISSION[3]

(Whatever little we have achieved was not because, but in spite, of the Planning Commission. It is time to wind it up and bury the five-year plans once and for all.)

Before denouncing the idea of winding up a 63-year old aging institution as preposterous and heretical, let's take a hard look at the facts. The Planning Commission was created by an executive resolution of the Government of India in March 1950. The Commission is not a constitutional body, but it enjoys the extra-constitutional authority to recommend the transfer of almost half of our annual budgetary allocations to states as plan grants every year. It is known to produce voluminous 5-year plans full of fantastic rhetoric and fancy jargon, besides generating a plethora of reports on every conceivable subject. It is also known to entertain the nation from time to time by generating astounding statistics, especially in relation to poverty numbers. Over the decades, the Commission has grown into a mammoth bureaucracy that needs about ₹100 crore of public funds annually to run its report-producing apparatus. For several decades, it has also become the major driving force behind doling out national resources in the form of ill-conceived and poorly-implemented Centrally Sponsored Schemes, through which the powers that be gain access to public funds, and are licensed to misuse these funds for political ends.

There is only one mechanism provided in the Constitution for the devolution of central resources to the states–under Article 275, through the agency of the Finance Commissions. However, the spirit of fiscal federalism in the Constitution was hideously defeated by the creation of the Planning Commission and by giving it exclusive powers, without any constitutional backing, to transfer huge amounts of central resources to states as plan transfers, while limiting the scope of the Finance Commission to only recommending non-plan transfers.

The creation of the Planning Commission necessitated classification of expenditure into "plan" and "non-plan" categories, which was done without

---

[3] Originally published in *The Statesman as* "Disband Yojna Bhavan", 24th July, 2014.

any constitutional sanction. The device used for plan transfers is Article 282, meant for dealing with exceptional situations. These transfers are discretionary in nature, vulnerable to being influenced more by political than economic considerations and enabling the Centre to arm-twist any state, given the huge amounts at stake. When this arbitrary discretion of the Centre over the transfer of these plan funds was sought to be limited by making these transfers based on the so-called Gadgil formula, the Centrally Sponsored Scheme was the innovation introduced by the Centre to retain its hold over public funds, and to allow it to misuse these funds on cheap, wasteful and supposedly vote-catcher schemes. The numbers of such schemes have since proliferated unabated on political considerations, creating aberrations in our public finances all the way. Most of these transfers are also made outside the state budgets, so they bypass the usual budgetary, accounting and legislative controls. More than one lakh crore of rupees are thus transferred every year to states outside their budgets, often leading to huge waste and leakages. Plan transfers have now become tied to these fancy schemes and their allocations have taken quantum jumps in recent years. In the process, states' fiscal spaces have shrunk, their autonomy has suffered and their flexibility to launch schemes specific to their needs has almost completely vanished. Other distortions followed as private sector investment naturally went to states with better infrastructure, thereby widening the economic imbalance and disparity among them.

Debate on what the first four and a half decades of our planning since independence have achieved is already passé. Despite high sounding rhetoric like achieving a 'socialistic pattern of society', *'garibi hatao'*, 'growth with stability and distributive justice', 'planning from below', and adoption of fanciful models of growth borrowed from US textbooks, outputs fell, prices soared, unemployment increased, poverty remained undented and growth continued to languish within the Hindu rate of 3.5 percent until 1991 when the economy was poised precariously on the verge of failure. This was, in brief, the story of the first seven plans. However, through it all, as more and more ambitious plans were introduced with ever more allocation of public funds, the bureaucracy of Yojna Bhavan flourished, becoming ever more powerful by doing the bidding of its political masters. Its style of functioning, however, became curiouser and curiouser, increasingly falling out of sync with a modern economy.

It determined what was to be produced in the economy, how much and by what means. After surveying the available resources, a growth target for each sector of the economy was fixed and investments were allocated to each sector, specifying the type of projects and even the specific production techniques as well. Naturally, this led to an economy characterised by extensive regulation, protectionism and a public sector supposed to dominate the 'commanding heights of the economy'. The government's size also grew in tandem; under UPA II, we had 53 blessed ministries overseeing every aspect of our lives. The extensive control only fuelled pervasive corruption all around and stifled growth. Vital sectors of the economy were nationalised, and the rest regulated by an elaborate system of licenses and red-tape that inhibited private investment, making the economy reel under this License-Permit Raj. This tyranny of the state only benefited certain entrenched groups but smothered individual entrepreneurship.

In such a collectivised, centralised planned economy, economic democracy, growth and productivity became the ultimate casualties, and the market–the driver of growth in a modern economy–was not allowed to flourish. As Professor P. R. Brahmannda insightfully observed, instead of attacking poverty through a wage-goods model, the authorities chose a number of anti-poverty and pubic distribution measures that were simply fire-fighting exercises with large leakages. The result was a forced impoverishment of the nation that earned it the nickname the "sick man of Asia". Add to this the growth of black money, an offshoot of corruption, and the heightened inequality and disparity, and the picture of an impending disaster was complete. *Time* magazine quoted a recent McKinsey Global Institute report suggesting that even in 2012, 'as many as 56 percent of the Indians–some 680 million people– could not afford [the] most basic needs like food, water, housing, sanitation and health care'. The economic reforms came after realisation dawned that it is the market, not the government, that should drive the economy. In recognition of this fact, the 8th Plan stated in its preface that the plan was only "indicative" in nature and that the state could at best be a facilitator for investment by the private sector. However, despite the declining share of public investment post-reforms and promotion of the PPP mode of investment, the role and importance of the Planning Commission did not diminish.

Its role as the most important extra-constitutional allocator of plan resources has long jeopardised centre-state relations. As the Commission on Centre-State Relations observed in its report (March 2010), "Following the introduction of economic reforms in the country, the role of Central planning seemed to have lost much of its relevance. There was a shrinking of the share of the public-sector investment. States saw an opportunity to regain ground lost to the Planning Commission. However, this hope was belied." As such, the command and control mindset continued.

Command economies invariably tend to get corrupt as, by concentrating economic power and authority, the normal decision-making process is neglected. Plans drawn on the basis of insufficient information were approved and implemented with disastrous results. As growth slowed, inequality was amplified, the rural-urban divide widened, resource allocation to different sectors remained lopsided and ad-hocism reigned supreme. The evils that distress the common man –inflation, poverty and unemployment– remained uncontrolled and unfettered. One is reminded of what Frederick Hayek wrote in *The Road to Serfdom* in 1944: "There could hardly be a more unbearable and more irrational world than one in which the most eminent specialists in each field were allowed to proceed unchecked with the realisation of *their* ideals."

Our country certainly deserves better than to be led by a set of technocrats far removed from the ground realities but wielding unrestrained power and illegitimate authority. It is indeed time to realise that, in a diverse country such as ours, where skill, talent and entrepreneurship are abundantly available, centralised planning does not work. Whatever little we have achieved, it was not because, but in spite, of the Planning Commission. It is time to disband it and bury the 5-year plans once and for all. Responsibility for planning henceforth should be delegated to the elected representatives in respective states, where it logically and rightfully belongs.

(Afterword: The Planning Commission was wound up in August 2014, barely three weeks after this article was published. Subsequently the concept of 5-year plans was abandoned, and even the distinction between plan and non-plan expenditure was later removed. A new institution, the National Institution for Transforming India known as NITI Aayog, was set up under the Chairmanship of the Prime Minister, with the noted economist Dr Arvind Panagarya as Vice Chairman to advise the government on the developmental paths and programs, but without the power to allocate any resources.)

3. CHOICE OF INSTITUTION[4]

(Institutions have a life of their own, and once established, they cannot simply be wished away. If its replacement inherits any of the weaknesses that had made the Planning Commission such a dysfunctional and growth-obstructing institution, it will also continue to corrupt our governance system for a long time, like its predecessor. We ought to be very careful in resurrecting it in another form, without adequate thought and clarity about its intended role and purpose.)

"An institution is the lengthened shadow of one man", Emerson observed. Undoubtedly, the Planning Commission was nurtured under the overstretched shadows of the socialist ideals of Nehru. While the Modi Government's decision to consign it to the dustbin of history was most welcome, one cannot but look with apprehension at the government's consideration to create a replacement institution. Institutions have a life of their own, and once established, they cannot simply be wished away. If its replacement inherits any of the weaknesses that had made the Planning Commission such a dysfunctional and growth-obstructing, institution, it will also continue to corrupt our governance system for a long time. We ought to be very careful in resurrecting it in another form, without adequate thought and clarity about its intended role and purpose.

With its unrestrained powers and authority, the Planning Commission was serving powerful interests that ensured its survival for such a long time. Its abolition is no guarantee that these interests will let go of their privileges so easily; they are more than likely to stage a come-back, albeit in a different guise. This chain needs to be broken irrevocably, before history repeats itself. History is replete with examples of new incarnations of old institutions having inherited the character and shortcomings of those they have replaced. As a nation with an abundance of talent and entrepreneurial capacity, we need to consider if we really need another institution in place of the Planning Commission to guide the nation.

---

[4] Originally published in *The Statesman as* "Choice of Techniques", 6th October, 2014.

It may be interesting and instructive to draw from the experiences of other countries in this regard –for example, the BRICS countries India is often grouped with. In the erstwhile Soviet Union, the State Planning Committee, known as Gosplan, was responsible for central economic planning from its inception in 1923, until the dissolution of the Soviet Union in 1991. Gosplan was responsible for the creation and administration of a series of 5-year plans governing the economy of the USSR, much like the Planning Commission in India during 1950-2014, or the State Planning Commission in China during 1952-1998. However, after the break-up of the Soviet Union, the countries that rose from its debris have shifted determinedly from planned economies to market economies by adopting liberalisation, privatisation and globalisation as the only way forward, and some of these countries, like Estonia, have registered GDP growth exceeding 8 percent, transiting into advanced economies. Russia does not have a centralised planning system anymore; the state control that had marked six decades of overwhelming dominance of all investment, production and consumption decisions by the Communist Party is now a nightmare of the past. The country is grappling today with the decrepit legacy of its earlier centralised planning system.

Like the proverbial phoenix, China has risen from the ashes of the Cultural Revolution that ended in 1976. Chinese planning had initially followed the same Soviet model adopted by us. Before the economic reforms began under Deng Xiao-Ping in the late 1970s, private industry was virtually non-existent in China, and industry was dominated by state enterprises, and a rigid and coercive regulatory regime characterised by command and control. All resources–land, labour, raw materials and capital–were provided by the state, which determined the production and distribution plans and their final output. However, since the 1990s, as reforms heralding China's movement towards a market economy took firm hold, planning became more and more indicative, engaging only with projections, trends and bottlenecks, while allowing and encouraging private firms to grow and compete with each other and with state-run enterprises. As the state gradually withdrew from control of economic activities, in 1998, the State Planning Commission was restructured. It was merged with the Commission for Restructuring the Economic System, established in 1982, to direct economic reforms, and was renamed the State Development Planning Commission. In 2006, it was further rechristened the National Development and Reforms Commission (NDRC), omitting the word 'Planning'. This indicated a paradigm-shift to declare that China was no longer a centrally planned economy.

We may recollect that, at the end of the Seventies, India was ahead of China in terms of socioeconomic development. The early years of the present century saw India and China being bracketed together as 'Chindia', when our growth nearly matched China's. However, courtesy of the disastrous decade of UPA rule, China today is light-years ahead of us, and we are unlikely to catch up with it ever again. Nobody recalls 'Chindia' anymore, and comparison with China may be out of place. So, let us see how Brazil has fared.

Until the early 1990s, Brazil was mired in a web of crises, much like our own. About 40 percent of the population was poor, half of them sunk in absolute poverty characterised by severe deprivation of basic human needs. With a Gini coefficient measuring 0.6, it also had one of the highest income inequalities in the world. Poverty, exclusion and backwardness made the country a potential volcano, ready to erupt at any moment. Under its new Constitution of 1988, it undertook extensive reforms through the liberalisation of trade and financial sectors, decentralisation and deregulation, elimination of forex barriers, privatisation and enforcement of fiscal discipline. By bolstering the market to generate income and designing innovative social sector programs like Bolsa Família delivered through a system of conditional cash transfers, it had eliminated absolute poverty within just a decade. By 2012, its per capita income rose to $11690 and its poverty ratio shrunk to only 9 percent of the population. Today, the gap between India and Brazil is as wide as the distance that separates them. In 2012, India's per capita annual income was only $1440, and even at a much lesser poverty line drawn by our now-defunct Planning Commission, India's poor constituted 21.9 percent of the population.

South Africa, of course, was a different story because of its apartheid past that ended only in 1994, when its first democratic elections were held and the African National Congress came to power. It started with a Development and Reforms Program as the primary socioeconomic program, which ultimately was transformed into the New Growth Path (GNP) under the current President, Jacob Zuma. Under GNP, a National Planning Commission (NPC) was set up in 2009 to chart out a roadmap for development with a 20-year horizon. In 2013, it finally came up with the 'National Developmental Plans ~ 2030'. The NPC, however, is not a government entity, but a body of 26 experts from the outside appointed by the President to advise on matters impacting long-term development. It is perhaps too early to assess its impact and efficacy.

A central overarching body is thus not a necessary prerequisite for development. The 73rd Amendment to our Constitution provides for planning at the grassroots level of the villages, and for the consolidation of these plans all the way up. This way, a realistic plan can be made by considering the local needs and addressing the implementation bottlenecks, since people actually responsible for implementation will be involved in this bottom-up planning process. Planning must be a responsibility of states, and cannot be relegated to technocrats and experts on any pretext. It should be the priority and responsibility of the elected representatives who should drive the process through the consensus and involvement of all stakeholders, including experts. The process of consensus-based planning will ensure efficiency of the plan, and involvement of elected representatives will strengthen the accountability mechanism. If a think-tank is imposed upon the nation, the weight of the tank may sometimes become an obstruction, leading again to inertia and what can perhaps be called "fossilism". We need not cling to the old ways after life has completely departed from them.

(Afterword: NITI Aayog was set up in January 2015 in replacement of the Planning Commission. It was to replace the erstwhile one-way flow of policy from the centre states with 'a genuine and continuing partnership', while acknowledging that we need to find and adopt our own strategy for growth without depending on imported models. The stated objectives include providing a framework 'national agenda' to 'foster cooperative federalism through structured support initiatives and mechanisms with the States on a continuous basis, recognizing that strong States make a strong nation'. The Aayog is to develop mechanisms to formulate credible plans at the village level and aggregate these plans progressively at higher levels of government. The 13 objectives also include designing strategic and long-term policies and programs, monitoring and evaluating their implementation and progress, and the identification of required resources for strengthening delivery, while focusing on technology upgradation and capacity building for the implementation of programs and initiatives.

Chaired by the Prime Minister, it has a Governing Council comprising Chief Ministers of all states and Lt. Governors of all Union Territories; this will automatically render the existing National Development Council defunct. However, like its predecessor, NITI Aayog does not have any constitutional status and will therefore remain a think-tank of the government.)

4. EXPENDITURE REFORM[5]

(Niti Aayog should start its work by suggesting that it remove the distinction between plan and non-plan expenditure, and reduce drastically the number of centrally sponsored schemes.)

Hearty congratulations are due to Mr Arvind Panagariya for taking over the reins of Niti Aayog, the reincarnation of the Planning Commission of India, which had dominated and distorted the Indian public financial system for over six decades. As the newly appointed Vice Chairman of its new avatar, Mr Panagariya will have his hands full. We wish him good luck in first cleansing the system of the numerous aberrations that have crept into it over the decades and then driving it towards achieving real growth for the country. Thankfully, he comes with the belief that it is growth that has the potential to lift millions out of poverty by creating wealth and generating employment, as opposed to the sops and doles that formed the guiding philosophy of the previous regime.

The Union Budget 2014-15 had earmarked ₹575,000 crore as planned expenditure on various programs and schemes targeted towards the alleviation of poverty and the creation of employment, and for providing basic public services like education, healthcare, nutrition, drinking water and sanitation to the people of the country. These programs include the 17 flagship welfare schemes like NREGA, on which lakhs of crores of rupees are being spent every year without much visible improvement on the ground. Mr Panagariya will have to transform Niti Aayog into an effective instrument for monitoring and evaluating the implementation of these programs. On this will primarily depend whether NITI Aayog truly becomes what its name suggests: the **N**ational **I**nstitution for **T**ransforming **I**ndia.

Mr Panagariya would do well to begin by dusting off the "Report of the High Level Expert Committee on Efficient Management of Public Expenditure", which was appointed by the UPA government under the Chairmanship of Dr C. Rangarajan. The Committee had submitted its report in July 2011, but the Manmohan Singh Government had preferred to put it

---

[5] Originally published in *The Statesman as* "Planning Technique", 31st January, 2015.

in cold-storage, obviously because acting on the report would have meant undoing and unravelling the welfarist agenda of the Congress Party. The most important recommendation in the report was to abolish the distinction between plan and non-plan expenditure. Acting on it would have meant reducing the importance of the Planning Commission by removing the emphasis on welfare-oriented plan schemes of the government. The Planning Commission then would have been rendered powerless to allocate national resources under the guise of these plan schemes and confined only to the task of formulating 5-year plans. The regime, which believed that its electoral fortunes depended entirely on its ability to extend the benefits of doles and subsidies to the widest possible sections of voters, would naturally be loath to act upon such heretical recommendations.

The Rangarajan Committee Report stated: "Over a period of time, several issues have cropped up from the distinction between plan and non-plan, making it dysfunctional and an obstacle in outcome-based budgeting. Therefore, this distinction should go for both union and state budgets. On removal of plan/non-plan distinction in the budget, there should be a fundamental shift in the approach of public expenditure management - from a segmented view of plan and non-plan to a holistic view of expenditure; from a one-year horizon to a multi-year horizon; and from input-based budgeting to the budgeting linked to outputs and outcomes. This shift to a holistic view of expenditure would require, *inter alia*, changes in organisational structure, mandates and processes." These changes in the organisational structure of agencies concerned with the delivery of developmental programs and the necessary reengineering of the governmental processes and procedures have not yet been implemented.

In fact, the distinction between plan and non-plan expenditure has caused many more problems than mere segmentation of expenditure into the arbitrary 'plan/non-plan' classifications, fostering a rather limited and fragmented view of resource allocation. The Report noted that such classification has given rise to an inherent bias in favour of plan expenditure and against non-plan expenditure among the policy makers and officials across all levels, and enforced the notion that plan expenditure was good and non-plan expenditure was bad. This has led to a situation where the non-plan expenditure essential for the maintenance of valuable assets like roads, project assets, buildings and assets for the delivery of public goods and services created under the various plan schemes has systematically been neglected over the years, leading to a progressive deterioration in the quality of public services. "This has also led to a motivation for showing higher plan expenditure and higher plan sizes both at Central and State levels", the Report observed.

In addition to the poor quality of information that went into the making of successive plans, other problems in budget and accounting classification, inadequate information on transfers of resources to the states, unreliable and dated information on costing of services and the far-from-perfect Central Plan Scheme Monitoring System (CPSMS) generated data have always plagued our system of resource allocation, appraisal and monitoring of expenditure on plan schemes. These problems still remain unresolved and, unless effectively addressed, will continue to cause the sub-optimal utilisation of resources and short-delivery of outcomes. Removing the plan/non-plan distinction and realigning the budget and accounting classification would be the first step towards restoring sanity in our public financial system.

Once this distinction is removed, many things will automatically fall into place, and some others will have to be corrected, like the rationalisation of the endless mechanisms devised to finance the plethora of plan projects. A bewildering variety of these exist now: Normal Central Assistance for central plans and state plans; Additional Central Assistance for centrally sponsored schemes; Additional Central Assistance for externally assisted projects; Additional Central Assistance for programs funded by the Ministry of Finance but implemented by other departments/ministries; Special Central Assistance for special programs; and Advance Central Assistance for special and exceptional situations. In fact, there are so many of these that the normal human brain would struggle to grasp their astounding numbers and complexities. Until 2013-14, there were *only* 137 centrally sponsored schemes. Some semblance of reason was later sought to be brought in by restructuring these into 66 schemes, including the 17 flagship programs with significant outlays, for the remaining years of the ongoing 12th Plan (2012-17). It was also decided to abolish the direct transfer of funds for centrally sponsored schemes to agencies that were implementing these schemes in the states without routing the funds through their budgets. However, much more needs to be done, in terms of further integrating and streamlining these programs by coordinating, monitoring and directing their deliveries towards specific, target-oriented and time-bound outcomes. A suitable accountability architecture also needs to be created.

The newly-formed NITI Aayog is supposed to replace the erstwhile one-way flow of policy from the centre to states by '[a] genuine and continuing partnership'. It has been created with 13 laudable objectives, while acknowledging that we need to find and adopt our own strategy for growth without depending on imported models. The objectives include providing a framework 'national agenda' to 'foster cooperative federalism through structured support initiatives and mechanisms with the states on a continuous basis, recognizing that strong states make a strong nation'. The program is to develop mechanisms to formulate credible plans at the village level and aggregate these plans progressively at higher levels of government. The objectives also include designing strategic and long-term policies and programs, monitoring and evaluating their implementation and progress, and the identification of required resources for strengthening delivery while focusing on technology upgradation and capacity building. Strangely, there is no clarity or indication about how all these will be achieved or about the nature of the institutional mechanisms required, or indeed the changes that need to be affected in order to achieve the goals. The only machinery it hints at is a Governing Council comprising Chief Ministers of all the states and Lieutenant Governors of all union territories; that will automatically render the existing National Development Council (NDC) defunct. There will also be regional councils to address issues specific to each region. There is no guarantee that a Governing Council represented by all states and union territories would be more effective than the NDC even without the overbearing presence of a Planning Commission. The regional council would be a more appropriate forum for evolving a consensus-based policy. However, in keeping with the spirit of the 73rd amendment to the Constitution, a bottom-up planning process has now been institutionalised.

Like its predecessor, NITI Aayog does not have any constitutional status and has been envisaged to act only as a think-tank of the government, but, in reality, it will remain a political body of the ruling dispensation, like its predecessor. What role it will discharge and what purpose it will serve remain to be seen, but the lack of constitutional legitimacy, the absence of an accountability structure and the inherent political nature of the Aayog may present obstacles to its effective functioning. Mr Panagariya will need all the wisdom and tact at his disposal to ensure that NITI Aayog transcends these limitations and is truly perceived as an institution for generating ideas and innovations necessary for transforming a lower middle-income country like India (per capita income US$2074, 2013, World Bank) into an upper middle-income country (per capita income US $7598) within the next decade. For its intended transformational role, however, the bloated bureaucratic machinery it has inherited from the Planning Commission may prove to be dysfunctional unless trimmed.

(Afterword: The distinction between plan and non-plan expenditure was finally removed with effect from the budget of 2017-18. Five year plans were discarded after the 12th 5-Year Plan ended in 2016-17. The ventrally sponsored schemes were also restructured and streamlined into 28 schemes. Mr Panagarya has returned to his teaching position in Columbia University and Mr Rajiv Kumar was appointed as Vice Chairman of the NITI Aayog in September 2017.)

5. WILL FEDERALISM AT WORK LET POPULISM THRIVE?[6]

(The 14th Finance Commission has given a big boost to federal financial relations in India, but there is the danger that, with increased resources in their hands, states may now replicate the centre's populism.)

The recently released recommendations of the 14th Finance Commission will have far-reaching consequences for the states of the Indian Union, with 42 percent of the central divisible pool of resources now going to them, compared to the existing 32 percent provided by the 13th Finance Commission. In terms of resources now available to the states, it is indeed a quantum jump from the recommendations of all previous finance commissions which increased the states' share only in low incremental steps.

The divisible pool initially used to comprise only income tax and a part of central excise duties. Successive commissions increased the states' share of these taxes. The 11th Finance Commission (2000-05) expanded the divisible pool substantially by including in it the net proceeds from all taxes covered under Article 270 (income tax, corporation tax, central excise duty, customs duty, service tax and wealth tax) and making 29.5 percent of this pool sharable with the states. The next two commissions increased this share to 30.5 percent and 32 percent, respectively. Cess and surcharges are excluded from the divisible pool, which is entirely appropriated by the centre; this remains a sore point with all states. Aside from the devolution of taxes, the finance commissions also recommend grants-in-aid of revenues of states under Article 275.

The taxes are divided among the states on the principles of equity and efficiency, effectively transferring resources from the rich to the poor states on the basis of a formula that factors in population and area of a state, inter-state disparities in income, and fiscal and financial performance. From the 6th Commission onwards, governments have restricted the commissions to recommending only non-plan grants, the plan part being made the prerogative of the now-defunct Planning Commission. Plan transfers for the most part

[6] Originally published in *The Statesman as The Statesman*, 3rd March, 2015.

depended on the discretion of the central government; only a part was formula-based that progressively went on shrinking with the proliferation of centrally sponsored schemes. These discretionary transfers have now been reduced after the replacement of the Planning Commission by NITI Aayog, an expert body without any power of resource allocation.

However, the landscape of federal financial relations between the union and its states has really started changing since the recommendations of the 12th Finance Commission; before that, the commissions' recommendations were, by and large, accounting recommendations, a little more here, a little less there. These failed to address the perennial financial problems of the states which had revenue resources that fell far short of their revenue expenditure, let alone capital investment requirements, for which they had to borrow heavily. This led to the swelling debt burden of each state, and the nominal debt reliefs given by the successive finance commissions could hardly mitigate the crushing burden of their collective debt. Unable to manage this on the strength of their own resources, the states had to borrow from the centre just to be able to repay their debt instalments and interest; many states couldn't even manage that as the servicing of their existing debt exceeded their fresh borrowings. The successive Central Pay Commissions, especially from the Fifth Pay Commission (1996-2006) onwards, increased the salaries of central government employees, forcing the states also to give matching raises to the salaries of their own employees without having matching resources, this compounded their financial problems even more. After the Sixth Pay Commission recommendations (2006-16), the situations went absolutely beyond the control of most states, and they started sinking deeper and deeper in debt.

Meanwhile, the market rate of interest was going down, but Article 293 of the Constitution did not allow states to borrow from the market without the centre's permission if they were indebted to it, which they were. The centre continued to charge higher interest rates, which further worsened their indebtedness, making them fall into the viscous debt trap one by one, heading for sure disaster. It was in these circumstances that the 12th Finance Commission was constituted. It diagnosed the problem correctly, but departing from the incremental accounting approach of the previous commissions, came up with an outstanding out-of-the-box solution, forcing the states to control their unproductive expenditure by enacting the FRBMA (Fiscal Responsibility and Budget Management Act), which forced the states to contain their fiscal deficits within 3 percent of their income (GDSP) which, in return, freed them from the obligations of borrowing from the centre. They rewarded states that could generate surpluses in their revenue accounts by giving them a matching relief on their debt burden and more. As a result, most states, except a few indigent ones, were able to pull themselves out of their debt traps by generating revenue surpluses. These surpluses financed their capital expenditure, curtailing borrowing to that extent. Their debt burden was thus reduced as a consequence and their finances improved. The 13th Finance Commission further reinforced the states' improved financial positions and increased their share of the divisible pool to 32 percent. Even West Bengal and Sikkim, which had hitherto refused to enact the FRBMAs, were now forced to enact these legislations so as to obtain the benefits that could no longer be ignored for the sake of populism.

However, the recommendations of the 14th Finance Commission go far ahead – they have the potential to redefine and redraw the contours of federal finance in India by giving much more fiscal space to states to identify their own priorities and to spend thereon, instead of making them depend on an all-powerful centre to dole out resources through plan funds as per its own discretion, and in the process, jeopardise the process of growth and development of the country as a whole.

Centralised planning was a negation of the spirit of true federalism. The spirit of federalism is asserted when the centre and states are seen as equal partners in the nation's development, and not the former as a giver and the latter as recipients of common resources, as it has been until now. National interest must be supreme in any arrangement of federal transfer of resources, but the aberration of the badly implemented centrally sponsored schemes, often designed with dubious logic, has so far hideously defeated this objective. The number of these schemes has now been reduced from 347 during the ninth plan to only 66, but this is still far too many. Hopefully, the 14th Finance Commission's far-reaching recommendations will force the centre to consider scrapping some of these anachronisms and give the states the authority to spend taxpayers' money more judiciously, according to the right priorities and careful targeting so as to eliminate wastes, leakages and corruption.

The recommendations will have the effect of increasing the net flow of funds to the states by an extra ₹2.21 lakh crore during 2015-16 alone–the biggest ever jump in the states' share so far. During the award period of the Commission (2015-20), the tax share to states will exceed ₹44 lakh crore. In addition, 11 states with deficits in their revenue accounts will get grants amounting to ₹1.95 lakh crore during this period. Local bodies stand to gain significantly, with ₹2 lakh crore earmarked for Gram Panchayats and

₹87,000 crore for our almost dysfunctional municipalities – resources enough for transforming them, if used judiciously. The aggregate level of transfer of central resources –plan and non-plan combined– is estimated go up only by about 2 percent over the award period, but most of it will now be based on formula rather than on discretion and will not be tied to plan schemes of questionable usefulness. The Commission's methodology has been robust and estimates conservative, avoiding a high growth scenario in respect of taxes and GDP, which increases the credibility of their recommendations. By including forest cover as a new environmental factor and by giving weightage to inter-state migration since 1971 in population figures, it has taken into account the changing realities of the time.

For transfers outside the Finance Commission, it has recommended the setting up of a new institutional mechanism 'consistent with the overarching objective of strengthening cooperative federalism', by limiting discretion, improving design and giving adequate flexibility to the states. By recommending the exclusion of the states from the operations of the NSSF which were forced upon them, it has given them more liberty to manage their debt. It has also urged the centre to follow the true spirit of fiscal responsibility by dispensing the concept of 'Effective Revenue Deficit', ingeniously invented to circumvent the 3 percent limit on fiscal deficit. All these recommendations are likely to bring in transparency and accountability in the public finances of the union, as well as the states, heralding a spirit of federalism this country has not yet seen.

Of course, there is a danger lurking that the Commission ought to have considered and pre-empted. The mistakes that the Congress governments at the centre had made by resorting to unbridled populism at the cost of the nation's growth are now much more likely to be repeated with the increased resources available to the states. This is already in evidence in Delhi where the newly elected government has announced sops that will cost the exchequer about ₹1700 crore annually. They may be fulfilling their election promises, and Delhi, a union territory, may not be under the Finance Commission's jurisdiction, but such trends are irresponsible and dangerous. They are likely to be repeated by many states, especially those going to the polls within a few months, like Bihar, West Bengal and UP. The potential of subverting economic gains for populist purposes assumes serious proportions when political parties enter into opportunistic alliances forsaking all semblance of principles with an astonishing brazenness and when looters masquerading as leaders are in positions to drive governance in states, our politico-economic arrangements need serious introspection. These states will now find the increased resources a welcome bonanza to spend on ever more populism, squandering resources through unconstrained sops and doles in an election or pre-election year. A forward looking commission ought to have provided safeguards against these pitfalls.

(Afterword: The 14th Commission's recommendations have boosted the spirit of cooperative federalism in the country. However, not all the recommendations were accepted, especially those relating to reforming the existing system of fiscal transfers and the setting up of a new institutional mechanism for strengthening cooperative federalism. Meanwhile, it is almost time for the setting up of the 15th Finance Commission.)

6. MANAGEMENT OF PUBLIC DEBT[7]

(Deferring the decision to set up the Public Debt Management Agency was a retrograde step.)

An important step in clearing our institutional financial system of the cobwebs it has gathered over the years has now been reversed, with Mr Jaitley announcing to defer his plan to set up an independent public debt management authority, which he had promised in the budget presented earlier this year. Up until now, the Reserve Bank of India (RBI) has been managing the market borrowings of central and state governments, while external debt, which is vulnerable to the volatility of the forex market, is managed directly by the central government. While internal and external liabilities are thus managed by different agencies, no particular agency is responsible for overseeing the management of cash, investments and contingent liabilities of the union and state governments. The existing arrangement has created lots of aberrations including fictitious liabilities entering into government accounts, besides inept cash and debt management, with the result that governments are forced to borrow from the market to finance their fiscal deficits while sitting on piles of cash.

The level of public debt in the country stood at 66 percent of GDP in March 2013, more or less at the same level as in 1990-91 (69 percent). Domestic debt constitutes as much as 63 percent of the total public debt. As an agent of the union and state governments, while the RBI is empowered under Section 21(2) of the Reserve Bank of India Act, 1934, to manage the public debt of the union, it manages the public debts of the state governments by agreement with them, under provisions of the Government Securities Act, 2006. As debt manager to governments, it determines when government bonds are to be issued and their respective sizes, interest rates and maturity profiles, etc. However, its debt management objectives are influenced by its monetary policy interventions in the form of the Cash Reserve Ratio, Statutory Liquidity Ratio and the Liquidity Adjustment Facility, which

[7] Originally published in *The Statesman as* "That is Retrograde, Mr Jaitley", 30th May, 2015.

consists of a repo rate which the client banks pay to the RBI for short-term borrowings and a reverse repo rate which the RBI pays to the banks.

There are, in fact, too many conflicts of interest in the existing arrangements. The RBI is the regulator of banks. In addition to being the issuer of government securities, it is also the regulator of the securities market, in which banks are the largest purchasers. As the monetary authority of the country, it sets the interest rates for these securities. As the manager of domestic public debt, it can thus sell the bonds at higher prices by keeping the interest rates low and force banks –captive buyers in the securities market– to buy these bonds. This introduces an inherent inflationary bias in the monetary policy and prevents the market from determining the actual prices of these bonds based on their fundamentals that depend on the strength of finances of the central and state governments. Further, the government's ownership of more than 60 percent of the banking sector assets introduces further conflicts of interest, just as higher borrowings to finance larger fiscal deficits of the governments would have their corresponding monetary implications.

In fact, the RBI itself was the first to recognise these serious conflicts of interest, as pointed out by many of its in-house committees and working groups. The Committee on Capital Account Convertibility (1997), the Working Group on the Separation of Debt Management from Monetary Management (1997), the Advisory Group on Transparency and Financial Policies (2001), the RBI Annual Report (2001) and an Internal Expert Group (2001) all suggested the setting up of an independent and autonomous Debt Management Office. The Report of the Standing Committee on International Financial Standards & Codes (2002) observed that the RBI's responsibilities in the areas of monetary policy and internal debt management had "led to a situation of monetary policy function becoming somewhat subservient to debt management. Debt Management function puts the RBI in a situation of direct conflict of interest." Partially to address this, the FRBM Act of 2003 had prohibited the RBI from purchasing primary issues of the central government securities from 2006, preventing monetisation of government deficit.

In 2006, the Committee on Fuller Capital Account Convertibility recommended setting up an independent Office of Public Debt. Then, following the recommendations of the Percy Mistry Committee in 2007, in the union budget for 2007-08, Mr Chidambaram had proposed to set up an autonomous Debt Management Office (DMO) outside the RBI. As an interim step, a Middle Office was created in the Ministry of Finance pending transition to a full-fledged DMO.

The Internal Working Group on Debt Management (2008), headed by Mr Jahangir Aziz, suggested creating a 'National Treasury Management Agency', by combining debt and cash managements together with the management of contingent and other liabilities, and also to integrate these functions with risk assessment and other advisory functions. In the same year, the Raghuram Rajan Committee on Financial Sector Reforms also recommended establishment of an independent DMO.

Finally, in 2013, the Financial Sector Legislative Reforms Commission (FSLRC), headed by Justice B. N. Srikrishna, reiterated the recommendations of the 2008 Working Group Report to separate debt management from monetary management and to integrate the management of cash and contingent liabilities of the government with debt management, and making a single agency, called the Public Debt Management Agency (PDMA), responsible for all these functions. Accordingly, in the union budget for 2015-16, Mr Jaitley announced the creation of the PDMA by repealing the Government Securities Act, 2006 and amending the RBI Act, 1934 and other relevant legislations, thereby taking away the RBI's powers to regulate interbank repo and reverse repo rates and shifting the regulation of government securities and money market instruments to SEBI. Simultaneously, the RBI was given the task of inflation targeting under an MOU with the government. Inflation targeting, which should be the priority of the RBI as the monetary authority, would be impossible without dissociating it from debt management functions, as otherwise there will always be a conflict of interest between controlling inflation and keeping the interest rates low so as to reduce the cost of government borrowings. The RBI will of course continue to act as banker to all governments, while its debt management functions would stand transferred to the PDMA.

The setting up of an independent PDMA was one of the most welcome features of Mr Jaitley's budget. However, sadly, for reasons as yet unexplained, he has reneged on his promise and the entire process has now been put in reverse gear, on the grounds that a detailed roadmap needs to be set up. Political support was not lacking, and, with the PDMA being part of the Finance Bill which is a money bill, nor was there any fear of defeat in the Rajya Sabha. An independent PDMA would have sent strong signals about the government's intention to usher in serious reforms and create greater transparency in the domestic bond market, which could then be integrated into our vibrant capital market and derivatives market, unifying and creating a common financial market. Today, the banks hold much more in government bonds than required by the Statutory Liquidity Ratio; delinking the RBI from debt management would also have freed up resources for banks to increase their profitability through higher volumes of commercial lending.

There are of course defenders and sympathisers of the RBI who do not like to see a shrinking of its role and its diminishing importance in the administration of financial markets in the country. They cite the example of Greece and argue that debt management cannot be viewed as a routine function to be delegated to a separate agency and that the RBI has facilitated large borrowings of governments in a smooth and non-disruptive manner, which has led to improvements in securities trading and settlements with fewer risks and lesser transaction costs. They advocate a gradual and calibrated roadmap for separation of the functions, rather than setting up a PDMA straightway.

International best practices can probably serve as a useful guide in this contentious debate. Most developed countries like the OECS countries long ago removed debt management from the purview of their central banks. Emerging economies are also falling in line; Brazil, Argentina and South Africa have restructured their debt management and created independent agencies for managing their debts. None of these countries has so far reverted the debt management functions to their central banks. In any case, an institutional coordinating mechanism can be established between the RBI and the PDMA to prevent a Greece-like scenario, the possibility of which is rather far-fetched in the Indian situation; such coordination would also contain the fallouts from any future market volatility.

A large part of the country's infrastructure building requirements has to come from the bond market. However, the bond market, dominated by a limited number of players –mostly commercial banks and financial institutions– itself remains weak and undeveloped due to the same constraints of conflicting interests. Unless reformed, the bond market will not be able to attract the large pool of private savings which today are going elsewhere, such as to real estate. PDMA is the need of the hour, much beyond the jurisdictional considerations of the RBI or the Finance Ministry.

(Afterword: A PDMA has not yet been set up. The Monetary Policy Committee was set up in the Union Budget for 2016-17 by amending the Reserve Bank of India (RBI) Act, 1934. It gives statutory backing to the Monetary Policy Framework Agreement signed in February 2015 between

the RBI and the Government of India. The primary objective of the monetary policy is to maintain price stability, while keeping in mind the objective of growth, and to meet increasingly complex challenges. Under the Monetary Policy Framework Agreement, the RBI will be responsible for containing inflation targets at 4 percent (with a standard deviation of 2 percent) in the medium term. The Central Government will determine the inflation target in terms of the Consumer Price Index, once in every five years in consultation with the RBI. The Committee will decide any changes to be made in the policy rate (repo rate) for containing inflation within the target. The Committee will have 6 members. Apart from the RBI Governor who will be the Chairperson, it will have as members the RBI Deputy Governor in charge of monetary policy, one official nominated by the RBI Board and three experts nominated by the Government of India. The Committee is fully functional now.)

7. TAXING AGRICULTURAL INCOME[8]

(From time to time, people both from within and outside the government have talked about the necessity and feasibility of taxing agricultural income. There are no two opinions about the need for bringing this hitherto untaxed sector within the tax net and correcting the distortions it is causing elsewhere in the economy, as the agricultural sector remains a conduit for money laundering and the concealment of black income. Committee after committee has recommended in favour of taxing large agricultural incomes, but successive governments have shied away from this for fear of losing potentially large vote banks. While the loss of potential vote banks remains a myth, the available data clearly prove that the small and marginal farmers would not be affected by any tax imposed on agricultural income.)

In March 2016, in response to an RTI application, the Income Tax Department revealed that agricultural income earned by the 6.57 lakh people who had filed returns in 2011, stood at nearly ₹2,000 lakh crore, which was over 20 times the country's gross domestic product of over ₹84 lakh crore in that year. Subsequently, however, in January 2017, it was clarified that the shocking figures were primarily due to data entry errors, an assertion yet to be verified, but even extrapolation of the reduced income for all the identified cases implies that more than ₹4,000 crore of agricultural income was lying outside the tax-net.

Agriculture is exempt from income tax under Section 2(1A) of the Income Tax Act, which defines agricultural income as rent/revenue from land, income derived from this land through agriculture and income derived from buildings on that land. Further, unless there is a specific taxing entry in the union or state list under the 7th Schedule to the Constitution, no tax can be imposed by the Union or the State. The tax on agricultural income is listed under the State List (Entry 46), and hence the Central Government cannot tax such income. As such, Section 10 (1) of the Income Tax Act, a Central Act, excludes agricultural income from the computation of total income. Read with Section 2(1A), it implies that farmers who have no other sources of income are not required to file income-tax returns. It is only those farmers who derive income from sources other than agriculture who are required to

[8] Originally published in *The Statesman as* "Tax on the Farm", 25th November, 2017.

file returns. If their agricultural income exceeds ₹5000, and their total income is otherwise taxable, the agricultural income is to be added to the total income only for determination of their appropriate income slab for chargeability of tax, but no tax will be imposed on the income derived from agriculture.

Any decision to tax agricultural income by the centre will require an amendment to the Constitution. For that a taxing entry needs to be inserted in the union list and appropriate changes should be made in Part XII of the Constitution, dealing with Finances of the Union and the States. Of course, states have to be involved in the process, as presently they only can impose such a tax. It will be foolish to expect that states, already reeling under agitations by farmers, will take the plunge. For the centre also, it will be a contentious issue, with various lobbying groups trying to protect the interests of the big farmers. However, the danger of avoiding or postponing this will spell doom for the economy and defeat the government's earnest attempts to eliminate black money, as the untaxed agriculture sector will continue to absorb black money. It is also extremely unfair from considerations of equity and simplification of the tax administration.

In June 2016, at the Rajasva Gyan Sangam, an annual conference of tax administrators, the suggestion was made to the Prime Minister "on the need to target farmers with non-agricultural income above a certain threshold, an idea that was pitched as a low-hanging fruit that could potentially bolster ongoing efforts to widen the country's taxpayer base." It may be mentioned that of the 25 crore taxpaying households in the country, 15 crore households are designated as agriculturalists and the remaining 10 crores are non-agriculturalists, according to estimates produced at the conference. Even earlier, committee after committee appointed by the government had warned the government about the pitfalls of not taxing the agriculture sector. The K. N. Raj Committee (1972), Tax Reforms Committee (1991), Task Force on Direct Taxes (2002), and Tax Administration Reform Commission (2014) all recommended taxation of agriculture to plug the loopholes for evasion and the laundering of tax-evaded money. Despite pointing out the inherent inequity in exempting rich farmers earning more than salaried employees, nothing really happened. Actually, it is not even something unprecedented - agricultural income used to be taxed in India till 1886 when it was abolished. Income from tea, coffee and rubber plantations is taxed even now under Rules 8, 7A and 7B of the Income Tax Rules, 1962. However, with agriculture being the holy cow of the economy, any proposal to bring the sector as a whole under the tax net has always met with the strongest disapproval from the farmers' lobbies and the government on the consideration of loss of vote banks.

The vote bank consideration is based on myth. Even if the sector is brought under the tax net, it is only a miniscule percentage of the total number of agricultural workers who would be affected by such a tax. Even at present, hardly 2 percent of those who have been assessed declare any agricultural income. As mentioned, small and marginal farmers are not required to file any income tax returns as long as agriculture is their only source of income; even if the sector is brought under tax, their income will be well below the tax threshold.

From the Agricultural Census and 2011 population census figures, we can estimate that the number of small and marginal farmers in the country is around 118 million (93 million marginal, 25 million small) – they account for about 93 percent of the total farmers in the country and together hold 45 percent of the total area under cultivation. The remaining 7 percent of farmers who share 55 percent of the total cultivable land would be the target group for the incidence of any future tax on agriculture. They certainly do not constitute a major vote bank, though their voice may be loud enough for any political party to yield to their demands for continued exemption. It is also relevant that the agriculture sector contributes only 16 percent to our GDP. Its growth has been stagnant, the percentages of growth during 2012-13 to 2016-17 being only 1.5, 4.2, -0.2, 1.2 and 4.1, respectively. No significant capital investment has been made in agriculture during the past decades.

According to the Situation Assessment Survey of Agricultural Households conducted during January 2013 to December 2013, the average monthly income per agricultural households was estimated as ₹6,426. The net receipt from farm business (cultivation and farming of animals) accounted for about 60 percent of the average monthly income per agricultural household. The average monthly consumption expenditure per agricultural household was ₹6,223, while the income was ₹6,426. Only for the large farmers holding more than 10 hectares of land, the income was ₹41,388 per month, above the income tax threshold. These data show that only the large farmers who account for a miniscule 0.7 percent of the total operational holdings will be liable to pay any income tax. They also have substantial non-farm income, above the tax threshold.

Even the agro-companies growing crops are entitled to the same tax reliefs as individuals in respect of agricultural income, which defies all logic when we consider the scale of exemptions enjoyed by these companies. Let us take a few examples. More than four lakh taxpayers had claimed exemption for agricultural income in the assessment year 2014-15. The biggest beneficiaries were Kaveri Seeds, which claimed ₹186.63 crore as exemption, and the multinational Monsanto India, which claimed ₹94.4 crore as exemption, and they earned ₹215.4 crore and ₹138.7 crore profits, respectively, before tax. It may be mentioned that Monsanto is the company that sells the genetically modified Bt-Cotton seeds in the country and earns huge profits therefrom. If this is not inequitable and irrational, one wonders what is. According to an estimate, when taxing only the richest 4.1 percent of agricultural households, as much as ₹25,000 crore could be collected as tax.

Given that only 2.6 percent of the population paid any taxes in 2015-16 (39 percent in the USA for comparison), and only 25 lakh paid tax at the highest rate –90 percent of them from the organised sector where taxes are compulsorily deducted at source– if we are serious about expanding the tax base, this hitherto untaxed sector must be brought under the tax net. Of course, given the highly informal nature of business in this sector, tax administration will pose serious problems initially, but that is expected of any new domain. It should be ensured that the tax liability rests only on the shoulders of the rich farmers while insulating the small and marginal farmers.

In 1925, the Indian Taxation Enquiry Committee noted "[t]here is no historical or theoretical justification for the continued exemption from the income tax of income derived from agriculture. There are, however, administrative and political objections to the removal of the exemption at the present time." After more than 90 years these words still ring the same. It is high time for another disruptive and structural reform in this area.

(Afterward: Nothing has changed so far as taxation of the agricultural sector is concerned. Agriculture continues to be outside taxation.)

SECTION 2

SHAPING THE FUTURE: DISRUPTIVE REFORMS

1. Tectonic Purge: Changing the Growth Trajectory
2. A Cashless Future
3. An Inescapable Future
4. GST: Things to Learn from Other Pioneers
5. Petroleum Sector under GST – A Chimera
6. Treat the Disease, not the Symptoms

1. TECTONIC PURGE: CHANGING THE GROWTH TRAJECTORY[9]

(The recent demonetisation exercise undertaken by the Government will radically alter the growth trajectory of India in the coming years.)

Over the long weekend, I had planned to escape the toxic air of Delhi and flee to the tranquil hills of Uttarakhand to breathe some fresh air, but had to drop the plan abruptly for want of cash. For the same reason, we have not been able to buy any fish, fruit, vegetables or medicine since ₹ 500 and ₹ 1000 notes were withdrawn last week, and have been forced to survive only on roti and dal, of which we had a stock. Given the unending queues at the bank, the plight is likely to continue for some time. I am sure most of you are also being forced to go through this logistical nightmare. But I am not complaining. Reforms are always painful, and the pain is necessary to cleanse the body politic of harmful viruses. However, in its significance and potential benefits, this step was indeed a masterstroke. In one swift move, the government has eliminated most of the black money currently circulating in the economy, even though the growth in some sectors may suffer in the short term, bringing down the growth rate of GDP during the current fiscal period.

The measures were not unexpected though; they are the logical culmination of a series of relentless steps the government has taken over the last two years against black money – *Jan-Dhan Yojna* and the opening of bank accounts for everyone, renegotiating the tax treaties and automatic information exchange agreements with other countries and tax havens, the Black Money Act, 2015 and the Benami Property Act, 2016, nudging people to declare their undisclosed income through the Income Declaration Scheme, and some other measures. This demonetisation was only to be expected as the next logical step.

As is often misunderstood, black money is not necessarily generated through corruption, nor is all the black income necessarily cash income. Many normal business transactions legitimately generate large volumes of cash –for example, textiles, jewellery, luxury goods, household appliances,

---

[9] Originally published in *The Statesman*, 20th November, 2016.

etc. Professionals like doctors and lawyers also trade mostly in cash. Demonetisation may disrupt such businesses by curtailing consumer spending on these goods and result in their negative growth for some time. While businesses and people dealing with legitimate cash have nothing to fear, the ban on higher denomination notes is sure to hit those who are holding large amounts of black money in cash. Much of the black cash may never surface at all. We, the common men, will only suffer some temporary inconvenience, but no financial loss or harassment by tax authorities.

The total amount of black money currently circulating in the economy is anybody's guess. The size of India's black economy expanded rapidly over the 1970s and 1980s, but since then has been contracting slowly. A recent study estimated it at 20 percent of GDP or about ₹ 30 lakh crore. The majority of this black money is believed to be locked up in physical assets, such as real estate and gold. The withdrawal of higher denomination notes will certainly and severely impact the real estate sector, especially the secondary market transactions where a 60:40 ratio is believed to be the norm between legal and black money.

India's economy remains overwhelmingly a cash-driven economy. In 2015, 78 percent of all consumer payments in India were made in cash against 20-25 percent norm in developed economies. The total value of currency in circulation in India today amounts to ₹ 17 lakh crore, and 86 percent of that cash, amounting to ₹14.6 lakh crore, is only in ₹500 and ₹1000 denomination notes. While the total number of bank notes in circulation rose by 40 percent between 2011 and 2016, the circulation of ₹500 notes rose by 76 percent, and that of ₹1,000 notes by a whopping 109 percent during this period.

The most corrupt who have the largest stocks of illegal cash will obviously suffer, because they cannot easily deposit the money that would be under surveillance and risk going to jail. So, this money does not surface at all, and as pointed out by experts, since the notes are a liability on the account of the RBI even though the liability may be notional, the RBI's and hence the government's liability on this account is automatically reduced. The rest of the illegitimate cash will get sucked out of the black money market to enter the normal financial system, where it will contribute to tax, along with a 200 percent penalty.

Now think of the cascading effect of this. As the black money gets sucked out of the market, several sectors like real estate will be forced to correct their current prices, leading to a fall in inflation. All the money that will now enter into the formal financial system will continue its contribution to future taxes, as its tracking by tax departments will become easier. As inflation falls and taxes increase, government finances will improve. If the government uses this increased liquidity judiciously and does not squander it in useless populist schemes, the fundamentals of the economy will get stronger, and accelerated GDP growth will more than make up for the temporary loss we are likely to witness in the short term. As inflation drops and liquidity improves phenomenally, interest rates will certainly drop giving a significant boost to the economy, by far more than the RBI can ever hope to do through manipulation of its policy rates. There will of course be a transfer of investment from physical assets like real estate and gold to financial assets, as people will shift their investment preference to dollars or equity where they can still save taxes. Coupled with lower interest rates, this will in turn boost the corporate sector, hopefully creating badly-needed jobs. Excess liquidity with the bank will also help them manage their NPAs to some extent.

The black money market will of course spring up again; it definitely will, and high denomination cash will continue to be used as conduits for corruption and the hoarding of black money. However, there are two aspects to this. The first is psychological –people who have lost money now will think twice before hoarding cash. This psychological aspect can be a very important determinant of behaviour. The second is based on pure economic logic. The accumulation of black money can reach dangerous levels only over a period of time, and is triggered by retrograde economic relationships established through political machinations –retrograde because they hinder the normal operations of market forces. Left to itself, the invisible hand of the market has a way of wiping out anything that affects its normal operation. The current build-up of black money can perhaps be traced to those days when the marginal tax rates were as high as 97 percent and there were various other distortions arising from the faulty command and control economic model that we followed. The Janata Party's 1978 demonetisation of ₹1000, ₹5000 and ₹10000 notes did not help because in those days these notes constituted only a tiny fraction of the total value of currency (about 1.6 percent). Even in 2001, their value was only 25 percent against 86 percent now. Besides, the tax system today is much simpler, much more rational and taxpayer-friendly; it is poised to become even simpler in future, thus creating an in-built disincentive against black money. Governments today can also be expected to display more maturity and not to interfere in the market unnecessarily. When the cost of tax compliance becomes lower than the cost of tax evasion, generation of black money becomes uneconomical. Thus, in future it may take much longer to build up the stock black money to a level where it will start distorting normal economic processes. This step is truly a 'surgical strike' against black money that may change our growth trajectory for the next decade.

(Afterword: Almost 99 percent of the total cash in circulation had come back into the banking system as reported by the Reserve Bank of India in August 2017, enabling the tax authorities to follow the future trail of these deposits and recover taxes on them. The inflation rate has come down to its lowest level ever –six months after demonetisation, retail inflation stood at 1.54 percent in June 2017, while wholesale inflation touched an all-time low of 0.9 percent. Of course, there are other factors, but demonetisation must also have played its part in this. Real estate and gold have always been the biggest absorbers of black money. Real estate prices, however, have not yet reflected the expectations of a substantial drop after tumbling in the immediate aftermath of demonetisation, and gold prices also have not reflected any real change after demonetisation. GDP growth in the short term has decreased to 5.7 percent in the first quarter of 2017-18 (April-June, 2017), presumably as a result of the move, but is expected to surge after some time; even the IMF agrees with this. The most significant impact has been felt in terms of direct taxes; more than 91 lakh of new taxpayers have been brought into the tax net, and more than ₹23,000 crore of undisclosed income have been unearthed. There is no doubt that the cash-driven informal sector was badly hit and many lost jobs. However, in elections held in February-March 2017, when the memory of sufferings through the 50-day window given for depositing the high denomination notes was still fresh in the minds of people, the BJP managed to win a landslide victory in UP, a state where the informal sector was much more prominent than the formal one. It does not mean that the poor did not suffer, but probably that they had thought – and perhaps rightly – that the rich who became rich via black money had suffered more.)

2. A CASHLESS FUTURE[10]

(The recent demonetisation in India can nudge the country towards a cashless future in the foreseeable future.)

The demonetisation of the ₹500 and ₹1000 notes was indeed a surgical strike on the black money that would entirely change our economic landscape and significantly correct distortions. The resultant pain is associated with any surgery, but nowhere in the world have reforms been effected without the accompanying pain. This reform can lead to a much bigger change by nudging India towards a cashless economy. If we are determined, in a few years' time, we can transform ourselves into a cashless society.

Bank notes were first introduced in Sweden way back in 1661. Three and a half centuries later, today most cities in Sweden do not accept cash anymore. Public transport, small businesses, museums and even churches now accept only electronic payments through card readers or digital wallets. Even newspapers can be bought from street vendors using a card. Three out of four of Sweden's largest banks are phasing out the manual handling of cash in their branches. As per the statistics of the Bank for International Settlements, an umbrella organisation for the world's central banks, the cash-GDP ratio in Sweden is down to only 3 percent, compared to an average of 9 percent in the Eurozone, 7 percent in the US and 12 percent in India. The number of bank robberies in Sweden plunged from 110 in 2008 to only 5 in 2012, because most Swedish banks simply will not handle cash.

Other Scandinavian countries are also not far behind. Most stores in Denmark had dumped their cash registers from January this year; only essential services, hospitals, pharmacies and post offices, still accept cash until the time cashless transaction becomes a law. Norway is also making a similar transition. Scandinavians today rely on cash for less than 6 percent of all their payments, compared to an estimated 47 percent in the US. They are discovering and benefiting from the advantages of reduced handling and transport costs, increased security and a drop in cash-robbery cases. Card

---

[10] Originally published in *The Statesman*, 23rd November, 2016.

frauds have increased though; the total card frauds in Europe hit a record value of $1.4 billion in 2013, 8 percent more than in 2012.

Many other countries are also making a move towards a cashless society across all continents. Canada, where electronic payments constitute 70 percent of total payments as against the world average of 40 percent, has stopped printing new currency notes. By introducing a preferential VAT treatment for consumers who pay with cards, South Korea has significantly reduced the share of cash from 40 percent to only 20 percent in 10 years. Their central bank, the Bank of Korea, is issuing less and less currency every year, and is moving towards a planned 'cashless society' by 2020. Australia, Singapore and even Nigeria are thinking of a cashless future.

In Africa, Kenyans are increasingly flocking to mobile money M-Pesa, which has already registered 15 million subscribers in a population of 47 million. Even in Somaliland, an autonomous region of Somalia, one of Africa's poorest countries, a mobile revolution has created an informal electronic banking system with more efficiency and convenience than in many developed countries. Cash is disappearing fast and credit cards are becoming redundant because even street vendors accept payments by mobile phones. A survey in 2012 found that the average customer makes 34 transactions per month on their mobile phone, higher than in almost every other country.

These are but a few examples of countries across the world which are moving resolutely towards cashless regimes and whose number is increasing because of the potential benefits. According to a McKinsey report, a cashless society has the potential to cut costs equivalent up to 1.1 percent of GDP. The report further states that in countries where total cash payments constitute below 50 percent of total payments, the shadow economy can grow only up to 12 percent of GDP, but where cash use exceeds 80 percent of total payments, the shadow economy can surge up to 32 percent of GDP. Apart from restricting the growth of the underground economy, becoming cashless may also help in the monetary policy domain. To stimulate the economy by encouraging spending, some countries may adopt minus interest rates, which would not work in a cash economy. When cash becomes electronic, people will have to spend it to avoid losses from minus interest rates.

Cashless transaction is not an invention of the modern era; in fact, the origin of cashless transaction can be traced to medieval times. Ever since the birth of Christianity in Rome, every devout Christian has wanted to visit

Jerusalem, the Holy City, at least once in their lives. Even at the best of times, the journey from Europe to Jerusalem was hazardous, but the emergence of Islam in Europe increased the hazards manifold. Once Jerusalem had fallen to the Muslims in 637 AD, Christian pilgrims began to be harassed not only by the Muslim fanatics who massacred the infidels, but also by groups of ruthless bandits en route.

Starting in 1009, the Crusades spilled blood in the name of God for the next two centuries. In 1099, Christians recaptured Jerusalem and the Holy City would remain under their control for the next 130 years. In 1119, out of the Crusades emerged a most mysterious order of the Knights Templars, an army of monks superbly trained in warfare, to provide protection to pilgrims going to Jerusalem. They were fierce and fearless, willing to die for the scriptures, and were among the most feared knights of their times. By 1120, they had entrenched themselves in Jerusalem at the site of the Biblical Temple of Solomon, and had dug the area around to discover many holy relics and riches, as the legend goes, including even the elusive Holy Grail. As the Crusades raged on, Templars attracted recruits from the wealthiest families of Europe and became immensely powerful and rich, not only from the wartime loot, but also from donations of land and gold from nobles and kings of Europe. They acquired wealth beyond imagination, owned vast tracts of land, hundreds of castles and a full fleet of ships that traded goods and shipped pilgrims across the Mediterranean. They became the first well-equipped standing army of Europe since the fall of the Roman Empire.

From 1150, they had, however, stopped guarding the road to Jerusalem physically, finding instead a much better and efficient way to protect the cash and valuables of the pilgrims, which attracted the bandits and imperilled their journey. They devised an ingenious arrangement by which pilgrims deposited a lump-sum amount in advance with the Templar Commandery nearest their homes and were given paper scrolls or vouchers in exchange that recorded in ciphers the amounts deposited. On their way to Jerusalem, at places where such commanderies were available –there were quite a few– they could draw cash against the note to defray expenditure incurred on the way, by paying a fee for the services rendered. This was the origin of the modern banking system and of the credit cards and travellers' cheques of modern times.

Templars gradually became bankers to the European monarchs, and that brought about their ultimate end. In 1307, on Friday the 13th of October, hundreds of Templars were arrested by King Philip IV of France, who badly wanted their enormous treasure for his kingdom, which was impoverished by his wars. They were charged with unspeakable crimes including desecration of the holy relics, were tortured by the Inquisition and ultimately put to slow death by burning. However, the treasures were never found, and many Templars had also escaped unscathed to the safety of Swiss villages deep in the Alps. In Switzerland at around this time, the farming communities were gradually transforming themselves into banking communities, whose operations were covered by secrecy laws that replicated the secrecy surrounding the Knights Templars. They also proved suddenly to be transformed into a formidable fighting force, taking on foreign invaders successfully, unlike farmers elsewhere. It may not have been a mere coincidence that the Swiss flag incorporates the Templar Cross.

The cashless system was originally devised to save pilgrims from bandits. Today, it can save us from a much larger bandit, the black economy. India has already taken the plunge in this. Like in many European countries, high value cash transactions are disallowed in India, making it easier to track financial transactions and collect tax, and also curb high value illegal transactions.

A recent joint report by Google and the Boston Consulting Group highlighted that the rise in smartphone penetration and adoption of mobile wallets by small offline merchants will increase the size of the digital payments market in India nearly tenfold to $500 billion, or 15 percent of the country's GDP by 2020, when India's internet user-base will reach 500 million. JAM (Jan Dhan-Aadhaar-Mobile), United Payments Interface, Digital India and mobile wallets have already laid the foundations, and the recent demonetisation can further facilitate the movement towards a cashless India. With a firm resolve, we can even become the first fully cashless country in the world.

(Afterword: Since November 2016 when the demonetisation exercise was undertaken, digital payments have surged like anything. Between November 2016 and October 2017, the average daily transactions jumped from a paltry 10,000 to 23.36 lakh through the United Payments Interface (UPI) and Bharat Interface for Money (BHIM). The value of these transactions rose from ₹101 crore in November 2016 to ₹7,057 crore in October 2017. For the other platforms, the number of transactions increased from 12.06 lakh to 29.08 lakh through the Aadhaar Enabled Payments System (AEPS), from 8.96 lakh to 32.42 lakh through the Immediate Payments Service (IMPS), and from 46.03 lakh to 72.72 lakh through M-wallet. Since demonetisation, the use of debit and credit cards has gone up by as much as 65 percent. Official statistics indicate an 80 percent increase in the value

of digital transactions in 2017-18, with the total amount expected to touch ₹1,800 crore in the wake of the impetus provided by demonetisation. The value of digital transactions until October this year, at ₹1,000 crore, was nearly equal to that for the whole of 2016-17. It was a continuation of a trend, with June, July and August registering on average ₹136-138 crore transactions, according to the Ministry of Information Technology.

There has been significant progress in establishing the 'Jan Dhan-Aadhaar-Mobile trinity', with 118 crore mobiles, a similar number of Aadhaar numbers and 31 crore Jan Dhan accounts. There has been a 23 percent increase in the e-filing of income tax returns in 2016-17 as compared to 2015-16. Further, nearly 90 crore registered entities with the GST Network (GSTN) are filing online returns, facilitating their coverage under the income tax net.)

3. AN INESCAPABLE FUTURE[11]

(India already has the basic infrastructure in place for going cashless. It is now only a question of taking the plunge. The future of India is inevitably a cashless one.)

After my last article ("A Cashless Future", November 23rd) in these columns, many readers had reacted with understandable sense of outrage. While some thought the idea of a cashless economy insane in a country where more than half the population still defecate in the open and about a quarter of the population still remain illiterate, others pointed out that in a cashless economy, there is a cost for every digital transaction which will put an avoidable burden upon the poor. Yet others suggested that the country has to grow and evolve before we can think of a cashless future. This, in my opinion, will require an eternity.

The post-demonetisation nightmares people are still passing through and the prevailing confusion, being aided and abetted by the RBI's never-ending directives, have all added to a miasma of helplessness and frustration among the people. Going by the daily reports of raids and the unearthing of huge loads of cash including both old and new notes all over the country, the black money hoarders are probably exploring ingenious ways of changing the colour behaviour of their money with the 'Jugaad' mindset. The anger at these incidents and the ongoing discomfort may justifiably blur our objective reasoning at times.

What is relevant and important for a cashless economy is not the penetration of toilets or literacy, but the penetration of mobiles and financial inclusion. Increasing digitisation of transactions is also essential for the success of the GST which will have to be rolled by September 15th 2017, and this may have been a very important, if unstated, objective behind the move to demonetisation, as it will serve to improve direct tax collections.

As regards the transactional cost of digital payments, every transaction carries an economic cost, including cash. According to a Bloomberg report, merely transporting cash to and from the villages in India cost about $335

---

[11] Originally published in *The Statesman*, 31st December, 2017.

million last year, equivalent to about ₹2200 crore. This is a poorly targeted indirect subsidy benefiting both the rich and the poor, but the former obviously more than the latter. Once digital transaction becomes the norm, the economics of scale is sure to bring down the transaction cost of digital transactions, and if it still remains unreasonable, a similar amount of subsidy can be distributed through the Jan-Dhan accounts to compensate only the poor, reducing the inherent inequity of the present system.

For a digital transaction, all one needs is a mobile phone (preferably a smartphone with an internet connection) and a bank account. Coming to the mobile penetration, as per the latest data released by the Telecom Regulatory Authority of India on the 30th September 2016, there were 105 crore mobile subscribers in India (60 crore urban and 45 crore rural). Of India's estimated population of 133.6 crore in 2016, roughly 67 percent, or about 90 crore, are rural; thus, the distribution remains skewed between urban and rural subscribers, though it is reasonable to assume that most households have access to a mobile phone. With overall tele-density –the number of mobile connections per 100 of the population– at 84, the basic infrastructure is already in place. Of course, the tele-density shows wide variation across states, from 56 in Bihar to 119 in Tamil Nadu, but it is only a matter of time before this unevenness is diminished.

Internet connectivity is of course a different story. With only 46 crore internet connections, more than 70 percent of those in urban areas in June 2016, most of the rural population remains unconnected. There are also various infrastructure bottlenecks like the availability and reliability of connections, in addition to the availability of electricity in many rural outposts. With internet connectivity, Mobile Wallets and United Payments Interface (UPI) can enable seamless digital payments across banks, but, apart from the internet, they also require a smartphone, which may not be affordable to many Indians as of yet, even with their prices nose-diving sharply. However, the number of internet connections grew by 30 percent last year and the growth rate is likely to be sustained, at which rate penetration of the internet can be increased from the current 35 percent to 70 percent within 4-5 years, assuming a concomitant expansion of the attendant infrastructure.

However, technology has already addressed this problem and with the Unstructured Supplementary Service Data (USSD), even a basic mobile handset (feature phone) without internet connection can facilitate cashless payment, through the IFSC Code of the Bank and an Aadhaar-number. One can transfer money up to ₹5000 using only the recipient's IFSC code, mobile number and Aadhaar-number –83 percent of India's population is now covered by Aadhaar.

The last element is financial inclusion and it is indeed difficult to estimate. But still, let us try to make a reasonable guesstimate based on available data. Taking the 2011 Census figure of 4.45 for the average household size in India, there are about 30 crore households to be covered for full financial inclusion, which can be ensured if each of these households has at least one bank account amongst its members.

As per the latest RBI data, in March 2015, the total number of savings bank accounts with the scheduled commercial banks in India was 11.7 crore (a 19.6 percent growth over the previous year). These included multiple accounts in the name of a single individual, the precise number of which is indeterminate. Making an allowance for even 25 percent redundancy on this count, we have about 8.8 crore unique individual accounts. This will still include multiple members of the same households having separate accounts. Again, making an allowance of 25 percent on this count, we have roughly 6.6 crore savings accounts spread across different households as of March 2015. The growth rate of 19.6 percent would yield 9 crore separate household accounts by December 2016.

Under the Pradhan Mantri Jan Dhan Yojna launched in August 2014, as of December 2016, there were 25.98 crore Jan Dhan accounts, more than half of which have been opened since March 2015, and hence excluded from the 9 crore accounts computed above. Add to this nearly 3 crore "No Frill Accounts" with the Regional Rural Banks, when these accounts were converted to "Basic Savings Deposit Accounts" in August 2012 by the RBI. Many of these may be inoperative, but from these statistics, it is likely that at least 20 crore of the estimated 30 crore households have already been covered by the banking network. Account opening has also become much simpler, with the Aadhaar Card and a photograph being the only requirements. Thus, a substantial part of the infrastructure essential for going cashless is already in place, and India can leapfrog into a digital economy without major disruptions. It is no longer an impossible dream if we only dare to dream, despite 90 percent of our informal economy today being based on cash. In fact, it is this informal sector that is the target of demonetisation, and naturally this is the sector that has been hit the hardest; indeed, it is gasping for breath. If India is to become cashless, this sector has to be brought into the formal stream. This is also essential to expand our absurdly narrow direct taxpayer base.

Let us explore some hard facts: of the 52-crore strong workforce of India, 29 crore are engaged in the primary sector outside the tax net (using 2011 Census percentages). The rest (23 crore) employed in the secondary and tertiary sectors constitute our potential direct taxpayer base. Of this 23 crore, only 5 crore file tax returns, 1.5 crore pay taxes and only about 20 lakh people pay taxes at the highest slab rate of 30 percent, with annual income exceeding ₹10 lakh. Consequently 85 percent of the net national income goes outside the tax net and our tax-to-GDP ratio remains among the lowest even among the emerging economies. Add to this the substantial evasion in indirect taxes – excise, service tax and sales tax (VAT) – the evasion unearthed by the government in only the last two years amounted to ₹50,000 crore and the undetected evasion is anybody's guess. This evasion is enabled by the use of cash –the anonymous, fluid unit of transaction that leaves no trail and cannot be tracked. With such endemic evasion of indirect taxes, the GST, which subsumes most indirect taxes, does not stand an iota of a chance to succeed, unless the informal sector is brought into the tax net. Besides, with the GST being a technology-driven tax, the primary prerequisite is a substantial digitisation of most transactions.

Life will not be the same in India ever again. Not all of the ₹15 lakh crore withdrawn from the monetary system is ever going to be returned, and the withdrawal ceilings are also not going to be removed anytime soon. The government is pushing the envelope hard to prod the informal sector into cashlessness to enable the authorities to check tax evasion. Once that happens, tax rates may be lowered to assuage people's anger and generate votes. Demonetisation is basically a political decision with economic ramifications. It is not about curbing black money but eliminating the source of black money: cash.

(Afterword: Demonetisation has reduced the amount of citizens with cash and the cash to GDP ratio has come down from 12 to 9 percent as a result. Bank deposits have increased by 3-4 lakh crore rupees, improving their lending capacity substantially. It has added 7.6 crore new monthly digital transactions, creating a financial information infrastructure for the tax authorities and curbing the use of black money in the form of cash. The bank interest rate has come down by nearly 2 percent. Tax compliance received a significant boost; for the financial year 2016-17, 1.26 crore new taxpayers, including return filers and non-filers making tax payments, were added to the tax base of the country, though the benefit of such an addition has not yet translated into a significant rise in tax collection. The second volume of the Union Government's Economic Survey, released in August 2017, stated that the growth of taxpayers post-demonetisation was

significantly greater at 45 percent as against 25 percent in the previous year.)

4. GST:
Things to Learn from Other Pioneers[12]

(The GST has caused a fall in the growth rate and a spurt in inflation in the immediate aftermath of its launch everywhere in the world, and the experience is the same in India. However, in all countries, GSTs have delivered in the long run and there is no reason to believe that the same will not happen in the case of India. A GST has the potential of transforming the entire economic landscape of the country within the next 3-5 years.)

On August 31st, 2017, the CSO released GDP data pertaining to the April-June quarter of the current fiscal which showed GDP growth falling to 5.7 percent –the lowest in 3 years. The liberal economists joined the political opposition in painting a bleak picture of the imminent collapse of the Indian economy, blaming the fall in growth entirely on the disruptions caused by demonetisation and the GST. However, the decline of growth only confirmed the continuing downward trend of falling growth since the last quarter of 2015-16, long before the demonetisation period, while the GST was launched in only July 2017. As such, its impact would be seen more in the second quarter's results, which I guess would not bring much cheer. Behind the declining growth were factors like a steady deterioration in the export sector, stagnant credit growth and an underperforming banking sector, combined with weakened domestic demand caused by demonetisation.

The launching of a GST in India was indeed a bold step fraught with high political risks. A radical economic reform like this can make and unmake governments. The most striking example of this is Canada whose GST has many features in common with the Indian GST.

In January 1991, led by Prime Minister Brian Mulroney, Canada introduced a dual GST like India's, replacing a highly unpopular 13.5 percent Manufacturers' Sales Tax which was hurting its international trade and export competitiveness, and the government thought that a harmonised GST was the remedy. Introduction of the GST in Canada was rather messy; inflation soared and growth declined immediately and the GST could not raise the

---

[12] Originally published in *The Statesman* as "GST in India & the World", 9th and 10th November, 2017.

tax levels enough to contain the rising fiscal deficits. The economic slump led to widespread public resentment, and the GST became the object of public wrath. Mr Mulroney and his Progressive Conservative Party (PCP) had to pay a steep price for this. In the Parliamentary elections of 1993, the PCP's strength in the 295-seat House of Commons was reduced from 169 to only two seats. The PCP could never recover from the shock –it finally disbanded itself and merged with the Canadian Alliance to form the Conservative Party of Canada in 2004. The opposition Liberal Party under Jean Chrétien won the 1993 elections on the promise to repeal the GST, but instead of repealing it, it was rather strengthened and streamlined. Chrétien later apologised to the electorate for reneging on his election promise. Canada today administers a federal GST together with either a provincial sales tax (PST) or a harmonised sales tax (HST) levied by its different provinces. While the federal GST rate has come down from 7 percent in 1993 to 5 percent today, the HST attracts a uniform rate of 15 percent, while the PST rates vary between 6 and 10 percent.

A GST is a disruptive reform and needs to be managed carefully. Managing disruption is never smooth or easy. There are bound to be hiccups which can be very unsettling, both economically and politically. To be sure, the GST is not a miracle cure for everything that ails the economy. Prices take time to adjust in a market economy, and the effect of the GST can be seen only over time and not overnight.

Like in India, the GST everywhere followed the introduction of VAT. France was the first country to introduce VAT way back in 1954. As many as 160 countries today, including all OECD countries except the USA, have some form of VAT or GST. Many countries have introduced a GST by harmonising the taxes on goods and services, partially if not wholly, but very few of them have a federal structure –and hence the attendant complexities– like ours. Some of the countries which have harmonised the taxes on the sales of most goods and services include France, Italy, the UK, South Korea, Japan, Singapore, Sweden, Hong Kong/China, Austria, Malaysia, Canada, Germany, Russia and Australia; the last 6 being federations.

In Australia, a GST was introduced with effect from 1st July 2000. Although the idea had existed since 1975, it was always treated with a great deal of scepticism. The proposal was revived in the 1990s by the Liberal Party's leader John Hewson. However, after being asked by journalist Mike Willesee to explain the arithmetic of how the price of a birthday cake would be impacted by the proposed GST, it was given up on the assumption of being "too complicated". In that interview, to Willesee's statement, "You tell us in what you've published that the cost of cake goes down, the cost of confectionery goes up, there's icing and maybe ice-cream, and then there's candles on top of it", Hewson could only say, " To give you an accurate answer, I need to know exactly what type of cake to give a detailed answer", prompting Willesee to retort, "If the answer to a birthday cake is so complex–you do have an overall problem with the GST, don't you?"

In 1996, the Liberals won the federal elections after promising 'never ever' to introduce a GST. The 'never ever' lasted for only two years, when, under the leadership of John Howard, the Liberals fought the 1998 election on the issue of the introduction of a GST that would replace all existing sales taxes and apply to all goods and services. Despite a negative vote swing of 4.6 percent, they formed the next government and introduced the GST in 1999, replacing the federal wholesale sales tax system. Gradually many state and territorial government taxes, duties and levies such as banking taxes and stamp duties were abolished. The consequent budget shortfall was compensated for by the revenue earned from the GST that was shared with the states. Simultaneously, for greater acceptance, rates of federally levied personal income tax and company tax were reduced to absorb the shocks emanating from the GST. It was understood that the GST would take time to stabilise, and its intended consequences like reduced business costs which would spur consumer demands would flow over time, and no miracles could be expected in the short term. In the 2001 federal elections, the opposition Labour party made its rollback a centre-piece of its electoral campaign, describing it as a "bastard tax", but lost the election.

The Australian GST has a rate of 10 percent with a system of input credits, like in India. Like in Canada or France, here concerns were also raised that a GST would impact the poor much more than the rich, being a regressive tax, but the likely regressive potential was mitigated by adopting a set of measures like abolition of a federal wholesale sales tax, as well as some stamp duties and fuel taxes, besides effecting reductions in rates of personal income tax and state banking tax side by side with the launching of a GST.

However, the reactions and counter-reactions were very much like what we are witnessing in India today. The behaviours of businesses and consumers were also strikingly similar in the two countries. In the period leading to the introduction of the GST, consumption rose sharply as consumers rushed to purchase goods that they perceived would be more expensive in the post-GST period, and traders and businesses destocked and cleaned up their inventory by offering lucrative discounts, just like in India. Thus, immediately after the GST came into effect in July 2000, both consumption and economic growth declined. Inflation soared by as much as 2.8 percent in the quarter which ended in September 2000. In the first fiscal quarter of 2001, the Australian economy recorded negative economic growth for the first time in more than 10 years. The opposition, exactly like in India, cried foul and blamed the GST. Like in India, small businesses complained of cumbersome procedures and glitches faced in the online submission of quarterly Business Activity Statements to the Australian Taxation Office as required under law; one study in fact estimated that costs of compliance to the new tax system amounted to 3 percent of the annual turnovers of small businesses. But consumption soon returned to normal and growth picked up gradually. In each of the countries that had introduced a GST, the economy had underperformed in the year of its introduction, something that was anticipated and, in fact, is being witnessed in India today. One study pointed to the negative impact of a GST on the real estate market, projecting a steep rise in prices of new homes by 8 percent and a steeper fall in demand by 12 percent. However, the real estate market returned to boom between 2002 and 2004 with prices and demands both soaring, especially in cities like Sydney and Melbourne.

Ten years hence, the GST was recognised as a resounding success in Australia that had replaced inefficient taxes that imposed high deadweight costs while raising little revenue. As Professor Sinclair Davidson of RMIT University wrote, "The GST was the last great tax reform that Australia experienced. In the subsequent ten years we have become accustomed to tax cuts, not new taxes."

Short term inflationary impact has characterised the switchover to a GST in almost every country, and governments had intervened appropriately to arrest this, sometimes adopting extraordinary measures and policies for limiting price escalation by businesses like freezing prices and profit margins, price monitoring, publicity campaigns, enactment of anti-inflation laws and reduction of other taxes. When VAT was introduced in India from 1st April 2005, no such measure was adopted. As a result, there were either unexplained increases in prices, or businesses refused to reduce the MRPs despite a decline in the tax rates of their products, as pointed out by the CAG in 2010. We ought to be more proactive this time, having learnt from the past.

One particular concern in Australia as in India was to ensure that there was no undue profiteering in the implementation phase and that the benefit of reduced costs was passed on to the consumers to mitigate the immediate impact of a GST on prices. The anti-profiteering provisions of our GST Act derived some useful ideas from the GST Acts of Australia and Malaysia in which there are stringent anti-profiteering provisions.

Social acceptance of any new tax is vital for its success, and public criticisms and debates play a significant role in informing and moulding public opinion. The political risks and costs of introducing the GST are always high, but proper management of transition and follow up can always provide insulation to the risks.

Nearer home, Indonesia was the first ASEAN country to implement a GST in 1984. All eight members have a GST now in place, Malaysia being the latest to join the GST brigade in 2015. Malaysia had been toying with the idea of introducing a GST for a long time. When a GST Bill was introduced for the first time in 2009 in the Malaysian Parliament, it attracted mounting criticism from public and political opposition, and the bill had to be withdrawn. Finally, on 1st April 2015, a uniform 6 percent GST was launched, replacing the sales-and-service tax regime of indirect taxes. The effect of replacement of the single-stage sales and services taxes to a multi-stage GST was highly disruptive –inflation went up immediately, consumer confidence nosedived and public protests erupted. However, the timing of its implementation had coincided with the steep global slump in oil and gas prices between 2014 and 2016, and the successful implementation of the GST had helped the federal treasury to cushion the impact of lower oil revenues; by that time the public protests and opposition had also fizzled out. 12 months later, business confidence was restored and 70 percent of the businesses surveyed reported growth. As the Malaysian Prime Minister had rightly said, “the GST has been our saviour”.

Like in India, Malaysia also had a black economy problem, with estimates of it ranging from 9 percent-27 percent of GDP, and emphasising the need for a more efficient and effective tax enforcement regime. The World Bank has reported that the “hidden or informal economy” constitutes 31 percent of the Malaysian economy. Just like in India in the post-demonetisation period, the Malaysian post-GST implementation phase had also seen many searches and seizures to unearth black money. The procedural changes necessitated by the GST were phenomenal and it shook up the entire gamut of commercial operations in Malaysia. At the end of June 2016, there were over 7,294 GST appeal cases, indicating the extent of taxpayer grievances. But the government had created a social safety net in the form of monetary assistance to compensate poor households, along with a package of measures to mitigate the impact of the new tax, benefiting about 4.7 million households and 2.7 million single individuals, to address the adverse distributional effect of the GST. Despite this, the concerns of the small and medium enterprises (SMEs) were not properly addressed, about one-third of the firms audited by the Malaysian Customs during September 2016 was facing problems very similar to those SMEs are facing in India.[13]

The GST contributed about 18 percent to Malaysia's federal revenue in 2015, a share that is bound to increase substantially with an expanding economy. Share of GSTs varies widely from country to country, depending upon the structure of their tax systems and expenditure priorities, and the rates and threshold amounts also show wide variations. Thus, no horizontal comparison among different countries in respect of a GST will be valid. About 160 countries have adopted some form of VAT or GST, but most of these are vastly different from the dual destination-based system that Canada and India are following. Among the OECD countries, most of which had switched over to VAT/GST during the 1970s and 1980s, Chile raises as much as 55 percent of its total tax revenue from its GST, followed by Turkey (44 percent), and Mexico (36 percent), while Japan raises only 20 percent of its total revenue from its GST, as against the OECD average of 33 percent.

As regards the rate, it varies from 5 percent in Canada, 6 percent in Malaysia, and 15 percent in New Zealand to 19 percent in Germany, 20 percent in France and 27 percent in Hungary. Japan had introduced a consumption tax in 1989, the rate of which was increased from 3 to 5 percent in 1997. The effect was devastating and Japan went into recession. In 2013, the Shinzo Abe Government increased the rate to 8 percent, while postponing further the proposed increase to 10 percent until October 2019.

The GST experiences of these and other countries make one thing clear – that GSTs everywhere have followed more or less the same track and run the same course, causing similar ripples, disruptions and turbulence, but everywhere these distortions have proved to be transitory. Ultimately, the

---

[13] Just after his unexpected win in the general elections in Malaysia in 2018, the new Prime Minister Mahathir Mohamad had rolled back the GST in order to fulfil his poll promise, replacing it with a moderate sales-and-service tax. He had promised to scrap the GST as people were unhappy over the rising living costs. While the government hoped to bring down the rising inflation by this move, the credit rating agencies, like Moody's and Fitch, had warned of serious economic consequences, including higher budget deficit and fall in the revenue. However, since the crude price had reached $79 a barrel, the government was confident that it would be able to absorb the shocks likely to result from rolling back the GST. Malaysia is the only country to have rolled back the GST after having launched it.

new system has found its own equilibrium in every country where it was launched. Everywhere, there were initial spikes in inflation and economic growth took a beating in the immediate aftermath of the launch of the GST. Eventually growth had picked up greater momentum, and inflation could be controlled everywhere.

The Indian experience is a repeat of this universal trend and there is no particular reason for despondency at the developments that we are witnessing again. These are undesirable but not unanticipated outcomes, if we are to relate to the experiences of other countries in our connected world, because behaviour of the consumer and businesses remains identical everywhere. The transition phase we are passing through could be longer and more difficult than one might wish, especially in a complex and diverse country like India. It is crucial that this phase be carefully negotiated, by drawing lessons from the countries discussed above. As these experiences show, without exception, GSTs deliver in the long run, and by long run, I estimate a time horizon of 3-5 years. In the end, GSTs have been working well in every country.

Global experiences also tell us that our GST design may not be as imperfect as it is made out to be by its critics. In many countries, there are multiple rates and a wide variety of exempted goods and services, and essential supplies needed by the poor often attract a reduced rate. Real estate and petroleum are covered in some countries but excluded in others. There cannot be a one-size-fits-all solution; different countries have different systems at the national and sub-national levels. SMEs have been impacted negatively almost everywhere; apart from their genuine concerns about lack of capacity and technological weaknesses which need to be addressed urgently, a part of their problems also arises from a certain reluctance to comply with the new tax regime which makes tax evasion difficult. Awareness and public education are essential for the success of any new system, to make way for its acceptance and voluntary compliance, without which no tax system can ever achieve its objectives. There are many lessons to be learnt from the international experiences and the sooner we learn them, the better it will equip us to avoid the pitfalls.

5. PETROLEUM SECTOR UNDER GST: A CHIMERA[14]

(To bring the petroleum sector under a GST is not simple. It requires a carefully calibrated approach over a sustained period.)

Stung by the opposition attack on the rising prices of petrol and diesel despite a drastic fall in the global crude prices since 2014, the Finance Ministry has finally reduced the Basic Excise Duty on these fuels by ₹2 per litre with effect from 4th October and urged states to cut their levies on the fuels by 5 percent. After the cut, the retail prices of petrol and diesel in Delhi will be around ₹68 and ₹57 per litre, respectively, almost the same price level as in August 2017.

From 2010 until mid-2014, world oil prices had remained fairly stable at around $110 a barrel. However, since June 2014, prices started falling steeply, to below $50 a barrel (about 159 litres) by January 2015. It was due to the snowballing effect from many causes: weak global demand due to insipid economic growth, a surge in US production, and OPEC's decision not to cut on production. After touching an all-time low of $28 a barrel in January 2016, the price recovered somewhat and is now hovering around $50 again. However, this has not made any change to the prices of petrol or diesel in India; the drop if any has only been marginal, and in fact, prices have risen by 8 to 10 percent in the last 2 months. A litre of petrol and diesel cost ₹71.41 and ₹55.49 in Delhi in May 2014. Before the latest cut in prices, their prices were respectively ₹70.38 and ₹58.72 per litre. Thus, while the imported prices have fallen by more than half, the Indian price has remained the same. The reason is taxes, levied both by the centre and the states on all petroleum products, which has been attracting increasing criticism from the opposition, especially when the GST has created inflationary pressures on the economy affecting demand and consumption, and in turn slowing down the economy.

On October 6th, BJP-ruled Gujarat became the first state to announce a cut on the VAT on petrol and diesel. Other BJP-ruled states, such as Madhya Pradesh, Chhattisgarh, Uttarakhand, and Jharkhand, with the possible

---

[14] Originally published in *The Statesman* as "Petroleum Chimera", 27th July, 2017.

exception of Haryana, and states where it shares power, like Bihar, seemed likely to follow suit. While the GST has covered most sectors, the significant exclusions have been petroleum and real estate. The clamour is now becoming louder every day to bring these sectors under the GST. Petrol and diesel prices affect almost every sector and bringing them under the GST regime is expected to give a real boost to the economy at a time when it is widely perceived to be underperforming. The tax reforms must be extended to this sector, and if the states could agree on a mechanism to levy the GST for oil products and forgo their rights to levy the VAT on these products, with a suitable scheme of compensation being worked out by the centre, the prices of petrol and diesel can come down immediately. Unfortunately, there are formidable constraints and hurdles to be overcome before we can do this, and the solution is not so simple.

The centre earns a large part of its own revenues not only from excise and customs duty on petro-products, but also from a cess on crude oil and taxes on the profits of oil companies and dividends from oil PSUs. In 2015-16, it collected ₹2.58 lakh crore from these taxes, which accounted for 36 percent of the total indirect taxes collected during the year. This is more than the total central government expenditure of ₹2.04 lakh crore on all centrally sponsored schemes during or the total subsidy of ₹2.42 lakh crore paid for fertiliser, food and petroleum during that year. In other words, the oil revenue accounts for almost all of our welfare expenditure or subsidies. The petroleum sector contributes between 17 and 26 percent of the total VAT revenues of the states, which collected another ₹1.60 lakh crore from VAT on petro-products, cess and royalty on crude oil and entry tax, etc. The total contribution of the petroleum sector to revenues of the central and state governments in 2015-16 was ₹4.18 lakh crore, or 3.0 percent of India's GDP (the tax-GDP ratio in India is around 17 percent). Despite the latest duty cut, the centre's oil revenue is estimated to rise by more than 10 percent to 2.86 lakh crore in 2016-17. It is therefore only natural that neither the states nor the centre would agree to bring this sector under the GST and thereby risk losing their discretion to increase the taxes even when crude prices have fallen worldwide.

As of August 2017, a litre of imported crude oil cost only ₹20.19. After taking into account the operational, refining, transportation and marketing costs, as well as the margins of oil refining and marketing companies, the basic cost of a litre of petrol became ₹29.53. The dealer commission was ₹3.23, bringing the final cost to ₹32.76 a litre as against its market price of ₹68.88 (in Delhi). The difference of ₹36.12 per litre was on account of taxes: central excise duty (₹21.48) and state VAT (₹14.64). For diesel, the total cost including dealer commission of ₹2.17 per litre came to ₹31.29, and the final market price was ₹57.06 a litre after accounting for an excise duty of ₹17.33 and VAT of ₹8.44 per litre. Thus, the total taxes paid on the basic cost presently amount to 110 percent for petrol and 82 percent on diesel.

Next consider this; in June 2014, when the crude price was more than $100, the excise duty was only ₹9.20 per litre of petrol and ₹3.46 per litre of diesel. As the prices have dropped more than half since then, the excise duty on petrol has more than doubled, and that on diesel has risen by 5 times. Similarly, the VAT rates on petrol and diesel in June 2014 were, respectively, 20 and 12.5 percent of the basic price; in August 2017, these rates increased to 27 and 16.8 percent, respectively, in addition to cess of ₹2,500 per ton. Prices vary from state to state, as states charge VAT at different rates. Accordingly, the price of petrol varies from ₹68.9 in Delhi to ₹78 in Mumbai, and diesel varies from ₹57.1 in Delhi to ₹60.6 in Mumbai.

Given the implication of the petroleum sector taxes on the revenues of both the central and state governments, it is indeed difficult to bring this sector immediately under the GST regime, as both governments will then have to slash their welfare expenditure severely, which might have serious political and electoral consequences, or at least that is what the governments fear. The petroleum sector in fact receives an annual subsidy of ₹25,000 crore, mainly on account of subsidising the prices of diesel and cooking gas. Also, 42 percent of all excise duty collected by the centre passes on the states under the Finance Commission devolutions. Much of it is used by the states to finance populist schemes like loan waivers for farmers.

Based on the consumption and tax data provided by the Petroleum Planning and Analysis Cell, and taking only diesel and motor spirit into account, a crude estimate of the revenue neutral common rate for these 2 products works out at ₹32.95 per litre, including both the excise and VAT, in lieu of ₹36.12 for petrol and ₹25.77 for diesel. This will imply a tax rate of almost 100 percent on the current basic price of petrol and 105 percent of the current basic price of diesel after dealer commissions. The highest rate allowed by the GST today is 40 percent, though the highest rate being levied presently is only 28 percent on goods like tobacco or perfumes. Clearly, under the present structure, bringing this sector under the GST regime may not be sustainable if revenues are to be protected. The roadmap for such an eventuality must be carefully calibrated, first by equalising the excise on diesel and petrol. Obviously then, the price of diesel will go up, whereas the price of petrol will fall, but it will correct many distortions that afflict the present system, leading to reduced demand for diesel and diesel-driven vehicles, and a decline in diesel imports, reducing vehicular pollution. This should be followed by making the states agree to a uniform rate of VAT throughout the country, and the rates of both excise and VAT on these products should then be brought down in phases, in slow but sure steps. The resultant loss in revenue will be compensated by higher volumes of consumption until their ultimate integration into the GST framework.

The road will be long, but by eliminating the arbitrariness of the current mechanism open to manipulation by both the centre and the states, the goal of one common market will be promoted, in addition to reducing the inflationary potential of the economy.

6. TREAT THE DISEASE, NOT THE SYMPTOMS[15]

(While schemes for the direct benefit transfer of subsidies launched in India can eliminate many operational inefficiencies, they are inadequate in empowering the poor. We can draw lessons from conditional cash transfer programs, like Bolsa Família, which has helped transform Brazil's socio-economic landscape by empowering the poor and vulnerable. We can begin by reforming our dysfunctional Panchayat-run schools and primary health centres in villages.)

The administration of massive amounts of subsidies by the union and state governments for various purposes has always been plagued by pilferages, waste and corruption. To prevent this, the Government of India has launched the program for direct benefit transfer (DBT) of subsidies to the bank accounts of beneficiaries by linking these accounts to their AADHAR numbers. The scheme, as expected, has brought transparency into the system, while reducing corruption and leakages.

Starting initially with 20 districts and covering scholarships and social security pensions in January 2013, within 10 months, DBT was extended to 121 districts covering 21 schemes run by nine union ministries. These schemes pertained to the welfare of women and children, especially girls, besides providing scholarships to students, including those from disadvantaged sections of society. In November 2014, the Government of India launched a scheme for extending the DBT in respect of LPG subsidy in 54 districts in 11 states, whereby cash equivalents of subsidy amounts – the difference between market price and subsidised price of LPG cylinders– were to be transferred directly into the bank accounts of LPG consumers, while making the cylinders available only at a single market price. By January 2015, the scheme covered over 15 crore consumers across all 646 districts of the country, making it the world's largest direct subsidy roll-out scheme.

There is no doubt that the DBT scheme has increased the efficiency of subsidy administration beyond measure and it is hoped that the scheme will

---

[15] Originally published in *The Statesman* as "Directly Says It", 24th and 25th May, 2015.

soon be extended to cover the entire gamut of subsidies in the country. Here, the government has successfully leveraged technology to improve the economic lives of the poor, and achieved better targeting of beneficiaries while ensuring economical and efficient transfer of financial resources to poor households to 'expand the set of antipoverty tools the government has in its armoury', as the Economic Survey for 2015-16 has noted. The survey has claimed that such well-targeted cash transfers can boost household consumption and asset ownership, while increasing the effectiveness of the existing anti-poverty programs. The technological platform that can facilitate this in a less distortive manner has been named the 'JAM Number Trinity', covering the **J**an Dhan Yojana, **A**adhaar and **M**obile numbers, and the delivery mechanisms that have been identified are mobile money and post offices with their enviable network of 1.55 lakh offices reaching out to the most remote corners of the country, which can be used to extend the direct cash transfer benefits to people living in the furthest outposts of India.

Doubtlessly, cash subsidy is better than price subsidy, which distorts markets in various ways that ultimately hurt the poor, and there cannot be two opinions that DBT is a much better option for rolling out subsidies. There also cannot be any dispute that, in a country that still falters in defining poverty and fumbles in estimating the number of its poor, eliminating or phasing down subsidies cannot be an option. The poor, the marginalised and the vulnerable must be provided with an adequate safety net, with a view to ultimately empowering them with the income-earning capacity so as to obviate the need for any more subsidy. The question is about the route to such empowerment, and when this question is considered, the optimism exuded by the Economic Survey that by seamlessly linking the JAM Number Trinity, once all the subsidies are rolled into a single or a few monthly transfers, the *Nirvana* of real progress in terms of direct income support to the poor will be attained seems rather misplaced.

Subsidies, even if targeted carefully and transferred efficiently by eliminating leakages, may not necessarily transform overnight into an empowering and enabling mechanism, helping the poor to overcome the hopelessness of their situations. To emerge from poverty, the only viable option is employment which demands a skill-set. Such a skill-set can be imparted only by quality education, to which the poor have no access. Unless conditions are created for such empowerment, a subsidy will always remain what it is, a debilitating dole, making the poor permanently dependent on the government for their sustenance and thus making them a captive vote bank for any political party that holds out the promises of such doles, as we have witnessed in election after election in our country. It suits the political class to keep the poor in a permanent state of impoverishment, and empowering them in real terms by developing employable skill and knowledge is not in the interest of political parties, given the trends in our current socio-political discourses. The keys to such empowerment are education and health of the youth –both always go together. We have a plethora of schemes devised for extending doles to the poor in the name of anti-poverty intervention, but mechanisms necessary to create and augment the earning capacity of the poor to overcome poverty are singularly absent in these schemes.

Seven decades since independence from exploitative colonial rules and 11 5-year plans that have doled out lakhs of crores of rupees through countless anti-poverty schemes have failed to eradicate even absolute poverty characterised by severe deprivation of basic human needs. A quarter of the population still remains illiterate, and suffers from serious handicaps arising from a lack of quality healthcare, drinking water, nutrition and sanitation. Public infrastructure for primary, secondary and college education remains pathetic in most places, barring a few isolated islands in the elite institutions managed and funded by the central government. As the Annual Status of Education Report published every year by the educational NGO Pratham indicates, half the children in our primary schools are nowhere near their class-age appropriate learning levels. The delivery of merit goods and services like education and health remains dismal, if not non-existent, in most states. Thus, millions of graduates and post-graduates emerge every year from our temples of learning without acquiring any employable skill-set or knowledge. Public healthcare also presents a similar dismal scenario, with services available at most of the primary and secondary health centres remaining far below optimal. We cannot dream of achieving higher or double-digit growth rates touted by our leaders if the vast multitudes of our rural (non-city) dwelling people are left out of the growth trajectory, unable to afford the cost of private education or healthcare, and have access only to the mostly dysfunctional municipal/Panchayat schools or equally dysfunctional government dispensaries. The end result is that they remain permanently at the bottom of the pyramid, adding little value to the economic system, and getting little benefit and hardly any value in their lives.

The most serious problem that continues to plague our delivery system is the state's very limited implementation capacity to target and deliver services to the poor. It does not arise from any constraint of resources; in fact, the government spends about ₹3.78 lakh crore –more than 4 percent of our GDP– every year on providing subsidies on a few commodities and services like rice, wheat, pulses, sugar, kerosene, LPG, naphtha, water, electricity, diesel, fertiliser, iron ore and the railways. Compare this to the central government's total plan outlay of ₹4.26 lakh crore as per the revised estimates of 2014-15 to understand the magnitude of government subsidy-expenditure, which serves only a very limited purpose for a limited time-span. It is not simply the efficient allocation of resources which can be the route to the *Nirvana* as so consummately wished for in the Economic Survey. It is actually a question of outcomes, for which the focus needs to be shifted from the restructuring of economic reforms to the restructuring of our delivery system.

Some of the countries have successfully bridged the gap between the two by novel designing of the social welfare schemes and addressed their inherent structural incapacities, and in doing so, not only have lifted millions of their inhabitants out of poverty by empowering them in real terms, but also eliminated absolute poverty and boosted real disposable income in the hands of the people. Brazil and Mexico are often cited as examples of what a well-designed government program can achieve. Much has been said about Brazil's *Bolsa Família* program launched by Luiz Inácio Lula da Silva, the President of Brazil from 2003 to 2011. Successful implementations of social sector welfare programs like *Bolsa Família* to address the question of poverty and *Fome Zero* (Zero Hunger) to combat hunger were the major hallmarks of his presidency and have redefined the socio-economic landscape in his country, from which we also can draw lots of lessons.

Bolsa Família, meaning *'Family Allowance'* in Portuguese, is a part of the federal assistance program of the Brazilian Government. It is not simply a poverty-reduction strategy like our MGNREGA, but is meant to address the needs of the poor and fill in the existing gaps and inequities in the delivery and actual outcomes of education, health and social assistance programs of the government. To understand its role, we have to go back to Brazil's socio-economic conditions in the 1990s.

Up until the early 1990s, Brazil was mired in a web of crises, much like our own. About 45 percent of the population lived below the poverty line –half of them sunk in absolute poverty. With the Gini coefficient at more than 0.6, it also had one of the highest income inequalities in the world. Poverty, exclusion and backwardness made the country a potential volcano, ready to erupt at any moment. Under the new 1988 Constitution, the country undertook extensive reforms through the liberalisation of trade and financial sectors, decentralisation and deregulation, elimination of forex barriers, privatisation, and enforcement of fiscal discipline which together bolstered the market and generated additional income. The additional income was meant to be spent on a social welfare program and by the beginning of the new millennium; there was a horde of these programs, much like in our country, often with overlapping objectives and unclear goals. The elimination of hunger, reduction of poverty, improving the delivery of quality education and healthcare and ensuring gender equality, were the focuses of most of these programs. Different executing agencies, diverse spending modalities, multiple funding sources, as well as diverse information systems and duplication of efforts, were affecting the implementation of these programs, much like in our own plan schemes. Some of the programs also featured a component of cash transfer, like our DBT; some even transferred the cash on fulfilment of certain conditions, making it a Conditional Cash Transfer (CCT) as opposed to a DBT. These conditional issues were based on two objectives: (1) to alleviate poverty today, and (2) to increase the poor people's stock of human capital for tomorrow. To fulfil the first, identified poor families were given program payments in cash. The second was achieved by making those payments conditional to specified behaviours on the part of the beneficiaries, like compulsory enrolment and attendance of their children in schools and their compulsory immunisation and regular public health check-ups in government-run clinics.

After Lula da Silva became president in 2003, all these diverse programs were integrated and unified into *Bolsa Família*, with redefined vision, objectives and goals which focused on access to social services like health, education and social assistance as much as upon the outcomes of the programs on a sustained basis, by improving food and nutritional security and achieving a synergy between different government programs. As Soares (2011, 55) had said, "The evolution of *Bolsa Família* is the story of a fight for legitimacy in the sphere of social protection policies in Brazil." It also put a target to cover all the poor families, estimated at 11.1 million by 2011.

Under the program, cash benefits were extended to indigent families depending on their levels of income and impoverishment, but subject to certain conditions which included: (i) compulsory enrolment of all children in schools; (ii) their minimum 85 percent attendance every month to be reported by the schools; and (iii) regular visits to health centres and following the immunisation calendar of the Ministry of Health, to be reported by the health units at the municipal level. It thus provided a minimum income to poor and vulnerable families, while serving to lift their children out of poverty in future, by providing them with skill and knowledge and ensuring their health.

While the unification of various programs and redefining of the objectives streamlined the programs and processes, the constraints the nation faced in implementing the program were truly formidable. These basically arose from a lack of capacity, just like in our case. How does the government set up a quality infrastructure of hundreds of schools with qualified teachers and health clinics with qualified doctors to cover all the targeted families? Without the teachers, doctors and schools and clinics, the program would only remain on paper. Furthermore, setting up any kind of school will not do –quality was the keyword here, without which the objective of creating a stock of future human capital capable of adding to the productive capacity and earning incomes was unachievable. Side by side, a real-time information system had to be created for recording school attendance and clinic check-ups. Funds, however, were not a major constraint. International aid agencies also pledged their support to the program on the understanding that quality education would boost economic growth by raising incomes and also improve the quality of life. Besides, the program was inexpensive –total investment in the program was only 0.2 percent of GDP in 2003, which subsequently increased to 0.43 percent in 2012. Despite this, the creation of the requisite massive capacity was a daunting challenge not addressable in the short term; hence the program had to be rolled out in phases, starting with a few municipalities in 2003, and gradually extending after creating capacity in terms of the establishment of schools and clinics with qualified teachers and doctors, to cover the entire country by 2011.

In 2009, the ceiling of 11.1 million beneficiaries was revised upwards to 12.9 million families, also to include the non-poor but vulnerable families that ran the risk of sliding below the poverty line; this led to an increase in program expenditure to 0.43 percent of GDP. In 2012, the coverage was extended further to 13.7 million families comprising 56 million people, making it the largest CCT program in the world. The high coverage and good targeting of the program led to astounding results. Within a decade, by 2012, poverty in Brazil had fallen to just 9 percent of the population; extreme poverty almost disappeared as per capita income rose from US$3,000 in 2003 to US$13,000 in 2012. There were distinct improvements in the job market, the real minimum labour wage also increased, and consequently inequality was reduced. Besides, there was no negative impact on labour supply, unlike sometimes observed in the case of our MGNREGA. *Bolsa Família's* contribution to the reduction of poverty, inequality and extreme poverty was estimated to be very significant by all scholars and evaluators.

Other Latin American countries also replicated similar CCT programs with equivalent measures of success, like *Oportunidades* in Mexico or *Chile Solidario* in Chile for extending support to impoverished families. These programs focused on social and economic inclusion while facilitating easier access of the poor to the government's social sector programs. Since then, many developing countries had set up some kind of CCT programs. Nearer home, Indonesia has implemented an unconditional cash transfer programme called *Bantuan Langsung Tunai* to mitigate the impact of fuel subsidy reductions for over 19 million poor and near-poor households like our LPG subsidy program, while a CCT program called *Program Keluarga Harapan* (PKH) started in 2007 has now been implemented in all its 33 provinces, covering around 1.5 million - about a quarter of the very poor Indonesian households. The objectives of PKH are very similar to those of *Bolsa Família*, to reduce poverty in the short run by aiding immediate consumption of the poor households, while investing in future generations through improved health and education to develop future human capital for making the final frontal attack on poverty in the long run.

Can we emulate some of these initiatives in our country after making the necessary adaptations and modifications to increase the efficiency and effectiveness of the delivery mechanisms of our anti-poverty program? Can we make our village school and primary health centre something like a model school and a model health clinic? If we can, it will be a win-win situation for all.

As Brazil's example has taught us, successful implementation needs the building up of capacity at the levels of municipalities by sourcing local talent and resources, and to extend the program coverage in a phased manner only after the requisite capacity has been created in this manner. We have our village panchayats at the bottom of the pyramid which are in direct contact with the grassroots level. It will not be difficult to equip them adequately for exercising effective monitoring at the local level. Suppose the Panchayat schools are to be manned by local talent - qualified, trained and adequately compensated. For carrying out the basic immunisation and nutritional checks of students in these schools, we may not need full-fledged doctors; paramedics produced with lesser effort may suffice. Careful designing and planning can take care of both these requirements in the medium term. Once we launch a CCT program, say in a few Panchayats to begin with, after meeting these requirements, its coverage can be extended in a phased manner, concomitant with the creation of required additional capacity. This can then transform the rural landscape –with students coming out of Panchayat schools, with the knowledge and skill appropriate to their age, with health and hope, armed to combat poverty. This will also stop migration of local talent to cities and derive better synergy from the existing infrastructure. The total additional expenditure will only be miniscule compared to what we are spending today on our anti-poverty programs and interventions. We may not realise the results in the short term, but national objectives are always achievable in the long run. Will a government take the plunge and dare to set its vision far into the future? Will it ever think of an alternative strategy for alleviation of poverty other than doles that only create dependence?

(Afterword: As per data released by the government, the shift to DBT has led to savings of over ₹50,000 crores during the last three years. The transfers through DBT have been increasing continuously. In 2016-17, ₹74, 502 crore were disbursed through DBT, benefiting more than 33 crore beneficiaries, compared to ₹7,367 crore benefiting 10.71 crore beneficiaries in 2013-14.)

SECTION 3

SUBOPTIMAL DELIVERY

1. Ten Years of MGNREGA
2. Mid-Day Reckoning
3. Death of Austerity
4. Coalgate Revisited
5. Let's Fix and Not Escape
6. Educational Paradox
7. Work from Home to Save Our Cities

1. TEN YEARS OF THE MGNREGA[16]

(Despite making some positive impact, the MGNREGA could not address the structural issues that lie at the roots of poverty. It never addressed the basic issues of imparting quality education, health and employable skillset, a combination of which alone can make a dent in poverty through providing gainful employment. Despite its extensive outreach, the MGNREGA still basically remains a program of dole distribution.)

It is now 10 years since the Mahatma Gandhi National Rural Employment Guarantee Act (MGNREGA) was enacted by the UPA Government to eliminate poverty in India. While the Congress party, as well as a section of economists, believed that it had benefited millions and brought the party to power for the second consecutive time in 2009, many economists have accused it of draining our precious resources without getting concomitant benefits. Though the Prime Minister had criticised the MGNREGA as "a living monument" of the failure of the UPA Government because of which even "after 60 years of independence, people had to dig pits", considerations of realpolitik seem to have twisted the thinking among the NDA since then and its tenth anniversary was celebrated by the government and the Congress alike with a great deal of fanfare –with both claiming credit for its successful implementation.

At a seminar organised by the Rural Development Ministry, the Finance Minister had promised additional funds over and above the budget allocation for the scheme, which was understandable, since the country is still recovering from two successive droughts and the MGNREGA can justifiably relieve rural distress to some extent. No doubt, the MGNREGA also provides valuable rural employment during seasons when there is little farm-based activity. However, the central question is: does it end their poverty? Does it empower them with education, health and employable skills, a combination of which can alone lift them above poverty and bring permanent sunshine in their lives? The available evidence suggests otherwise –that it only helps the poor to subsist at a level below the poverty line and that the intended benefits do not always reach them.

---

[16] Originally published in *Economic & Political Weekly*, 1st August, 2017.

The Ministry of Rural Development claims that the MGNREGA marks a paradigm shift from all previous allocation-based wage employment programs and is unlike any other in its scale, architecture and thrust with its focus on transparency and accountability. The MGNREGA combined several anti-poverty employment generation programs and was launched with the objective of bringing livelihood security of households in rural areas by providing at least 100 days of guaranteed wage employment in every financial year to every household whose adult members volunteer for unskilled manual work. The MGNREGA is a demand-driven, right based program in which the government is obligated to provide employment to everyone demanding it, and provision of work is triggered by demand for work by job-seekers. Creation of durable assets and strengthening the livelihood resource base of the rural poor were other important objectives of the scheme. The work was to be provided at the minimum wage rate and close to the applicant's village. The principal implementing agencies of the scheme were the Gram Panchayats. The MGNREGA emphasised community participation in planning, implementation, social audit and transparency and placed a complete ban on the use of contractors. By 2008, the MGNREGA's outreach had extended to the whole of rural India. Funding was in the ratio of 75 percent to 25 percent between the centre and the implementing states. The durable assets that were actually created were limited mostly to the building of mud roads and embankments or cutting the overgrowth on road margins or desilting of tanks or reclamation of fallow land and the like. They have very limited long-term effects and were labour intensive, but required no special skill. They can hardly be called rural investment in the sense that no income generating assets were created out of the funds.

₹34,699 crore were earmarked for the MGNREGA in the Union Budget for 2015-16, and in the current fiscal period ₹38500 were allocated to the scheme. Similar amounts were provided every year throughout the last decade, and more than ₹300,000 crore have thus been fed into the MGNREGA so far, but their effect in making any significant reduction of poverty for the country as a whole still remains to be seen, despite contrary claims by its hardcore supporters. The issue has become so emotive that even a mild criticism of this program evokes the strongest and loudest chorus of condemnation from its defenders, and the high pitch of emotions often silences the demands for a dispassionate and objective analysis of its benefits vis-à-vis the costs.

The NDA government did not reduce the budget allocation for MGNREGA after coming to power, but unlike in the earlier years, the funds meant for this program are now being routed through the state budgets, direct transfer of funds having been abolished, thus giving states more control over the use of these funds. However, the capacity of the states to utilise the funds productively remains a crucial issue –and these capacities vary widely across the states.

It is undeniable that the MGNREGA has helped alter the rural scenario in India over the last decade to a large extent. Studies have noted a positive impact of MGNREGA funds on household income and monthly per capita expenditure. Most significant has been the impact of the MGNREGA on rural demand and wages, especially in agriculture wage rates. The MGNREGA-notified wages have increased significantly across all states since 2006. Studies have also highlighted the benefits to women and Adivasis, not only in terms of income-consumption effects or enhancement of choice and capability, but in correcting the gender-skewedness.[17] Socio-economic variables, like annual per capita income, monthly per capita expenditure on food, annual per child expenditure on education, per capita savings, condition of the dwelling houses, access to healthcare facility etc., have improved as a result of this scheme.[18] Seasonal migration of rural labour has come down significantly due to the opportunities of employment provided under the scheme, while the benefits by way of additional incomes were used by the rural households primarily for food security, education of dependents, healthcare and debt repayment.[19]

But it is also equally true that many studies conducted over the years pointed to the sub-optimal performance of the scheme due to a number of factors. These studies indicated that the scheme was becoming supply-driven and top-down in nature, instead of remaining demand-driven and bottoms-up as envisaged[20] and that the average number of days of employment per

---

[17] Pankaj, Ashok & Rukmini Tankha, "Empowerment Effects of the NREGS on Women Workers: A Study in Four States", *EPW*, Vol. 45, Issue No. 30, 24th Jul, 2010

[18] Sarkar, Prattoy, Kumar, Jagdish & Supriya, "Impact of MGNREGA on Reducing Rural Poverty and Improving Socio-economic Status of Rural Poor: A Study in Burdwan District of West Bengal", in *Agricultural Economics*, Research Review Conference Number, 2011

[19] Kareemulla K, Ramasundaram P, Kumar S, Rama Rao C. A., "Impact of National Rural Employment Guarantee Scheme in India on Rural Poverty and Food Security". *Curr Agri Res* 2013; 1(1):13-28. http://dx.doi.org/10.12944/CARJ.1.1.02

[20] Mukhopadhyay, Abhiroop, Himanshu & M R Sharan, "NREGS in Rajasthan", *EPW*, Vol. 50, Issue No. 6, 7th Feb, 2015

household was declining over time[21]. However, its impact on rural poverty has at best only been modest.

The central question is whether any such right and entitlement-based program can really address or reduce poverty, without integrating capacity development as an essential element of strategy. While such programs may reduce the intensity of poverty in the beneficiary households in a limited scale, the impact of such a scheme on poverty alleviation will always remain sub-optimal as it does not address the essential question of development of skill-based capacity which alone can ensure gainful employment along with economic growth.

Money spent on any social welfare program obviously has an opportunity cost, and given the huge resources being spent on the MGNREGA, questions will inevitably be raised on the opportunity cost of these humongous funds. The utility of programs like the MGNREGA or Food Security, which consume enormous sums but whose assumptions, methods of implementation and outcomes have all along been suspect and remain unsubstantiated by hard evidence, should engage our policy makers and thinkers into introspection and serious objective analysis. The UPA regime has launched quite a few of these schemes through the enactment of right-based legislations like right to work, right to food and right to education. Huge sums of money are being spent on these right-based schemes, but the cost to secure these rights and the cost of administrative mechanisms to extend these rights to the intended beneficiaries were never given much consideration. The now-defunct National Advisory Council which promoted and advocated many of these schemes never had to bother about the costs, since it was not directly or indirectly accountable to the taxpayers. Its task was to provide inputs in the 'formulation of policy by the government' and bring a 'special focus on social policy and the rights of the disadvantaged groups', and it made regular recommendations to the government on multiple and diverse areas, such as improvements in the rights to education, strengthening of Panchayats in tribal areas, livelihoods of small-holder farmers, development of the North East and rights of the disabled.

It has been pointed out by many commentators that their interventions were often guided more by electoral reasons than by concerns of growth and development. The result was the colossal leakages of public funds, weak or almost non-existent vigilance and monitoring over the use of these funds

---

[21] Gaiha, Raghav & Raghbendra Jha, "NREGS: Interpreting the Official Statistics", *EPW*, Vol. 47, Issue No. 40, 6th Oct, 2012

and sub-optimal achievement of their outcomes, evidence of which can be found aplenty in the reports of the Comptroller & Auditor General of India (CAG). An earlier CAG Report on the Performance Audit of the MGNREGA in 2008 had pointed out some serious deficiencies, such as non-transparent recording of employment demand, deficiencies in the planning and implementation process, poor record maintenance demonstrating the lack of reliability and the authenticity of the reported figures.[22]

The CAG's last report on the MGNREGA –Report no. 6 of 2013[23]– observed that even though the average wage cost or wages paid was rising, the benefits to a rural household were negated by the decline in employment provided per household. While the average wages increased from nearly ₹80 to 120 per person day between 2007-08 and 2011-12, the employment per household increased from around ₹40 per person per day to ₹60 in 2009-10, and then again declined to around ₹40 in 2011-12. The report also found that, while representation of women increased to around 48 percent during the last 3 years, the share of both SCs and STs continued to decline from around 30 percent to less than 20 percent for the STs, and a little more than 20 percent for the SCs during 2007-12. Since SCs/STs comprise the most vulnerable sections of the rural poor, their exclusion meant that the benefits were not reaching the poorest among the rural population.

About the so-called 'durable assets', the CAG report has observed that while the number of works taken up increased steadily from about 20 lakh in 2007-08 to more than 80 lakh in 2011-12, the number of works actually completed increased from about 1 million in 2007-08 to only about 2.5 million in 2010-11 and then declined to 2 million in 2011-12; most of the funds were still locked up in works-in progress. An asset is created only after the corresponding works are completed, and 80 percent of the works taken up under the MGNREGA remained incomplete.

However, the most damning finding of the CAG report was that there was hardly any correlation between the number of rural poor in a state and the number of households given employment under the MGNREGA. There are, of course, some notable exceptions like Andhra Pradesh, Chhattisgarh, Rajasthan, Tamil Nadu and West Bengal which seemed to have made better utilisation of MGNREGA funds, but Bihar, Odisha and Uttar Pradesh –the three most poverty-stricken states of the country– had shown very poor utilisation of MNGREGA funds along with Maharashtra. It is also

---

[22] Report No. 11 of 2008 of the Comptroller and Auditor General of India

[23] Report No. 6 of 2013 of the Comptroller and Auditor General of India

noteworthy that while in the poorer states, not all the poor households could be covered, in richer states most of the households covered were not poor. Thus, in Bihar, only 19 lakh households could derive the benefits, while the number of poor was nearly 5 crore. In contrast, in Tamilnadu, 58 lakh households were covered under the MNGREGA, while there were a total of 78 lakh poor people in the state. Rajasthan gave employment to 53 lakh households, while it accounted for 1.3 crore poor. In West Bengal, almost the same number of households (52.8 lakh) were provided employment under the MGNREGA, while there were 1.8 crore poor people in the state. Only a few states could cover almost the entire population of poor households, notably Assam, Odisha, Gujrat and Punjab. Thus, the benefits did not go to the poor as intended, but largely went to the non-poor.

Poverty Levels and Average Annual Number of Households Provided Employment in States

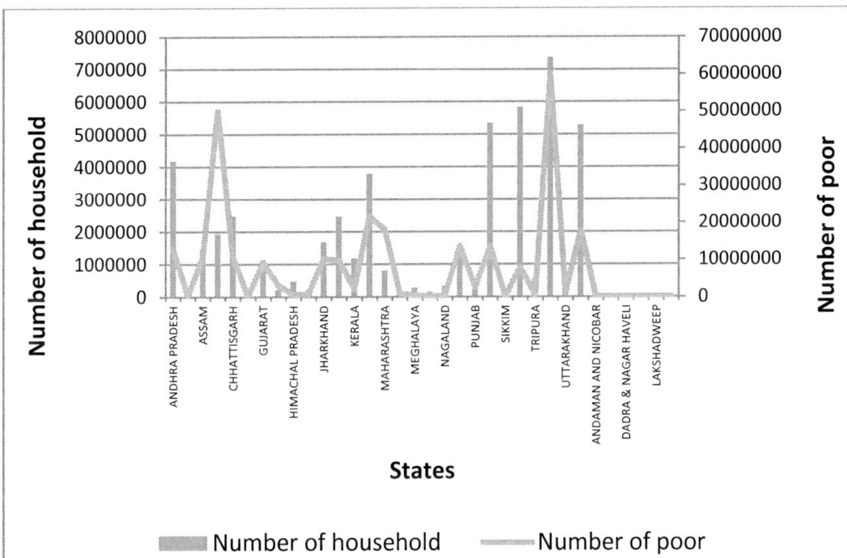

Source: CAG Report no. 6 of 2013-Union Government (Ministry of Rural Development)

The report also noted that Bihar, Maharashtra and Uttar Pradesh accounted for 46 percent of the rural poor, but could utilise only 20 percent of the MGNREGA funds; consequently only 20 percent of total households were provided employment under the scheme. In fact, only 4 states (Andhra Pradesh, Madhya Pradesh, Rajasthan and Uttar Pradesh) accounted for 50 percent of the total expenditure made under the scheme. There was thus little correlation between poverty level in a state and the implementation of the MGNREGA. As the CAG report states categorically, "the poorest of the poor were not fully able to exercise their rights under MGNREGA". This directly contradicts what the advocates of the scheme have always been claiming to justify its continuance in the same form.

The CAG report is silent on the reasons for the observed lack of correlation between the MGNREGA and poverty levels, but they are not difficult to divine. The poor do not get to overcome their poverty until they are empowered to do so, and empowerment comes only through education, health and acquisition of an employable skill-set. Programs like the MGNREGA do not facilitate any of these and merely provide subsistence-level aid, which may alleviate their poverty only temporarily. In fact, instead of addressing the roots of poverty, they only perpetuate it by denying the poor the only tools –education, health and skill– that can eradicate poverty through the generation of wealth in the economy and providing productive employment while ensuring economic growth. These programs only endeavoured to keep them below the bottom of the development ladder by ensuring mere subsistence without any real empowerment. Actually, in the name of employment, the MGNREGA is a scheme for the distribution of doles, and one that is poorly targeted. It is only a palliative cure, and one that works sub-optimally too while draining precious resources that could have been utilised to create assets, capacity and skill.[24]

In fact, as the experience with other similar anti-poverty schemes has shown, such dole-schemes never work. Maharashtra had a similar scheme, the Maharashtra Employment Guarantee Scheme (MCBIEGS), which guaranteed work for anyone who demanded it. As observed by the columnist Swaminathan A. Iyer, comparison of the rates of decline in poverty in various states did not show that Maharashtra's rate of decline was any faster than the national average. It had failed to make any dent in poverty and it was not due to the corruption and leakages that afflict the MGNREGA in most states. This was not only bad economics, but also poor politics. As Mr Iyer had pointed out, Narasimha Rao's Employment Assurance Scheme of 1994 –of which the MGNREGA was a replica– had provided 100 workdays per family in 200 backward districts. Rural employment rose from 875 million person-days in 1990-91 to 1,232 million in 1995-96. Despite this, the Congress was thrashed in the 1996 elections.

---

[24] Bhattacharjee, Govind, "Treat the disease, not the symptoms", in *Indian Economy: A Roadmap Towards Development*, Ed. Prof V. V. Singh, Flying Pen, Jaipur, 2016.

The success of the UPA in the 2009 elections need not necessarily have flowed from the MGNREGA.

The CAG report also cites numerous instances of leakages, corruption, inefficiencies and poor internal controls with very poor monitoring in the implementation of the MGNREGA. A randomly-selected snapshot of these observations may provide some interesting insights:

- Obtaining a job card was no guarantee for employment when demanded by the beneficiary. The CAG detected over 47,687 cases where beneficiaries were not provided employment on demand, and CAG audits check only a small sample of the total eligible population.
- Even after receiving employment, the CAG detected widespread instances of non-payment and delayed payment of wages in 23 states. As the report notes with alarm, "The scale of inadequacies in providing livelihood security could not be fully ascertained in view of the pervasive and extensive deficiencies in record maintenance at all levels. Non-maintenance or incorrect maintenance of basic records was noticed in 18 to 54 percent of the test checked Gram Panchayats. In such a situation the legal guarantee of 100 days of employment on demand and other aspects of the implementation of the Scheme were not fully verifiable."
- Works of ₹2,252 crore which were undertaken under the scheme were not permissible. The expenditure on works for ₹6,547 crore did not result in the creation of durable assets. The CAG detected diversion of MGNREGA funds for other uses in a large number of states. The statutory 60:40 wage-material ratio was also not maintained. The Ministry itself relaxed this provision.
- Monitoring was by and large absent. The CAG noticed large gaps in the envisaged monitoring mechanisms in a large number of states. MGNREGA Guidelines require the states and the Panchayati Raj Institutions to monitor the implementation of the scheme in various ways; the CAG noticed significant shortages in each of these mechanisms. Accounting for funds left much to be desired. Necessary records were not maintained.

No wonder, therefore, that the delivery and outcome of such schemes would always remain sub-optimal, and instead of reducing poverty, they would only perpetuate it while draining precious resources, despite the loud protestations of its supporters.

However, even a poorly designed scheme like this could have been implemented much better through appropriate convergence with other poverty alleviation schemes in an imaginative manner. Let us consider the example of the Pradhan Mantri Gram Sadak Yojna (PMGSY). The PMGSY was launched by the Government of India in 2000 to provide all-weather connectivity to unconnected habitations with populations of 500 each in plains areas and 250 in hill areas as part of the government's poverty reduction strategy, and to set uniform technical and management standards to ensure sustainable management of the rural roads network. It is a 100 percent Centrally Sponsored Scheme financed by a cess on high speed diesel. Monitoring and quality assurance in this scheme are provided by the National Rural Road Development Agency (NRRDA).

About 1.67 lakh unconnected habitations were eligible for coverage under the program, including construction of about 3.71 lakh km of roads for new connectivity and 3.68 lakh km under upgradation. The work was to be awarded to road contractors after following the usual tender procedures. To avoid overlap, it was stipulated that the same work could not be taken up under the MGNREGA and the PMGSY, which was unnecessary because the PMGSY links villages with expensive asphalt roads, while the MGNREGA, with a ban on contractors, builds only mud roads. Both need only unskilled labourers, while under the PMGSY they work under the supervision of skilled or semi-skilled workers.

Until March 2014, ₹1.14 lakh crore had been spent under the PMGSY and 4.0 lakh km or 54 percent of all-weather roads including upgradation were constructed, providing all-weather connectivity to 97,838 or 50 percent of eligible habitations. Though way behind initial targets, it has been reasonably successful in building up a large, all-weather rural road network in the country and at the same time provided productive employment while building up capital assets and capacity in the economy. Roads facilitate transportation of rural produce to the market and hence the development of markets. By giving access to health and education to people living in remote areas, it includes them in growth and development. In short, it builds for the future. In contrast, the MGNREGA only provides for subsistence and could hardly build any durable assets, though spending more than twice the amount spent on the PMGSY during the same period. It was possible to synergise between the two schemes by making the labour component of the MGNREGA available to the PMGSY, to the effect that rural households could get the intended employment while helping create durable assets, and achieving a judicious balance between capital intensive growth and labour-intensive poverty-alleviation measures. Similar convergence with other schemes run by other ministries is essential for the creation of durable and productive assets.

There are also other imaginative ways also to utilise the MGNREGA, as the example of a village in the Nanded district of Maharashtra has shown recently. MGNREGA funds are being used in the Tembhurni village to construct soak pits, called 'magic' pits by the locals, behind every house in the village. As reported by the Times of India, the four-foot-deep pits dug make the usually overflowing open drains redundant, thus depriving mosquitoes of their breeding grounds. They are covered with a cement pipe that has four equidistant holes at the top. A layer of sand and fine gravel is spread under and around the pipe to allow the water to percolate slowly into the ground that sucks in the waste water. Within a year, it had rendered the village free from mosquitos, against the backdrop of dengue, malaria and various other mosquito-borne diseases that severely continue to plague rural Maharashtra. Water flowing into the 200 soak pits gradually drains down into aquifers, recharging the ground water level, and thereby eliminating water scarcity in the village. This again proves that if used innovatively with appropriate technology, the MGNREGA can be a highly potent tool for promoting sustainable development and strengthening of rural infrastructure, both physical and social.

Vision and statesmanship are closely linked with imagination. There are many imaginative ways to make the MGNREGA deliver, not by providing doles as it is mostly being employed for, but by addressing poverty by building capacity, protecting the environment, improving health and sanitation, by providing drinking water, building networks for irrigation, roads and creating other assets in the rural areas which are so starved of these. It only requires a vision to rise above the narrow considerations of vote bank politics.

(Afterword: Budgetary allocation for the MGNREGA was increased to ₹48,000 crore in the 2017-18 budget, from ₹47,499 crore in the revised estimates of 2016-17 (actual expenditure in 2015-16 was ₹37,341 crore). The Ministry of Rural Development (MRD) has since introduced some reforms in the implementation of the program to combat agrarian distress, especially in the drought-affected areas to create assets linked with augmentation of irrigation potential. The household entitlement was increased from 100 to 150 days of work in drought-affected regions of ten states in 2015-16, which according to the Ministry had benefited 20.48 lakh households. According to a report released by the State Bank of India in March 2017, based on a study undertaken by it along with CMIE,

MGNREGA works allocated to households had increased from 83 lakh in October 2016 to 167 lakh households in February 2017.

In collaboration with National Remote Sensing Centre, ISRO and National Informatics Centre, one crore of the estimated 2.82 crore assets created under the MGNREGA have been geotagged for better monitoring, transparency and accountability. To cut the delay in payment of wages, MRD also tagged it to the National Electronic Fund Management System (NEFMS). Some cosmetic measures like introducing awards for convergence with other livelihood schemes and for effective implementation were also introduced in September 2016. However, the structural weaknesses pointed out in the article remain unaddressed.)

2. MID-DAY RECKONING[25]

(As the latest report of the Comptroller & Auditor General of India, the Mid-Day Meal Scheme has once again vindicated, education is about quality, not food.)

Instituting systems that are designed to fail or falter and then adapting to such dysfunctional systems has been the specialty of the Indian state for a long time. This has been the driving force behind the philosophy of our centralised welfarism, which has translated into a plethora of central and centrally sponsored plan schemes. Most of these schemes are 'one-size fits all' structures designed by the mandarins of the now defunct Planning Commission. Because they provided a ready source of finance to the cash starved states permanently on the lookout for resources, these schemes took no time to gain acceptance and popularity among the states. One such scheme was the Mid-Day Meal Scheme (MDMS). Now a report of the Comptroller and Auditor General of India has busted the myth of its so-called usefulness and presented concrete evidence of its lop-sidedness, something that we always had suspected. The truth is always difficult to accept, but ultimately it sets us free and enables us to exercise judgment with an open mind.

The MDMS, otherwise known as the National Program of Nutritional Support to Primary Education, was launched in August 1995 under the UPA-I Government to boost the government's continuing programs on universalisation of primary education by increasing enrolment, retention and attendance in schools, while simultaneously ensuring the adequacy of nutrition levels of children. Universalisation of primary and secondary education has always been a debilitating weakness of our democracy. There are two vital aspects to such universalisation–increasing the enrolment and improving the retention and pass-out percentage. Quantity and quality will both remain the essential complementary aspects for any measurement of success in achieving the universalisation of education. Quality again has two components, the hard component of infrastructure and facilities and the

[25] Originally published on www.ourstories.org, 25th February, 2016.

soft component of quality of teachers and of the instructions imparted to students.

The Planning Commission experts, while looking at such schemes through the prism of populism that has always suited the ruling dispensation, have laid excessive emphasis on the quantity and provisioning of infrastructure while ignoring the quality aspect so essential for any education. Governments in India spend about 3.5 percent of our GDP on education and individual states spend about 10 percent of their budgets on elementary education. But the sorry state of government schools in respect of the quality of teachers as well as the minimum infrastructure and basic facilities like drinking water and sanitation hardly show any sign of improvement. The outcome therefore remains dismal, as the Annual Status of Education Report (ASER) 2015 conducted by the NGO Pratham Education Foundation showed. About 33 percent of children in class II in government schools cannot recognise letters of the alphabet when they are expected to readily understand simple sentences. More than 50 percent studying in class V cannot read class II textbooks. About 40 percent of rural children studying in class III do not recognize numbers up to 100. Rural government schools are unable to impart these very basic educational skills at the primary and secondary levels. That was precisely why, in 2014, 30.8 percent of rural children aged 6-14 went into private schools. Absence of emphasis on quality makes education not substantially different from un-education. It is in the above context that the CAG report on MDMS assumes importance.

The MDMS, on which the government spends about ₹10,000 crore every year, now covers all children till the upper primary stage in government, local body and government aided schools as well as recognised Madrasas supported under Sarva Shiksha Abhiyan. The scheme lays emphasis on providing cooked meals with a minimum of 400 calories and 12 grams of protein to every child, along with essential micronutrients and de-worming medicines, and has a special focus on children belonging to disadvantaged sections of society.

The CAG report highlighted that despite emphasis on the meal component, the enrolment of children in the schools covered under the MDMS had consistently declined over the years, from 14.7 crore in 2009-2010 to 13.9 crore in 2013-14. In contrast, the enrolment of children in private schools went from 4.02 crore to 5.53 crore during the same period. Thus, MDMS in itself was not incentive enough to retain children in schools, and this is the crux of the issue. As the report spells out in no uncertain terms, “there is a growing section of [the] population which prioritises quality education over free meals…it also shows that a free MDM, by itself is not a sufficient condition to retain children in school, unless accompanied with improvement in teaching/learning outputs. It is time to realise that the meal is a means to an end, serving the larger purpose of education. Clear trends were noticed, which demonstrated that the meal served its purpose only when the expectations of parents, with respect to good education for their wards, were fulfilled."

This is what we were always afraid to speak out for fear of being branded as 'anti-poor' and 'elitist' by the pioneering welfarists of our country, even though in our heart of hearts we had always felt that education is not only about facilities or food, but about quality, character and content. That is what makes a person useful to society, gets him/her a job from which he/she finds not only livelihood and sustenance but also derives meaning and purpose for life. Quality is what brings wholesomeness into the personality, without which life becomes too humdrum–a mere existence without purpose.

Governance is all about delivery, and efficient and effective delivery calls for careful planning and monitoring. The CAG report found evidence galore on the absence of purposeful planning or monitoring. All government schemes suffer universally from wastefulness, leakages, financial misappropriations, and institutionalisation of corruption, which together render the outcomes of such schemes far below the optimal. Databases are always the weakest links in the chain of delivery, because ensuring the integrity of databases alone has the potential to reduce, if not altogether eliminate, the leakages. The CAG report highlights that the mechanism in place for assimilating data on the number of children availing MDM was seriously compromised. The percentage of actual number of children availing MDM as gathered from various sources was consistently lower than that furnished by the states to the ministry for claiming cost. There were many instances of exaggeration of figures of students availing MDMs as well as irregular diversion or theft of food-grains, submission of inflated transportation costs, and fudging of data pertaining to supply of food-grains, leading to spiralling losses, leakages and misappropriations in the scheme.

Most schools lacked infrastructural facilities like kitchen sheds, proper utensils, availability of drinking water facilities etc. There were numerous instances of food being prepared in the open in unhygienic conditions exposing children to serious health hazards. Tragedies are not uncommon, the latest on which we had shed the tears of our wrath being as recent as July 2013, when 23 students had died and scores became ill at a primary school in the village of Dharmashati Gandaman in the Saran district of Bihar after eating a midday meal contaminated with pesticides.

It is time our planners and program designers realise that feeding children and imparting quality education to them are two entirely different objectives that are disjointed and not complementary. Realisation should dawn upon them that the only thing that can ensure retention of children in government schools is the quality of instruction imparted, and not the quality or quantity of food provided. To pretend that food will help attract children reflects a shrinking of imagination and a refusal to transcend the transactional. As a nation, would we ever strive to extricate ourselves from the quicksand of populism into which we have been sinking slowly and irretrievably, discarding common-sense as well as the wisdom of our forefathers?

3. Death of Austerity[26]

(Blanket waivers of farmers' loans by various state governments are not going to solve their problems. It will only make the finances of the states unsustainable, besides destroying the credit discipline.)

As Finance Minister of UPA, Mr Chidambaram had to handle many difficult situations, and he managed most of these with an élan expected of a person well-versed in finance and economics as befits the Finance Minister of India. But the one instance where he had abjectly surrendered his objective judgment and financial prudence to populism, presumably at the command of his political bosses, was when he waived a whopping ₹52,000 crore of farm loans in his 2008 budget, ahead of the 2009 general elections that returned UPA to power. The loan waiver may or may not have played any part in UPA's election victory, but a dangerous precedent was created which had the potential of shaking our entire financial edifice. Indeed, it is precisely doing that now, for which the blame squarely falls on Mr Chidambaram's shoulders.

One thought that with Congress rule being a thing of the past, the period of peak populism was over. But the genie had already been unleashed, and it is proving impossible to bottle it again. GPS has waived ₹36,359 crore of farm loans up to ₹1 lakh, each after the new government had assumed power, putting its finances in serious jeopardy as its fiscal deficit had already breached the 3 percent limit set by its FRBM Act in 2015-16. Maharashtra followed suit with a similar farm loan waiver, also up to ₹1 lakh, that would cost the state exchequer ₹34,000 crore. In a competitive populism by sacrificing all fiscal prudence, Punjab then announced farm loan waiver for double the amount, up to ₹2 lakh each, which would cost the state more than ₹10,000 crore. Both Punjab and UP are among the most highly indebted states in the country. When it comes to populism and pampering of the vote-banks, no political dispensation wants to be left behind. Haryana, Madhya Pradesh, Gujarat and Rajasthan are waiting in the wings too.

[26] Originally published on www.scroll.in, 6th August, 2017.

Gujarat, Karnataka and Himachal Pradesh will face the electorate within a year and are sure to promise waivers on farm loans, and maybe more. The race for populism will only get hotter, because Chhattisgarh, Madhya Pradesh and Rajasthan will go to the polls before January 2019. Banks are already complaining that in anticipation of waivers, famers have already stopped repayment of the loans, which is only to be expected. Courts have also jumped into the fray, with Madras High Court directing the Tamil Nadu government to extend its crop loan waiver scheme to all farmers, including those with land holdings exceeding 5 acres–an order the Supreme Court recently had to stay. The domino effect will spread among all states very soon, throwing our state finances back to the olden days, before the Twelfth Finance Commission, when states had to borrow just to be able to repay, with repayments exceeding the borrowings for many. A recent Bank of America-Merrill Lynch research report estimated that the total farm loan waivers in the run-up to the 2019 polls can total 2 percent of India's GDP, amounting to $40 billion. The contagion is spreading like a cancer in our body-politic, with competing populism forming the economic and political agenda of all parties. The days of austerity and fiscal prudence seem to be over.

Not that Mr Chidambaram's loan waiver had solved any of the problems of distressed farmers. The 2008 UPA loan waiver scheme was audited by the CAG, whose report revealed huge gaps in delivery, besides serious lapses and corruption. It was also bad in design, being limited to bank borrowings only. According to the NSSO 70th Round Survey, the majority of small and marginal farmers were indebted to informal or non-institutional sources like local money lenders, traders, or bigger farmers; they will not get the benefits of these loan waivers. The smaller the land holding of a farmer, the less likely he is to get a bank-loan. Thus 85 percent of marginal farmers with less than 0.01 hectare of land borrow from non-institutional sources, mainly money-lenders (64 percent). This percentage gradually decreases to 35 percent for small farmers with holdings of 1-2 hectares. Thus, the intended objective of providing relief to small and marginal farmers in distress will remain a myth. All such waivers achieve is to vitiate the credit culture and loan discipline, and consequently worsen the banks' already precarious NPAs. By encouraging wilful default in expectation of a future bailout, they disincentivise repayment and promote a culture of irresponsibility all the way.

Bad economics is never good politics and political parties need to realise this sooner rather than later. According to the just-released RBI Report on "State Finances - A Study of Budgets" (2016-17), the states that cumulatively exercised more fiscal prudence than the centre until about 3 years ago are now sliding into a regime of higher deficits. Relaxations in market borrowings given by the Fourteenth Finance Commission (FFC) had led to an increase in the debt burden of the states and the consolidated fiscal position of states had deteriorated sharply between 2014-15 and 2015-16. Uttar Pradesh and Punjab are not even eligible for additional market borrowings, not having fulfilled fiscal prudence norms prescribed by the FFC. For Uttar Pradesh, the fiscal deficit would rise to ₹49,960 crore in 2016-17, i.e. 3.9 percent of GSDP, while for Punjab it would ₹13,090 crore or 2.9 percent of GSDP, as per the budget estimates. The actual figures are likely to be far higher.

The states, boosted by 10 percent extra devolution provided by the FFC, have now taken to indulging in the kind of populism that was earlier a prerogative of the centre under the UPA regime. The GFD-GDP ratio in 2015-16 breached the FRBMA ceiling of 3 percent for the first time since 2004-05, and is likely to worsen in 2016-17. Even though the centre has reversed the trend of profligacy so visible during the previous regime, as per the RBI Report, the combined fiscal deficit of the centre and the states could soar to 7 percent or even higher due to the swelling state deficits.

Apart from the farm loan waivers, another contributing factor is loans and advances for power projects related to the Ujwal Discom Assurance Yojana (UDAY) scheme, under which the states had to own over 75 percent of the outstanding Discom debt –50 percent in 2015-16 and 25 percent in 2016-17. Only 8 states had borrowed ₹98,960 crore under UDAY during 2015-16 alone, hiking the states' consolidated GFD: GDP ratio by 0.7 percent during the year. The borrowing is done through UDAY bonds, the interest on which becomes an additional liability for the states. States would also have to discharge additional liabilities in case these Discoms continued to incur losses. There is also the problem of guarantee commitments of state governments in respect of state public sector enterprises. Though a contingent liability, these are emerging as a major source of potential risk to debt sustainability of the states.

Austerity and old conservative ways are seemingly dead. But they will need resurrection, before it is too late.

4. COALGATE REVISITED[27]

(The recently conducted auction in respect of allocation of coal blocks only confirmed the CAG's estimates of a loss of ₹1.86 lakh crore due to the opaque policies followed by the earlier government.)

The auction of 33 of the 204 coal-mines whose allocation were cancelled by the Hon'ble Supreme Court has just been completed. The auction has brought the government a 'windfall gain' of ₹2.07 lakh crore for 19 operational blocks and 13 about-to-open blocks, which were put under the hammer, as against ₹1.86 lakh crore estimated by the CAG. The phrase 'windfall gain', first quoted from the noting made by the then Secretary of the Coal Ministry in the CAG Report no 7 of 2012-13 on the allocation of coal blocks, had at that time caused a lot of rancour in the UPA government and invited the wrath of all concerned, the decision-makers, as well as the beneficiaries of a totally opaque allotment process. As recommended by the CAG in his report, the NDA government has now resorted to a completely fair and transparent e-auction process for allocation of the coal blocks. It has proved, beyond all doubts, that auction is the best process, simple as well as transparent, for allocating scarce natural resources, especially for a polluting fossil fuel like coal. High bid prices incentivise faster and higher production for cost recovery and also serve as a carbon tax.

The CAG Report of 2012-13 had stated that since July 2004, 194 coal blocks with total reserves of 44,440 million tons were allocated to various government and private companies following the existing process of allocation that completely lacked transparency, objectivity and competition. 75 of these blocks were allocated to private parties. Of these, 57 allocations were for open cast or mixed mines–partly opencast and partly underground. In the absence of reliable data for underground mines, those were excluded from the CAG's calculations which were based on the net gain from estimated extractable reserves in respect of these mines. The estimates came to ₹186,591 crore (1.86 lakh) crore. Very few of these were producing coal by March 2011; many of them were deliberately waiting for future price gains for selling the blocks at a premium instead of producing coal and using it for power production. The entire process of allocation was mired in such

---

[27] Originally published in *The Statesman*, 29th March, 2015.

opacity and arbitrariness and created such huge controversy that finally the Supreme Court had to cancel all but four of 218 coal block allocations, just as it had cancelled all the 122 spectrum licenses issued earlier as "unconstitutional and arbitrary". The nation had to pay a heavy price for such indiscretion; the power sector suffered for want of coal, and despite sitting on one of the largest global reserves of coal estimated at more than 300 billion tons, the nation was forced to import coal at the cost of precious foreign exchange, pushing our already high current account deficit further into the red. Economic growth was the ultimate casualty and ultimately UPA had to pay a terrible price for such gross indiscretion.

It will still be fresh in the public memory how the CAG report was widely criticised, pilloried, ridiculed and lambasted by very senior functionaries of the ruling government. Their virulent criticism was unceasingly directed against the institution of the CAG. And not only politicians, some 'learned economists' had also joined the bandwagon of maligning the institution, calling the estimates wild. Their argument was that the estimates ignored the net present value (NPV) of the reserves that takes into account the present value of future benefits, by discounting all future benefits at the prevailing interest rates and thereby arriving at the true value of benefits calculated at today's prices; had this been considered, the estimates would have been significantly lesser than the 'astronomical figure' cited. The same argument is being advanced even now that this ₹2.07 lakh crore the bids have fetched the government is to come over the next 30 years and its NPV would be much, much less. Mr Vinod Rai, the then CAG, had countered this argument in his book *Not Just an Accountant* by saying that estimating the NPV would have required a lot of assumptions without supporting data; in any case, it would not have made any substantial difference in the estimates because the discounting rate at which NPV is to be estimated would have been annulled by the increase in sales price of the extracted coal which is expected to go up in line with global price trends.

Even now, from time to time, the CAG is being advised not to quote 'astronomical figures' in his reports. As things stand now, the estimates seem not astronomical at all, but rather conservative. When all the 204 blocks go under the hammer in a transparent manner as the current process has been, it is anybody's guess what will be the final aggregate figures collected from all bids, given that the price of coal may increase once the global economic downturn reverses, of which signals are already emanating from the USA.

It will be instructive to recall a little bit of the sordid history of coal allocations to remind ourselves about the need to follow transparent, objective policies in regard to the allotment of natural resources of the nation. In 1991, Manmohan Singh and P. V. Narasimha Rao had dismantled the License Permit Raj, opening up the economy to entrepreneurs. But any enterprise would need land and natural resources like coal and other minerals like iron. As demands for these spiralled, so did corruption. The nexus of politicians, contractors and bureaucrats now started taking maximum advantage of the opaqueness and discretion prevalent in the system to misappropriate land and other national resources for their own benefits; many of them never used these resources for productive purposes, but later bartered them for earning windfall gains, which many a time, were truly astronomical. Raghuram Rajan, the present RBI Governor, rightly analysed the situation in an article, "India's corrupt elites had moved from controlling licenses to cornering newly valuable resources like land. The Resource Raj rose from the ashes of the License Raj." Exercising unfettered discretion with total lack of accountability and transparency were the defining characteristics of this 'Resource Raj'.

Demand for coal had increased substantially after 2003, when the government had resolved to provide power for all by 2012 (we are light-years away from this, even in 2015). Given that 70 percent of India's power needs are supplied by thermal plants operating on coal, assured supply of coal to all producers, public and private, was an essential prerequisite of this vision. The domestic shortfalls were estimated at 70 million tons of coal by 2011-12, and imports were costly. Under the Coal Mines Nationalisation Act, 1973, mining of coal was the monopoly of Cola India Limited. An amendment to this act made in June 1993 allowed private companies engaged in the production of power, iron and steel the right to mine coal for captive use.

Till 1993, there were no criteria for allocating coal blocks for captive mining, allotments being made on the basis of the state government's recommendations. Since 1993, the Coal Ministry has started the allotment of coal blocks on the basis of recommendations of an inter-ministerial screening committee set up for the purpose. The committee scrutinised all applications received by the Ministry and its recommendations were approved by the concerned minister. The deliberations of the screening committee were shrouded in utmost opacity, there being no records of such deliberations except the final recommendation that a certain coal block was to be allotted to a certain applicant.

The CAG report and Mr Vinod Rai's book together chronicle how the PMO and the then coal secretary tried their utmost to bring in transparency in the process by introducing a transparent bidding process, and how all their efforts were repeatedly stonewalled, on grounds that were extremely flimsy, by the then Minister of State for Coal, Mr Dasari Narayana Rao and the Coal Minister Mr Shibu Soren during his brief sojourn in the Ministry of Coal, in between a jail term and another conviction, both on charges of murder, while a helpless PM merely watched in silence. Today the former PM, an architect of India's economic reforms, is paying the price for his uncanny silence, having been summoned by a special CBI Court as an accused in the coal scam case. No one in the entire nation doubts his personal integrity or intention, but he is being forced to humiliation for presiding over a bankrupt system whose hallmarks were opacity, arbitrariness and crony capitalism. He had apparently intervened in the allocation of the Talabira II coal block, reserved for the public sector, facilitating its final allocation to Kumarmangalam Birla's Hindalco in preference to the state-owned Neyveli Lignite Corporation, after acting on the recommendation by Odisha CM Navin Patnaik, while 'ignoring words of caution put forth by PMO officers', as the CBI judge had stated in his order, indicating 'a conscious effort on his part to somehow accommodate Hindalco in Talabira II'. While the nation prays and hopes that he will come out clean, the process once again has demonstrated the absolute necessity of following a completely transparent policy in regard to the allocation of national resources. As the Hon'ble Supreme Court has held, the state should get the full value from allocation of natural resources for which purpose, 'adoption of means other than those that are competitive and maximise revenue may be arbitrary and face the wrath of Article 14 of the Constitution'.

Side by side with coal-block auction, open bidding for 800, 900, 1800 and 2100 MHz spectrum is also going on, and the process has already generated ₹1.07 lakh crore. It is imperative that the Government resorts to open and transparent bidding in respect of all minerals, not simply coal and telecom spectrum. But that is not apparently happening anytime soon. As reported by the *Hindustan Times* on March 17th, the proposed amendment to section 11 of the Mines and Minerals Act, now before the Rajya Sabha's Select Committee, allows only one category of mining leases–the new grants–to go through the auction route. 'For the rest, the government has succumbed once again to the pressure of mining lobbies and opted to continue with the policy of renewing expired leases, bypassing auction, and thus forgoing the possibility of enhanced or maximum earnings.' Should we keep crucial reforms at bay till history is repeated once again? Hasn't the country already paid enough?

5. LET'S FIX AND NOT ESCAPE[28]

(The decrepit public-school system in India cannot be fixed simply because the people responsible for running it and fixing its problems can and do opt out easily.)

Allahabad High Court passed an interesting order last month, directing the Chief Secretary of the UP government to ensure that from the academic year beginning in 2016, children of all officials serving with the government, including judiciary, local bodies and representatives of people, must send their children to study only in government primary schools, failing which the fees paid by them to private schools should be deducted from their salaries and paid to government accounts. "Only then would they be serious enough to look into the requirements of these schools and ensure that they are run in good condition," the Judge observed. Responding to a series of writ petitions on the procedures for appointment of assistant teachers in the state's primary schools, Justice Sudhir Agarwal directed the Chief Secretary to take necessary steps within 6 months to implement the above order and to submit a compliance report immediately after the lapse of 6 months. The government's response is not yet known.

Taking note of the deplorable conditions in many of the government-run primary schools, the Judge had observed that although 90 percent of the state's children study in these schools; their conditions remain 'shabby' because officials responsible for running these schools treat them in a shabby manner. The Court's logic was based on the simple common sense that government schools have become the 'last refuge of only the poor', since officials responsible for running them have the liberty to opt out and send their own children to better managed private schools without trying to fix the ills that universally afflict the government schools. If they did not have this liberty, the schools possibly would have become more functional. Officials, no longer being stakeholders, have become completely apathetic to the system.

[28] Originally published in *The Statesman* as "Let's Fix the System Instead of Opting Out", 27th September, 2015.

Governments in India spend about 3.5 percent of the nation's GDP on education. Individual states spend about 10 percent of their budgets on elementary education; for UP, it comes to a whopping ₹20,000 crore a year. But the sorry state of government schools in respect of the quality of teachers as well as the minimum infrastructure and basic facilities, drinking water and sanitation, hardly shows any sign of improvement. The same can also be said about the state-run hospitals and dispensaries, especially in rural areas where most of the populations live and where private health facilities are almost absent. Another judge will hopefully pass a similar order in respect of government hospitals someday.

Let the academics and legal luminaries debate whether the order is tenable or constitutional, whether it infringes on the fundamental rights of the government servants to send their children to schools of their choices or whether it was another case of judicial overreach into executive or legislative territories. Let us leave it to their higher wisdom to decide upon these issues. Let the talking heads on TV, if and when they find time from other pressing issues facing the nation like the Indrani Mukerjea case, decide whether revision of the terms of appointment of government servants by requiring them to send their children only to government schools in future would render it legally valid and binding on their part to do so. Let us also forget for a moment that the present set of government employees may not be held entirely responsible for the abysmal deterioration in the government-run schooling system. Let us also overlook the fact that such a relief was not prayed before the Court by the petitioners either. Let us instead try to understand and appreciate the judge's frustration and anguish.

I and my brothers, like most others belonging to our generation, attended government schools. Five decades ago, private schools were far fewer in number and most parents were not affluent enough to afford them; even many of those who could often chose to send their children to government schools. Education in government schools did not incapacitate us to compete at the all-India level, and nor did it undermine our ability and intellect in any way. One went to the school for the quality of education rather than for nice buildings and facilities; these considerations probably are true even today. But government schools have ceased to be the temples of knowledge they used to be earlier. People do not send their children to these schools any longer–I did not send mine–only those who have no option are forced to avail of their non-existent services, and they constitute the majority of our rural population. It is here that the judgment becomes relevant.

Five decades ago, the infrastructure of government schools was as pathetic as it is now, possibly worse. But there were teachers, ill-paid, but qualified, dedicated, committed and proud of their jobs. They used to administer severe corporal punishments if one did not perform, and also offered their assistance free of cost to make learning a little easier for those who could not cope or keep up with their lessons. Private coaching was not unheard of but not quite as pervasive as now. Government teachers are today better paid than their counterparts in most private schools and many of them remain equally knowledgeable, dedicated and committed to their jobs, but their numbers are fast diminishing. It would be unfair to hold only teachers responsible for the decay; they are perhaps equal victims of a dysfunctional system. Besides, decay has not remained confined to government schools only; nationwide, the system of delivery of public services as a whole has crumbled almost beyond repair, along with the general erosion of values. We can of course blame the politicians, bureaucrats and others who have hijacked the system by interfering in recruitment and transfer of teachers and for leakages from the education budget–but blaming them does not help in restoring the integrity and value of the system.

Enrolment in India so far has been a success story, with that in primary schools reaching over 90 percent since 2009, and girls making up more than 50 percent of the new students between 2007 and 2013. But to keep the students in school is another story–29 percent of children drop out before completing 5 years of primary school and only 42 percent complete high school. With 1.4 million children aged 6-11 out of school, India has the dubious distinction of ranking among the top five nations for out-of-school children. Infrastructure remains a huge problem–primary schools are short of about 700,000 teachers, only 53 percent of the schools have functional girls' toilets and 26 percent have no access to drinking water. But when we talk about the quality of education in government schools, the situation becomes really ugly. The judgment was precisely aimed at this aspect, rather than the need for improved infrastructure.

The Annual Status of Education Report (ASER) 2015 conducted by the NGO Pratham Education Foundation brings out some startling facts. 32.5 percent of children in class II in government schools cannot recognise letters of the alphabet when they are expected to understand simple sentences easily. More than 50 percent studying in class V cannot read class II textbooks. About 40 percent of rural children studying in class III do not recognise numbers up to 100. Rural government schools are unable to impart these very basic educational skills at the primary and secondary levels. That was precisely why, in 2014, 52.8 percent of rural children aged

6-14 in UP went to private schools, the corresponding all-India figure being 30.8 percent.

The huge gap between expectation and delivery is both the cause and effect of the corruption that runs through the entire system, eroding its value at every stage. Last year, more than 50 principals in the Kaimur district of Bihar were suspended after they were found guilty of misappropriating funds meant for building classrooms. About 10,000 primary school teachers were dismissed last year after they failed a mandatory competency test, not being able to name the president of India and the planet closest to the Sun, among other things. 23 primary students died after consuming contaminated free mid-day meals. In Bihar, during the last decade, the appointment rules were relaxed to fill 3.62 lakh vacancies in the state's 73,000 primary schools on presentation of degree certificates attested by government officials without having to write any competitive examination. After reports had surfaced that about 20,000 of them had forged their degree certificates, 779 teachers were dismissed after investigation.

This was of course not the first time that such a scandal had erupted, and not only in Bihar. The story continues to be repeated in state after state, in degrees of malfeasance that compete with each other. The officials responsible for running the system have completely abdicated their responsibility and are not affected by it, having the option of sending their children elsewhere. If they did not have this easy option, the system would certainly not have been allowed to become so decrepit. The judgment, no doubt born out of deep anguish and a sense of helplessness, only seeks to restore their accountability that has been hopelessly lost, though nothing probably will come out of it.

6. EDUCATIONAL PARADOX[29]

(It is high time we address the question of quality of education and introduce a uniform national or state-level exit examination for all degrees to be awarded by all universities that will serve as a template for auto-ranking of the universities and institutions.)

The Global Competitiveness Report prepared by the World Economic Forum, which is best known for its annual meeting in Davos, Switzerland, assesses the competitiveness of 140 economies, providing insight into the drivers of their productivity and prosperity. The report remains the most comprehensive assessment of national competitiveness worldwide. The Competitiveness Index computed by them is a composite index based on 12 pillars of competitiveness, which are grouped in 3 dimensions : (1) Basic Requirements based on four pillars - Institutions, Infrastructure, Macroeconomic Environment and Health and Primary Education; (2) Efficiency Enhancers based on 6 pillars - Higher Education and Training, Goods Market Efficiency, Labour Market Efficiency, Financial Market Development, Technological Readiness and Market Size; and (3) Innovation and Sophistication Factors measured by the twin pillars of Business Sophistication and Innovation.

The 2016-17 report has just been published. India ranked a commendable 39 on overall raking (China is ranked at 28), as against 55 last year. While India has performed well in respect of other pillars of competitiveness, its overall ranking still remains depressed due to the dismal performance in respect of Health and Primary Education (ranked 85 among 140 countries), Higher Education and Training (ranked 81), Labour Market Efficiency (ranked 84) and Technological Readiness (ranked 110). Worse still, there has not been much movement in respect of these pillars compared to the last year except for Labour Market Efficiency (last year's rank was 103). These pillars have to do with the quality of education which we have not been able to improve so far.

The Human Development Index (HDI) measured by the United Nations is another composite index built from indicators pertaining to three key

[29] Originally published in *The Statesman*, 7th October, 2016.

dimensions of human development: Health, Education and Standard of Living, measured respectively by the average life expectancy at birth, mean years of schooling vis-à-vis expected years of schooling and per Capita GNP. In respect of education, which is a major determinant of economic development and quality of life, and which in turn determines whether a country is developed or underdeveloped, India's performance is nothing to be cheerful about.

In 1980, India ranked 105th among all the nations with an Education Index of only 0.24 (maximum score 1.0). Its rank in terms of the Education Index has progressively been sliding ever since, dropping to 113 in 1990, 127 in 2000, and 146 in 2010 (index 0.46). As per the 2014 report, India's overall ranking was 135 among 187 nations, but its education ranking had slipped further to 145 (index 0.47), behind Vietnam, the Congo, Zimbabwe, Cambodia, Uganda, Rwanda and Angola–countries that were torn by strife and turmoil not very long ago. This should have served as a wake-up call to our political leaders, but they continued to live in their make-believe world of complacence, denial, identity politics and social justice.

As of July 2016, India had as many as 759 universities, which includes 47 central universities, 350 state universities, 123 deemed universities and 239 private universities. These institutions produce more than 50 lakh graduates and postgraduates every year in all streams. Most of these universities find no place among the first 1000 universities of the world. As per the Times Higher Education Survey, 2016, only 17 of these universities came within the first 800 global rankings, and none featured within the first 250; among them were the Indian Institute of Science, 7 IITs and 9 other universities.

Our political leaders try to evade responsibility by questioning the ranking methodology which gives higher weightages on international students and faculties that disfavour the Indian universities, but that does not cut much ice. Whichever survey one looks into, the results are equally dismal and distressing. As per the widely-used "Webometrics Ranking of World Universities" conducted by the *Consejo Superior de Investigaciones Científicas* (CSIC), a research organisation attached to the Spanish Ministry of Education, only 9 Indian universities were ranked between 500 and 1000. Even within Asia, India is a laggard in higher education. As per the QS World University Rankings for Asia, 2016, only 9 Indian universities (IISc, 7 IITs and Delhi University) came within the first 100.

The low ranking reflects the poor quality of education in the country, the natural result of which is the increasing unemployability of our graduates and postgraduates. According to a study of more than 150,000 engineering students who graduated in 2015 from over 650 colleges (Aspiring Minds National Employability Report, January 2016), 80 percent were unemployable. Another study by ASSOCHAM in April 2016 found that, barring a handful of top business schools like IIMs, most of 5,500 B-schools in the country were producing largely unemployable graduates earning less than ₹10,000 a month, if they could find any placements. The vast majority of 93 percent of the 500,000 management graduates turned out by these B-schools annually have no employable skills, like basic linguistic and numerical ability, logical reasoning and problem-solving ability, besides communication and leadership abilities.

An education system that cannot inculcate these basic employment skills is decrepit and dysfunctional by all measures, and that implies that the entire eco-system of our higher education should be revamped drastically, and urgently; 'Make in India' will otherwise remain a chimera. Ours is a paradoxical ecosystem in which a few centres of excellence share space with hundreds of dysfunctional institutions without any quality control. As Lant Pritchett of Harvard's Kennedy School of Government observed, India produces about 100,000 students a year in the global top 10 percent and simultaneously churns out millions with zero skills. An educational commission chaired by S. Radhakrishnan in 1948 declared that "education is a universal right, not a class privilege." Unfortunately, even after 70 years of independence it remains very much the exclusive preserve of the elite and the privileged. Universities that should be places for creativity, debate, dissent and experimentation with ideas exist only as degree-manufacturing-shops that beget no value to the students' lives.

The rot starts with the schools. In 2009, the UPA government enacted a thoughtless piece of legislation that masquerades as the Right to Education (RTE) Act. Section 16 of the Act, considering its backbone, prohibits schools from detaining or expelling any student up to class VIII, ostensibly because this could demotivate a child to drop out altogether. In the absence of any other mechanism to test the learning of students and correct deficiencies therein, this naturally led to a situation where a class VIII student was unable to read class V textbooks, and a class VI student was unable to work out class II arithmetic.

A Group of Experts at the Niti Aayog, however, has come up with a template for medical education in the country, which if implemented with seriousness, has the potential to change the educational landscape. Both medical education and medical practices in our country have been plagued with endemic corruption, complete opaqueness, unscrupulous extortion and unlimited greed. Now under a Supreme Courts directive, from the next year onwards, there will be a single-entry examination for admission to all medical colleges in the country, public as well as private. Medical education in India is controlled by the Medical Council of India (MCI), which is an exclusive club of doctors from corporate hospitals and private practices with deeply-entrenched vested interests. Niti Aayog has now recommended replacement of MCI by a National Medical Commission (NMC), to be advised by another parallel body, the Medical Advisory Board, which will have representatives from all states and union territories. Disbanding a corrupt and decaying MCI would be freeing medical education and practices from a Medical Inspector Raj. The NMC will conduct a single national entry examination for all medical colleges and the quality of education imparted by them will be certified by an exit examination, also conducted nationally, without passing which no aspiring doctor can get a license.

Entry in higher education, by and large, is still guided by merit, and performance in the entry exam guides who gets admission in which college or university. But the quality control stops here. If there is a single exit examination for all graduate and post-graduate courses in the country (or to begin with, within a state) taught by whichever institution, this will also measure the learning imparted by these institutions, and hence determine their relative rankings. This will make and break these institutions–good ones will prosper and bad ones will be forced either to close or improve. It will usher in a self-regulating educational ecosystem in which the quality of education imparted will become the sole determinant of students' and parents' informed choice. Universities will then only teach, but not be allowed to conduct examinations for awarding degrees, which can be done by a board represented by all universities and stakeholders including the government.

No system can ever be perfect and such a system too will have its own pitfalls, which will have to be addressed. But it is time to be obsessed with quality in education over any and every other consideration.

7. WORKING FROM HOME TO SAVE OUR CITIES[30]

(Telecommuting may be a viable and a more effective alternative to save the city environment from vehicular pollution than an even/odd registration number formula.)

We are literally inhaling poison in Delhi. I do not normally have a sinus or coughing problem, and I am highly exercise-dependent for my mental and physical well-being. But every year during the three winter months, I do not dare to venture out for taking a walk or jogging, even though I live in an area that is reasonably green. During the dismal winter months of Delhi, I keep myself hermetically sealed within the 4 walls of my house, refusing to step out except for an emergency and barking at anyone who dares to open a window. But this year, none of this is helping me. I have blocked noses, sore throats, sleepless nights and what naturally follows as a consequence, a depressed and sterile mind. It is the same with my wife; you can well imagine what happens when 2 depressed souls are locked within a house that increasingly resembles a gaol in a city that the Delhi High Court has aptly described as a "gas chamber".

So, it was cheerful news that at last the AAP government focused its attention away from the Lt. Governor towards the Aam Admi of Delhi for a change. Alarmed by the rising air pollution that has assumed unseemly proportions with no one having any clue about how to combat it, the Delhi government has announced its intention to allow the plying of private vehicles bearing odd and even registration numbers to alternate days only in the national capital from 1st January 2016. A motorist will now be able to drive his vehicle only for 15 days in a month. Several other measures were announced along with this, like shutting down the Badarpur Thermal power station, moving the National Green Tribunal to close the Dadri power plant in Uttar Pradesh, carrying out a massive plantation drive along all arterial roads across the city to curb the spread of dust and vacuum-cleaning of roads by the PWD from April, besides allowing trucks into the city only after 11

---

[30] Originally published in *The Statesman* as "It Isn't Even Odd to Work from Home", 9th December, 2015.

pm. If even only half these intentions could be translated into actions rather than being exercises in tokenism, the city indeed would be a different place to live in, instead of the lethal toxic cocktail it is at present.

The odd/even number scheme is nothing new. Cities like Beijing and Singapore have already tried it. The question is whether it is practicable in Delhi, where the public transport is clearly unequipped to carry the additional load. Thankfully, it would not restrict the Chief Minister's movements, who has 2 cars numbered 0001 and 0002, or the rich people who can afford to buy a second vehicle–usually a used one –to beat the scheme and thereby contribute to increasing rather than reducing vehicular pollution. As always, it will be the Aam Admi Government wanting to help that will be hurt the most. It is still unclear how the scheme will be implemented, what would be the penalty for violators and how it would be enforced, or how the government would regulate the vehicles coming from outside. Considering all these, the scheme seems not to have been thought through. It looks more like a knee-jerk reaction; for a scheme like this to succeed, all stakeholders including the public have to be taken on board beforehand, which obviously was not the case.

A scheme like this can at best be a quick fix rather than a permanent solution, as experiences of different cities across the world prove. Beijing used it for the first time during the 2008 Olympic Games. It did curb its notorious smog level by 20 percent, the concentration of PM 2.5 (fine, respirable particles) by 31 percent and asthma-related doctor visits by 50 percent. Now the ban is enforced for only a day every week, and it restricts not one but two last digits–one odd and one even, say 3 and 4–so that to beat the scheme, one has to have a third vehicle carrying a different number. In 1989, Mexico City started its *Hoy No Circula* (today you can't drive) program based on the even-odd formula to fight smog, which only resulted in giving a boost to the automobile sector, sharply increasing the sales of vehicles. Bogota's *Pico y Placa* (Peak and [License] Plate) program reduced private vehicle use by up to 40 percent on weekdays, but the effect on the city's pollution was only marginal. For a scheme like this to succeed, we also need an effective system of public transportation which is just not in place in most of our cities.

Other cities have tried other methods linked to pricing which are more effective but may not be palatable in a country with a baggage of socialistic pattern of society and a history of dole culture practiced and promoted as national welfare. Transport Demand Management methods linked to pricing like parking restrictions and congestion pricing have accrued long term benefits which are more helpful than short term emergency measures like an even-odd formula. London introduced congestion pricing in 2003 by imposing a tariff of £5 for vehicles entering Central London areas–in the first 3 years, it reduced vehicle traffic by 16 percent and journey times by 14 percent, with significant reduction in the levels of toxic gases and particulate matter. The fee was hiked to £10 about 5 years later, followed by restrictions on the entry of buses and trucks in Greater London areas, which led to a reduction in the level of PM 2.5 by 20 percent. Singapore follows a similar Electronic Road Pricing system based on high-pricing using technology like GPS.

Delhi had 84.75 lakh registered vehicles as on 31st March 2015, out of which 57.26 lakh were 2-wheelers. Every year, 6 lakh new vehicles are registered in Delhi, more than 1,600 vehicles per day. There is also an unknown number of vehicles registered in neighbouring states of Haryana or UP plying in Delhi. It is estimated that on any given day, there are about 40 lakh 4-wheelers plying on Delhi roads–more than the total numbers of vehicles in Kolkata, Mumbai and Chennai put together. For all its good intentions, the AAP government's move may add to this number by forcing commuters to buy additional vehicles. This cannot be a lasting solution to the city's woes. Let us therefore think of a more viable alternative.

Telecommuting is a term coined by Jack Nilles in 1973 which is increasingly being used in the developed world, and is not unknown in some private sector organisations in our country too. It means remote work or telework, i.e. technology-assisted work–an arrangement that allows employees not to commute to a central place for work; they are 'work-at-home' employees. In addition, there are 'nomad workers', who use mobile telecommunications technology to work from cyber cafes or other locations. The government and companies are increasingly using these concepts to attract and retain workers. These are not only welfare measures, but also smart economics as well. The General Services Administration of USA estimates that if federal employees telecommute at least one day every week, federal agencies could boost productivity by more than $2.3 billion annually.

Wikipedia reports the results of a Reuter's poll, according to which approximately "one in 5 workers around the globe, particularly employees in the Middle East, Latin America and Asia, telecommute frequently and nearly 10 percent work from home every day". The guiding motto behind this is: "Work is something we DO, not a place that we GO". According to Wikipedia, over 50 million US workers–that is, about 40 percent of the working population–could work from home at least part of the time. The number of employees reported to have actually worked from their home on their primary job in 2010 was 9.4 million. In that year, the US Federal Government passed the Telework Enhancement Act 'in order to improve Continuity of operations and ensure that essential Federal functions are maintained during emergency situations; to promote management effectiveness when telework is used to achieve reductions in organisational and transit costs and environmental impacts; and to enhance the work-life balance of workers'.

The 2011 Federal Employee Viewpoint Survey indicates that in 13 government departments, more than half the employees reported teleworking, including 69 percent from the Department of Education, 74 percent from the Office of Personal Management, and 76 percent from the National Science Foundation. Forrester Research's US Telecommuting Forecast reports that 34 million Americans work from home and 'the number is expected to reach a staggering 63 million–or 43 percent of the U.S. workforce–by 2016'. Cisco reports that the company has generated 'an estimated annual savings of $277 million in productivity by allowing employees to telecommute and telework'. In the UK, in 2012, over 4 million employees out of a total workforce of 30 million were teleworkers.

Let us look at the potential benefits of telecommuting should we introduce it in India. It would allow employees to better manage their work together with family obligations. It would lead to more freedom, more resilience, greater productivity, improved staff retention and lower operating costs. The most significant impact would, of course, be on our city environment. Think of Delhi, with a population of 18 million and a working population of about 6 million; even if a third does not have to report to the office every day, this means 1 million fewer vehicles on the roads. Think about the impact of this on vehicular pollution.

Many government departments and ministries, public sector organisations, think-tanks, IT/ ITC industries, design and development organisations, taxation departments etc. can seamlessly shift to such a work culture by appropriate planning and reengineering of their works. Only those employed with organisations whose business involves dealing with the public, like banks, academic institutions, trading and business, transportation and the like will have to commute daily, but they commute faster since the roads will be decongested. Life for everyone will be simpler and freer, and the air purer to breathe.

SECTION 4

INDIA AND THE WORLD

1. A New Global Financial Order?
2. China's Tawang Conundrum
3. Exploiting the Synergies of the Indian Ocean Rim Countries
4. The UN at Seventy: High Time to Reform
5. SAARC Summit: Another Missed Opportunity
6. End of Jobs
7. Demonetised Living

1. A New Global Financial Order?[31]

(The Bretton Woods System that established the IMF and the World Bank is now being challenged by the emerging economies in a possible reconfiguration of the financial order in a changing world.)

In July 2014, at the Brazilian seaside city of Fortaleza, leaders of the five most populous nations, which are also the most important emerging-market economies–Brazil, Russia, India, China, and South Africa, collectively known as BRICS–took a momentous decision to create 2 new international financial institutions: A New Development Bank (NDB) and a joint monetary fund, to 'reconfigure the system of international economic governance', as Brazilian President Dilma Rousseff said. The NDB, with a capital base of $50 billion, contributed equally by the 5-member states irrespective of the sizes of their population or economy and having equal voting rights, will finance their infrastructure and development projects. The bank, to start lending from 2016, will be headquartered in Shanghai. India will be its first president for 5 years, followed by Brazil and Russia. The new bank reflects the growing importance of BRICS, which account for almost half the world's population and about one-fifth of the global economic output. But its capital base of $50 billion, which might eventually rise to $100 billion, cannot rival the World Bank's capital base of $232 billion or even the Manila-based Asian Development Bank's $165 billion.

The 5 leaders also agreed to establish a Contingent Reserve Arrangement (CRA) of $100 billion to help member states in financial emergencies, especially in the event of acute balance of payment crises. The BRICS countries have the world's largest foreign currency reserves, led by China, and the new institution can invest these savings at a profit. China contributed $41 billion to its capital stock; India, Brazil and Russia each paid in $18 billion, and South Africa paid $5 billion. Each member nation has the right to withdraw different amounts from the CRA: China $20.5 billion; Brazil, Russia, and India $18 billion each; and South Africa $10 billion. The 2 institutions ushered in a new era in global financial power structures.

---

[31] Originally published in *The Statesman*, 20th October, 2014.

In another July, 70 years ago, 730 delegates from 44 allied nations gathered at the Bretton Woods Resort in New Hampshire, USA, to evolve a new international monetary and financial order that could address the needs of reconstruction in the war-ravaged European nations that were, moreover, staring at the impending demise of their colonial empires and the consequent loss of their own economic might.

Led by the USA, they established a new financial system–the Bretton Woods system–to prevent recurrence of the problems that had beset the world since the Great Depression of the 1930s, which had given rise to protectionism, with nations controlling access to foreign currencies which they were using to manipulate trade and build a surplus to be used for the purposes of war. The Bretton Woods conference made all currencies freely convertible at fixed exchange rates, while linking the dollar, and hence all currencies, to gold at a fixed exchange rate of $32 an ounce. To help European reconstruction, the World Bank was established with 28 members; today it is a 188-member body that works for their socio-economic development. To protect countries against devaluation of their currencies, the International Monetary Fund (IMF) was set up, from which members could borrow. The IMF is financed by contributions from member states, but decisions are not based on one-country one-vote; voting instead is determined by the level of contributions. Thus, the USA controls 16.75 percent of the votes, the European Union collectively commands 30 percent, and their friendly powers control about 12 percent. BRICS collectively controls only 11 percent of votes, with China alone contributing 5.76 percent. In this scenario, western countries always prevail over the developing nations. Leadership of the World Bank has also been reserved for an American and that of the IMF for a European.

The Bretton Woods system worked well till the early 1970s and despite devaluation of various currencies, managed the exchange rates rather successfully. But while the current account transactions were more or less free from currency controls, controls over capital account transactions continued unabated till the 1980s. Throughout, however, the US dollar retained its competitive advantage and US multinationals continued to invest abroad, leading to steady accumulation of capital in the hands of American financial institutions. As speculation built up against the dollar, in 1971, convertibility of the dollar was suspended, and following its devaluation soon afterwards, the fixed exchange rate regime had collapsed by 1973. As weaker developing nations increasingly faced balance of payments crises, the IMF extended finances to them, but in doing so, it actually protected the interests of international financial institutions, to the disadvantage of these countries. IMF loans came with trademark conditions of privatisation, steep increases in taxation, government deregulation and deep cuts in governments' social spending on the poor, on the pretext of stabilising their fiscal and monetary policies. These conditions unfairly opened the vast markets of developing countries to western business interests by removing tariff barriers, in the process destroying local business enterprises and exposing their people to acute hardships.

Every financial crisis is accompanied by high inflation and large government expenditure and corrections are always painful. But the severity of the IMF's pro-market conditions in the name of 'structural adjustments' often went much beyond what was necessary to restore equilibrium, making these countries surrender their own development strategies in order to borrow. For implementation of this strategy, authoritarian conditions were required even in a democracy, what Naomi Klein called shock therapy in her book *The Shock Doctrine*. The therapy was applied repeatedly under the authoritarian regimes of Chile, Russia, China, Argentina, Indonesia, Poland, Iraq and across many other countries, often under extreme coercion by an iron-fisted leadership. Growth at the cost of extreme income inequality, poverty and economic exclusion of large swathes of the population often resulted from these IMF-dictated policies.

Every nation has the right to pursue their own national interests and international organisations exist only for as long as they serve that purpose collectively. The problem arises only when interests of developed and developing nations clash and the latter, being in economically weaker positions, are forced submit to the will of the rich. Thus, when the IMF granted \$23.5 billion to Greece, \$22.9 billion to Portugal, and \$19.4 billion to Ireland, the BRICS countries had little to gain in bailing these Euro-area countries out as these countries' shares in their own trade balances were negligible. Discontent and frustration have been brewing among the developing nations against the hegemony of rich nations in the IMF or World Bank for quite some time. But the US Congress refused to ratify the IMF reform proposal of 2010 to redistribute voting rights by hiking the share of developing nations only by 6 percent, which would have seen India's quota rising marginally to 2.75 percent from the existing 2.44 percent. Now with the BRICs bank, international economic power might undergo a real gradual shift from the developed to the developing world.

Sceptics argue that apart from being major developing countries, the BRICS have little else in common and a BRICS Bank will be non-functional. But there is the precedent of Latin American development bank Corporación

Andina de Fomento, founded in 1970, which is successfully operating without US influence, and approved $12.1 billion for projects in 2013. Taking a cue from the BRICS Bank, India has gone a step further. The eighth meeting of the South Asian Free Trade Area ministerial council in Thimphu in July 2014 approved the proposal, first mooted by India, to establish a SAARC Development Bank to provide access to low-cost capital for financing infrastructure in the eight SAARC countries. There is already an SAARC Development Fund with a paid-up capital of $300 million to provide financial assistance to social sector and infrastructure projects which can be integrated with the new bank. Last month, the government set up a committee to examine this proposal due for final approval during the SAARC summit in Nepal next month.

This is a welcome step and may spur other regions to come up with similar institutions to break the dominance of developed nations in a changed world order.

After the collapse of the USSR, in his 1989 article, "The End of History?", Francis Fukuyama celebrated the 'triumph of the West' and 'Western idea', arguing that 'the end-point of mankind's ideological evolution' had been reached 'in an unabashed victory of economic and political liberalism', in deregulated markets and western democracy. That world is already cracking, and unless the West is ready to accommodate the emerging nations, Fukuyama's imaginary world will turn upside down.

2. CHINA'S TAWANG CONUNDRUM[32]

(Historical realities cannot be changed by rhetoric and muscle flexing. China should realise that it is now dealing with a different India.)

Tawang in Arunachal Pradesh caused a flutter in the Beijing roost. Wary of the fall-out from the Dalai Lama's visit to the picturesque 17th century Twang Monastery, which to Tibetans is next in importance after the Potala Palace in Lhasa, the erstwhile abode of the Dalai Lama, China has severely warned India that the Dalai Lama's visit "to the contested area will inflict severe damage on the China-India relationship". In a reversal of its earlier timidity and nervousness while dealing with China, India has of late also become more assertive, sensing correctly that in order to make its big neighbour more sensitive towards its own concerns like the United Nations Security Council, NSG or Masood Azhar, it has to aggressively confront China on issues like Tibet and the One-China Policy, which for China are non-negotiable. In fact, the Dalai Lama's visit may just provide some extra ammunition to India, which it may leverage to its advantage both at the political and diplomatic levels.

Since the 1962 war, not a single shot has been fired along the nearly 3500 km disputed border with China, but the Chinese position on the border has remained unyielding. China claims the entirety of Arunachal Pradesh as its own territory, being 'Southern Tibet'. But the Dalai Lama's visit to Tawang undermines Chinese claims and instead strengthens Indian position by imparting legitimacy, which riles China.

The origin of the dispute goes back to the early 20th century. The 885 km long northern boundary of Arunachal Pradesh, today known as the McMahon Line–a bone of contention between India and China– takes its name from Sir Arthur Henry McMahon, Secretary to the Government of India (1911-1914).

At the beginning of the 20th century, the Qing dynasty of China was in decline. China at that time exercised only limited control over Tibet, which was autonomous in every respect except foreign policy and international

---

[32] Originally published in *The Statesman*, 12th April, 2017.

relations which were determined by China. However, taking advantage of the failing powers of the Qing emperor, Tibet started asserting its independence. In a last desperate attempt to reassert its authority, the Qing Government sent military forces to Tibet in 1910, before it itself finally collapsed in the wake of the 1911 Republican Revolution in China, prompting the Thirteenth Dalai Lama, the spiritual and temporal leader of Tibet, to expel all Chinese officials and troops from Tibet and proclaim the independence of Tibet from Chinese occupation. Tibet sought international recognition for its new freedom in 1913.

A conference was therefore held in 1914 at Simla between Tibet, India and China to settle the frontier and other matters relating to Tibet. While India was represented by Sir McMahon, Mr Ivan Chen represented China and Lonchen Ga-den Shatra Pal-jor Dorje represented Tibet. The accord signed on July 3rd, 1914, known as the Simla Convention, provided that Tibet would be divided into "Outer Tibet" and "Inner Tibet": "The Governments of Great Britain and China recognising that Tibet is under the suzerainty of China, and recognizing also the autonomy of Outer Tibet, engage to respect the territorial integrity of the country, and to abstain from interference in the administration of Outer Tibet (including the selection and installation of the Dalai Lama), which shall remain in the hands of the Tibetan Government at Lhasa." Outer Tibet covered approximately the same area as the modern Tibetan Autonomous Region, while "Inner Tibet" would remain under the jurisdiction of the Chinese government. Article 9 of the Convention stated: "For the purpose of the present Convention, the borders of Tibet, and the boundary between Outer and Inner Tibet, shall be as shown in red and blue respectively on the map attached hereto."

The red line, defining the boundary between Tibet and China, coincides approximately with the McMahon Line, which ran along the highest ridges of the Himalayan ranges following the watershed principle of map making. The only exception was at Tawang, the birthplace of the 6th Dalai Lama, which was on the Tibetan side of the watershed; but the British negotiated to shift the McMahon line north of it, thus including Tawang in India for protecting its trade and political interests.

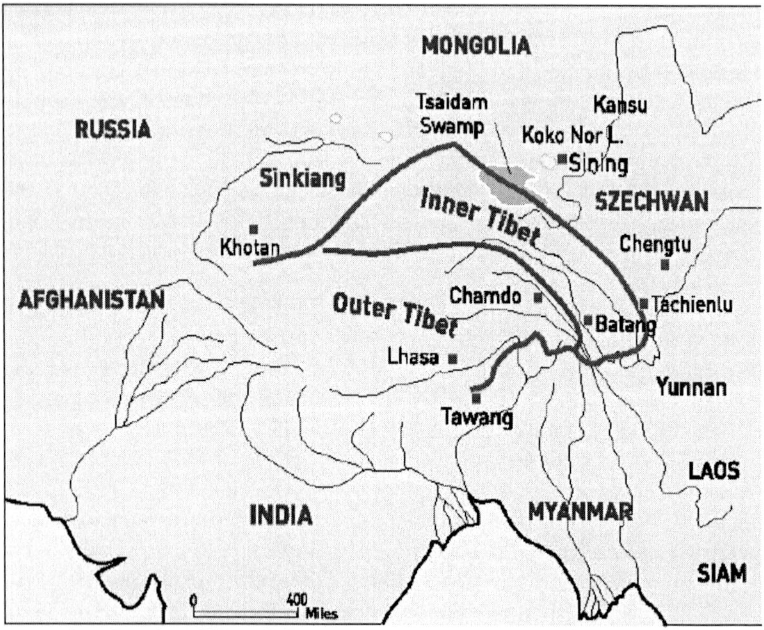

Outer boundary of Tibet with Tawang. Line dividing Inner and Outer Tibet.

Boundaries of Tibet and Inner and Outer Tibet as shown on the map appended to the Simla Convention of July 3, 1914. Tawang is shown clearly to the south of the Line.

The draft Indo-Tibetan boundary was formally confirmed in March 1914, and submitted at the 7th full meeting of all the delegates on 22nd April, 1914, along with the map signed by the Chinese Plenipotentiary, Ivan Chen, on 27th April, 1914. The final accord of 3rd July, 1914, lacked any textual boundary description, but attached an identical map. Delegates from India, China, and Tibet agreed on this frontier, but the talks broke down on the issue of the boundary between Inner and Outer Tibet. Two days later, the Chinese government disavowed its delegate and refused to sign the Convention.

However, the Tibetan and British representatives went ahead with the Agreement and declared that "We, the Plenipotentiaries of Great Britain and Tibet, hereby record the following declaration to the effect that we acknowledge the annexed convention as initialled to be binding on the Governments of Great Britain and Tibet, and we agree that so long as the Government of China withholds signature to the aforesaid convention she will be debarred from the enjoyment of all privileges accruing therefrom." China refused to sign the Convention and emphatically stated that any bilateral agreement between Tibet and Britain would not be recognised by it, since Tibet not being independent could not have independently signed treaties; further as per the Anglo-Chinese (1906) and Anglo-Russian (1907) conventions, any such agreement would be invalid without Chinese assent. But Chinese rule on Tibet had effectively ceased by then and China was too weak to challenge the might of the British Empire in India; hence no one challenged the authority of Tibet to sign the agreement. The Survey of India finally published a map showing the McMahon Line as the official boundary between China and India in 1938.

Much is made by scholars like Melvyn Goldstein, Alastair Lamb, Neville Maxwell and others of the fact that the Simla Convention was not signed but only initialled by the Chinese delegate and hence lacked legality. The fact remains that the map of 27th April 1914 showing the India-Tibet boundary bears the full signatures of the Tibetan Plenipotentiary and the Chinese Plenipotentiary. Mr McMahon initialled the map of 27th April 1914, while he and the Tibetan Plenipotentiary had signed the map of 3rd July 2014. To deny historical reality, one needs stronger grounds than initials and signatures.

The historical reality is that China has never protested against this position until 90 years later in 2006. Both Chou En Lai in his discussions with Nehru in 1960 and Deng Xiaoping in 1985 refrained from referring to Tawang; Chou, in fact, conceded that, while the McMahon Line was "undecided and unfair", it had become "an accomplished fact", and that "there was no better way than to recognise this Line". India and China have since held 19 rounds of border talks and signed 5 confidence-building agreements, in 1993, 1996, 2005, 2012 and 2013. The Sept 7th, 1993, agreement categorically stated that "Pending an ultimate solution to the boundary question between the 2 countries, the 2 sides shall strictly respect and observe the line of actual control between the 2 sides" which was reiterated in all subsequent agreements. The 2005 agreement further asserted, "In reaching a boundary settlement, the two sides shall safeguard due interests of their settled populations in the border areas." As *The Economist* then noted, this "implied that China had dropped its historical demand for Tawang".

The first time Tawang entered the official discussions was in March 2006, when Dai Bingguo, the special representative for boundary discussions, insisted that the eastern sector including Twang be made the focal point in border discussions, followed by the Chinese envoy, Sun Yuxi, claiming the whole of Arunachal Pradesh, including Twang, as Chinese territory. This was clearly going against the spirit of the 2005 agreement to leave areas with settled populations undisturbed. In 2007, the Chinese Foreign Minister, Yang Jiechi, told the then Indian Foreign Minister, Mr Pranab Mukherjee, that the mere presence of settled population would not alter Chinese claims. Since then there has been very little progress in negotiations between the 2 countries which have practically become stalled, and relation between the countries has become strained, moving from 'dispute settlement to crisis management'. India has effectively junked the "one-China policy" intensifying its interactions with Taiwan, and connecting it with China's acceptance of a "one-India policy".

China should realise that diplomacy and international relations depend on reciprocity. India is not overly disturbed over Chinese activities in Aksai Chin which was India's territory as a legacy of history, neither has it engaged in robust diplomacy to counter Chinese involvement in the POK, through which China is building its China-Pakistan Economic Corridor. It is time China realised that it is now dealing with a mature, strong and confident India.

3. EXPLOITING THE SYNERGIES OF THE INDIAN OCEAN RIM COUNTRIES[33]

(India must renew its historical and maritime trade links with the Indian Ocean Rim countries to exploit the full economic potential of the entire Indian Ocean region. It must provide leadership, besides economic and diplomatic support to the group of Indian Ocean rim countries to strengthen the age-old historical ties. India must exploit the cultural, historical and economic synergies of the Indian Ocean Rim countries dating back to two thousand years of connections through maritime trade.)

I

Apart from membership of several global and transcontinental organisations like the United Nations, Commonwealth, G-20, G-77, BRICS, etc., and being a full dialogue partner of ASEAN and an observer in the Shanghai Cooperation Organisation, India also features as a member of several prominent regional associations and supra-regional groupings, like SAARC, the ASEAN Regional Forum, Asia-Europe Meeting (ASEM), Bay of Bengal Initiative for Multi-Sectoral Technical and Economic Cooperation (BIMSTEC), East Asia Summit (EAS), South Asian Free Trade Area (SAFTA), Mekong-Ganga Cooperation and the Indian Ocean Rim Association for Regional Cooperation (IORARC). Some of these, like ASEM, EAS or IORARC, have not seen much activity in recent times, and some, like SAARC, have achieved practically nothing in so many decades of their existence, except indulging in occasional exercises in symbolism and tokenism. After isolating Pakistan last year, the forum itself has now become practically defunct. SAARC has never been a great integrating force within South Asia; in fact, the kind of integration that has transformed the socio-economic and political landscapes in Europe and other continents still remains a distant dream in South Asia, despite having an almost infinite potential for cooperation in infrastructure, creation of energy grids and transport networks, for erecting common architectures for handling intra-

[33]Originally published in *The Statesman* as "Oceanic Destiny", 29th & 30th January, 2017.

regional security and harnessing river potentials to improve the lives of people.

The time has indeed come to explore and harness the strengths of other supra regional groupings, by tapping into the synergies that flow from historical and cultural bonds. For India, one such group that is vital to our geo-strategic and economic goals is the group of Indian Ocean countries. However, caught in the stranglehold of stagnation in thinking, political leaders and opinion makers have so far neglected to examine the socio-cultural and economic bonds of these countries with India–bonds that were forged by history through centuries of maritime trade, as well as religious and political affiliations. These bonds remain strong and vibrant, and are cherished in many of these countries. As the former external affairs minister Mr S M Krishna had stated in 2011, the Indian Ocean remains "an integral part of our collective destiny, and we need a holistic vision for a co-operative response to the challenges in the region".

There are 59 countries in the rim of the Indian Ocean spanning a total length of 63,000 kms, of which 21 countries now constitute the Indian Ocean Rim Association for Regional Cooperation (IORARC)–with 7 more countries (including USA, China, UK, France, Japan and Germany) being the dialogue partners. These 21 countries, which include India, Australia, Indonesia, Iran, Thailand, South Africa, Malaysia, Bangladesh, Sri Lanka, UAE, Myanmar, Tanzania, etc., together form an economic powerhouse generating among themselves an annual income of more than US$ 7 trillion. As the former UN Secretary General Ban Ki Moon had articulated in propagating the compelling vision of a "United States of Asia" in 2007, the Indian Ocean Region has the potential to transform itself into a free-trade zone, and may even work towards adopting a common currency.

The region has immense geostrategic and geopolitical significance. It is home to 2 billion people spanning 3 continents–Africa, Asia and Oceania, with 3 strategic naval chokepoints at the Strait of Hormuz, Bal-el-Mandeb and the Strait of Malacca, connecting the Indian Ocean region with the Persian Gulf, the Red Sea and the South China Sea respectively. The Indian Ocean accounts for the transportation of the highest tonnage of goods in the world, with almost 120,000 ships transiting its expanse annually, and carrying two-thirds of the world's oil shipments, one-third of bulk cargo traffic and half the world's container shipments. It accounts for more than 20 percent of global trade. An estimated 40 percent of the world's offshore oil production comes from the Indian Ocean.

The IORARC, which is the only Pan-Indian ocean grouping that brings together diverse countries from three continents, had its origin in the 1990s, thanks to the initiatives taken by India and South Africa. It was set up in 1997 with the stated objectives of economic cooperation for sustainable growth and balanced development, and liberalisation and removal of impediments towards freer trade with free flow of goods, services, investment, and technology within the Indian Ocean rim. The apex body of the IORARC is the Council of Foreign Ministers of the member countries. Its Secretariat is located at Port Louis, Mauritius, which is probably not the best place to exploit its full potential.

As Jivanta Schöttli from the South Asia Institute of Heidelberg University has pointed out, the forum has suffered from a lack of visionary leadership and various other drawbacks since its inception. The sheer diversity in geography, culture and economic development of the members have made it somewhat an unwieldy entity. The track record indeed has very little to show in terms of tangible gains achieved. Projects taken up either faded away or collapsed, in the process leaving behind a number of parallel organisations, like the Indian Ocean Rim Academic Group, the Indian Ocean Rim Business Forum and the Working Group on Trade and Investment whose only job purportedly is to provide inputs to the apex body of the fledging organisation.

The 3 players who could have made a difference are India, South Africa and Australia. As Schöttli pointed out, Australia's enthusiasm dwindled after the second ministerial conference in Maputo in 1999 had ruled out voluntary trade liberalisation. South Africa's priority shifted towards African organisations after the election of Thabo Mbeki as president. India's interest waned as the forum failed to open up new regional space to stimulate investment and trade. The irrelevance of the forum was highlighted when the tsunami of 2004 had failed to elicit any large-scale cooperation for relief and rehabilitation of the thousands of hapless victims. Other groups and events have since taken over–BRICS, the Asian Infrastructure Investment Bank, and developments in the South China Sea areas for example. The forum is now practically dysfunctional and nothing is known of its activities except occasional meetings. Hardly covered by media, it could never generate much interest among the Indian intelligentsia and most are oblivious of its existence or purpose. The forum needs to be invigorated.

In recent years there has been a reorientation of our strategic focus in foreign relations in which the essential elements are maritime security, modernisation of the Indian Navy and co-operation with major naval powers such as the

United States, Japan and Australia, while asserting our presence in the Indian Ocean only as a 'catalyst for peace, tranquillity and stability'. But the rules of the game are changing slowly, in a marked departure from the past when benign rhetoric used to define and determine our policy on the Indian Ocean. The 26/11 Mumbai carnage in 2008 rattled us into reckoning and revising the Maritime Doctrine first formulated in 2004. The doctrine, revised in 2009, highlighted threats arising from maritime terrorism, piracy, coastal security and the heavy presence of extra-regional forces including the world's most powerful fleets in the Indian Ocean to safeguard their strategic interests. It identified, among the primary elements of our maritime doctrine, the oil wealth of the Persian Gulf region, which is home to 7 million expatriate Indians, the importance of key chokepoints in the Indian Ocean, while the Southern Indian Ocean region, including Antarctica, South and East China Seas, Western Pacific Ocean and the Mediterranean were identified among the secondary areas of our maritime interest.

Weariness about China's aggressive naval expansion and the fear of being surrounded by the so-called "string of pearls"–the network of Chinese military and commercial facilities and its muscle-flexing in the Indian Ocean region led India to forge closer maritime ties with the USA and Japan, and emboldened it into active engagement with Vietnam in a "comprehensive strategic partnership". It was a stark departure from our favoured policy of non-alignment we had practiced for decades without much tangible result.

It must be remembered that India's public and private-sector companies, especially in oil and power sectors, have heavily invested in foreign countries, such as Sudan, Yemen, Iran, Iraq and Myanmar. Security of such investments and considerations of our energy security, given that 80 percent of our oil imports are routed across the Indian Ocean, will continue to dominate our maritime policy demanding robust naval capabilities, and not only for deterrence purposes. Equally important are commercial considerations and safety to our trade vessels negotiating the ocean.

Prime Minister Modi also repeatedly underlined that the Indian Ocean region is one of India's 'foremost policy priorities', while projecting a vision for 'SAGAR', which means ocean and stands for "Security and Growth for All in the Region". India is now ready to mark its presence in the wider Indo-Pacific region and may even consider building military bases outside. India's interest in developing the Chabahar port in Iran is a reflection of this new-found determination to break from the passivity and hesitations of the past. But we need a vibrant organisation to back up and stimulate these efforts, so as to optimise the outcomes. This is why the IORARC needs to be actively and energetically engaged with.

II

In his book *Monsoon, The Indian Ocean and Future of American Power*, the American author Robert Kaplan argued that the geopolitics of the twenty-first century will be decided by events in the Indian Ocean rim which is emerging as the new geopolitical centre of the world. Kaplan's narrative rests on the premise that the Indian Ocean's regular monsoon winds, which carried traders across the ocean since antiquity had established cultural and economic patterns which are still very much in action. There has been little research conducted so far on issues relating to security, stability and sustainability of the Indian Ocean region and its future potential from the geopolitical and strategic perspectives of the 21st century. The concept of proactively promoting and engaging in a broader Indian Ocean grouping still lies at the periphery of our national objectives and geopolitical goals, ignoring the advantages conferred upon us by history. We are still unmindful of what Nelson Mandela prophetically said in 1995: "The natural urge of the facts of history and geography should broaden itself to include the concept of an Indian Ocean Rim for socio-economic co-operation and other peaceful endeavours."

One of the earliest works on the subject, *Histoire ancienne des états hindouisés d'Extrême Orient* published in 1944 (translated as *The Indianized States of Southeast Asia*) by the French archaeologist George Cœdès explores the dharma-dhamma continuum evidenced even today in the thousands of Hindu-Buddha temples practically all over South East Asia–Malaysia, Indonesia, Thailand, Cambodia, Vietnam, Laos and Myanmar. India's relations with these countries date back at least to the 1st millennium AD or even earlier; even countries on the eastern and southern coast of Africa and in the middle-east share thousands of years of close socio-cultural interaction through maritime trade links with India.

In 1947, K. M. Panikkar observed, "Millenniums before Columbus sailed the Atlantic and Magellan crossed the Pacific, the Indian Ocean had become a thoroughfare of commercial and cultural traffic." That was one of the earliest globalisations on record. Sanjeev Sanyal, in his book *Ocean of Churn*, mentioned that the Middle East and Iran had had trade links with the Indus valley people since the Harappan times, and that the merchant ships from Gurjrat used to sail along the Makran coast trading along the way, past Gwador and Sutkajen-dor (now near the Iran-Pakistan border). Discovery of Harappan artefacts and seals as far as Southern Iran suggests a continuum of economic and cultural trails throughout the region. The trail survived even in modern times–till the 1960s, the Indian rupee was legal tender in most Middle-East countries including Bahrain, Qatar, Oman and UAE. They resorted to their own currencies only after the sharp devaluation of the rupee by the RBI in 1966. The supreme living trail is of course the hundreds of thousands of Indians who live and work in the Gulf countries in the Middle East, especially from the south–a reminder of a vibrant ancient connection when hundreds Arab merchants used to flock to the Malabar and Kerala coasts in the course of maritime trade.

Sanyal narrated how seafarers from Odisha and Bengal had started visiting Sri Lanka from the sixth century BC. The first Indianised kingdom emerged in Vietnam's Mekong delta around the 1st century BC, established, according to legend, by a Brahmin named Kaundinya, to whom both the Chams of Vietnam as well as the Khmers of Cambodia trace their ancestry. By then, Indian mariners had learnt enough about monsoon winds and ocean currents to follow the north eastern monsoon to sail to Sri Lanka in mid-November, an event that is still commemorated in Odisha on the day of Kartik Purnima when ladies place paper boats with lighted diyas on waterbodies, a distant reminder of the times when their men-folk would sail away leaving them to take care of their homes for months. After replenishing the fresh water and provisions in Sri Lanka, mariners would set sail again in January, following ocean currents to Sumatra, then known as Swarnadwipa, and from there continue their voyage past the Malacca Strait on to the Malay Peninsula, Borneo and Vietnam, or southward along the western coast of Java, then known as Jabadwipa, and on to Bali. After trading for 2 months, by mid-March they would start their return journey to reach Sri Lanka in time to catch the south-west monsoon that would take them back home.

With more knowledge about ocean currents and monsoon winds, Indian seafarers became more adventurous. They sailed not only from Odisha and Bengal, but also from Andhra and Tamilnadu. Cotton was the most important export, and Indian cotton carried the seeds of Indian culture, language and religion into the lands of South East Asia. Hinduism and Buddhism spread within a few centuries, and Mahabharata and Ramayana struck deep roots along with Sanskrit in the soil of South East Asia, which have survived the onslaught of Islam and colonial rule by the Portuguese, the Dutch and the British till today. Hinduism is still dominant in Bali and Buddhism in Myanmar. The 9th century Buddhist temple of Borobudur and the 10th century Hindu temples of Prambanan in Indonesia and the 12th century Hindu temple of Angkor in Cambodia still attract millions of tourists from all over the world. The Indian links are remembered with a great deal of warmth, and I have myself experienced extraordinary affection in these lands just because I happen to hail from India.

The Hindu Srivijaya dynasty in Sumatra and Malay Peninsula (7th-13th centuries), Angkor (Khmer) in Cambodia (9th-15th centuries), Majapahit in Java (13th-16th centuries) and Kingdom of Champa in Central and Southern Vietnam (2nd-17th centuries) remained enduring powers in the region, before the gradual spread of Islam from the 14th century onwards after which colonisation by Europeans would eclipse their glory.

Along the west coast of India also, merchant fleets from Arabia negotiated the waters of the Arabian Sea, sailing south hugging the western coast of India, past Saurashtra and the Gulf of Khambhat, through the estuary of Narmada to the modern port of Bharuch, then Barygaza. The Arab merchants would reach the shores of Kerala within a few centuries. It was following this route that groups of Christians and Parsis fleeing persecution in Iran would reach India, making it their home for ever.

It is indeed paradoxical how the adventurous, seafaring people of India gradually turned inward-looking and lost their strength before succumbing easily to foreign invasions, and how even crossing the sea (*Kalapani*) became stigmatised in society. In his seminal work, "The Influence of Sea Power upon History, 1660-1783", American naval strategist Alfred Thayer Mahan had argued that control over the seas is essential for national greatness. The history of the colonisation of Asia, Africa and the Americas by European powers seem to vindicate much of Mahan's thesis. Seas provide excellent means for communication and exchange between nations, and an enemy can be neutralised by barring it from the use of the sea. Mahan's theory can be viewed in the perspective of current reinforcement naval power in the Indian Ocean by India, China and the USA. A strong navy that can bolster commercial interests, protect trade and control the strategic checkpoints would be the key elements in any race for supremacy of power in the Indian Ocean region, a region that will become the epicentre of global power-play in the 21st century.

"Project 'Mausam': Maritime Routes and Cultural Landscapes" was launched as a transnational project by the Ministry of Culture of India in 2014, to rekindle the long-lost ties across nations of the Indian Ocean-world and to forge new avenues of cooperation and exchange. The project, launched by India in partnership with member states, will enable a significant step in recording and celebrating this important phase of world history from the African, Arab and Asian-world perspectives. But to regenerate the economic links is even more important, and a sustainable way to achieve this is through the “Blue Economy”.

Gunter Pauli's 2010 book, *The Blue Economy: 10 years, 100 innovations, 100 million jobs* promises to “shift society from scarcity to abundance ‘with what is locally available’, by tackling issues that cause environmental and related problems in new ways”. It relies on the design of sustainable systems to fuel "blue growth" which address the problems of resource scarcity and waste disposal, while focusing on sustainable development in a holistic manner. The Blue Economy holds immense promise for the Indian Ocean region which has a treasure of vast untapped natural resources. Development of the Blue Economy in the Indian Ocean region has the potential to offer many benefits, from utilising the untapped marine and mineral resources of the Indian Ocean to interconnecting, boosting and synergising the coastal national economies of the region. It can also revive the IORARC as an ocean-based, close-knit and vibrant community. In fact, the IORARC has already adopted the Blue Economy as a top priority, and identified eight priority areas for cooperation between the member states including fisheries and aquaculture, renewable ocean energy, seaports and shipping, seabed exploration for minerals etc. One only hopes that the ideas are translated into actions, because, like in the past, what happens in the Indian Ocean now will determine the course of human history once again.

4. THE UN AT 70: HIGH TIME TO REFORM[34]

(The configuration of power distribution in today's world is quite different from what it was seventy years ago. If the UN cannot find a way to reflect this reality in the UNSC and its other organs, it runs the risk of gradually sliding into irrelevance and oblivion.)

The United Nations (UN) is celebrating its 70th anniversary this year. It was founded on October 24th 1945, in the aftermath of the devastation wrought by World War II. The United Nations Security Council (UNSC) was established as one of its 6 organs with primary responsibility for maintenance of international peace and security and "to save succeeding generations from the scourge of war". Mercifully, the world has not seen another global war and the likelihood of one too appears to be small, but the world is far from becoming free from the scourge of war, conflicts and violence. There are too many trouble-spots in the world today–Syria, Ukraine, Nigeria, Sudan, Mali, the Middle-East and Afghanistan, to name but a few– where the UNSC is powerless to stop innocent blood from getting spilled. The UNSC, instead of brokering the resolution of conflicts, is often reckoned as a part of the problem. The conflicting interests of its five permanent members (P5) often hold it hostage to take a decision in the interest of securing peace, as we have seen in the case of Syria in recent times, where China and Russia have repeatedly halted resolutions against Damascus. Arguably, the UN no longer commands the collective respect of the international community, making one wonder if it will fade into history as an 'ineffective, irrelevant debating society', as President George Bush once mocked. It has also ceased to represent the global power configurations in today's world.

The UN was founded on 2 principles: the sovereign equality of all member nations, as reflected in the principle of "one state, one vote," and the responsibility of major powers to maintain global stability and peace. The UNSC is the only agency with the right to adopt resolutions which are

[34] Originally published in *The Sunday Statesman* as "Three Score & Ten: Time to Reform the Security Council", 17th May, 2015.

legally binding on all UN members for maintaining and enforcing international peace, stability and security, if necessary, by authorising the use of economic sanctions, or even force. At the birth of the UN, the UNSC consisted of five permanent (P5) and 6 non-permanent members. Permanent members were represented by the major powers of the world at that time. The criteria applied for their election included population and territory, economic and military power and intellectual resources, which restricted the number of potential candidates to only a handful of countries–the same handful who continue to dominate the UNSC even today, irrespective of the erosion of their military, economic and intellectual capabilities, and in total disregard of the emergence of other competing powers possessing substantial demographic, economic and intellectual capitals.

In 1963, the numbers of non-permanent members in the UNSC was increased to 10, on the basis of regional representations: three from Africa, two each from Latin America, Asia and Western Europe and one from Eastern Europe. They are elected by the United Nations General Assembly for a term of two years each, on the basis of their contribution to the maintenance of international peace and security and also to the objectives of the UN Charter.

The decision threshold in the UNSC is nine affirmative votes. Each permanent member has a veto with which they can block any decision; often a decision is prevented by the mere threat of a veto. All UN member states are obliged to comply with the decisions of the UNSC. While nine affirmative votes suffice for a decision on procedural matters, other decisions–like establishing peace-keeping operations or application of coercive measures against a state–also require concurrence (at least non-opposition) by each of the P5.

There have been endless debates and extensive disagreements about reform and reconfiguration of the UNSC. Apart from Japan and Germany, the second and third largest contributors to the UN budget after the USA, emerging powers, like Brazil, India, South Africa and Nigeria, have staked strong claims for permanent seats in the UNSC. They have also served for considerably long periods in the UNSC as non-permanent members: Japan has served in the UNSC for 35 percent of the total time it has been a UN-member, Brazil 30 percent, Germany 25 percent, Argentina 24 percent, Pakistan, Italy, India and Columbia each above 20 percent, and Nigeria about 15 percent. Only South Africa, because of its apartheid past, served the UNSC for only 2 terms.

If the criteria for membership that was applied for electing the P5 countries at the birth of UN in 1945 are recomputed and reapplied today, the top 5 countries would include USA, China, Japan, Brazil and Germany, followed by Russia, India, France, UK, Italy, Spain, Canada, Australia and South Africa, in that order, calculated on the average of the their relative world rankings in respect of their shares of: (1) world population, (2) contribution to the UN regular budget and (3) GDP on purchasing power parity basis, all pertaining to 2014 IMF and UN data. Obviously, the configuration of power distribution in today's world is quite different from what it was 70 years ago. If the UN cannot find a way to reflect this reality in the UNSC and its other organs, it runs the risk of gradually sliding into irrelevance and oblivion.

To effect any change in its structure, the UN Charter needs to be amended. As per article 108 of the UN Charter, an amendment will need ratification by two-thirds of the members of the UN General Assembly (UNGA), including all permanent members of the Security Council. This is obviously a tedious process testified by the fact that the UN Charter has only been amended four times during the last seventy years of its existence. There is an alternative provided in Article 109 of the UN Charter, which is even more tedious–it entails convening a general conference of all member states and ratifying the proposed amendment by two thirds of the UNGA membership, in addition to ratification by 9 of the 15 UNSC members including all the P5. No wonder Article 109 has not been used so far!

Any P5 member has the power to block any reform proposal by casting a veto, but even the regional groups within the UN have the clout to block such proposals. Currently, African and Asian countries together constitute 56 percent of the total General Assembly membership–more than what is required for a majority. An amendment will thus necessarily need the political support of the majority of all regional groups of the world. This is not an easy task, given the delicate balances that need to be struck between conflicting interests of power and requirements of legitimacy and justice in a world where these are increasingly becoming rarer.

At the 2005 World Summit, Mr Kofi Annan had highlighted the need for urgent UNSC reforms. Several reform proposals have since emerged envisaging expansion of the UNSC. The G4 proposal put forth by Germany, India, Brazil and Japan seeks to expand the size of UNSC to 25 by adding 6 permanent seats without veto power including 2 from Africa, and 4 non-permanent seats. A second proposal was presented by the group 'Uniting for Consensus' (UFC) that includes the regional rivals of G4: Italy, Spain,

Pakistan, Mexico, Columbia, Argentina and South Korea; it sought to expand the UNSC to 25 members with 10 new, rotating, non-permanent members without veto rights. The African Union presented a proposal suggesting the addition of 6 permanent seats with veto power and 5 non-permanent seats. In 2012, a group of 69 small and middle-sized developing countries (L69), including Brazil, India, Nigeria and South Africa, presented another proposal seeking permanent membership with veto powers for these 4 countries, besides adding 8 new non-permanent members, thus expanding the size of the UNSC to 27 members. But none of these proposals ever got the backing of the required majority, and the resulting status quo embodies the formidable hurdles and contentious divisions. All P5 members except China have pledged support to India's candidature for a permanent seat in the UNSC which is fiercely opposed by Pakistan. China and South Korea oppose Japan's permanent membership, while Argentina and others oppose Brazil's and Spain and Italy that of Germany. Hope for a consensus is still a long way off.

As regards contributions in UN Peacekeeping operations, India, Pakistan and Nigeria have been among the top 5 troop contributing countries, followed by South Africa and Brazil. Italy, Argentina, Germany, Japan and China have also contributed significantly in this.

The real bone of contention is the permanent membership and veto rights. Mr Kofi Annan has recently attempted to break the gridlock by proposing a category of new members in place of permanent members, with much longer terms and eligible for immediate re-election, thus making them de-facto permanent members. He has also advocated that the P5 should cast their veto only in the interest of world peace and not just to defend their own strategic interests; they should pledge not to allow their disagreements to stand in the way of preventing atrocities being committed upon people, as in Syria. Given the fragmented vision that guides geopolitics today, such hope seems to be rather utopian. There are too many obstacles, diplomatic and political, and too many differences to overcome. The world will perhaps remain a divided place for a long time, with increasing violence, conflict, suffering and deaths of innocents. The UN might lapse into history unobserved, negotiating only fragile ceasefires and abandoning the ultimate objective of saving the world from the scourge of wars and conflicts.

5. SAARC SUMMIT: ANOTHER MISSED OPPORTUNITY[35]

(The recently concluded SAARC summit was another missed opportunity to transform the SAARC into a dynamic forum.)

It seems that the most important take-away from the recently concluded SAARC summit in Kathmandu was the belated handshake between Prime Ministers Narendra Modi and Nawaz Sharif. In concrete terms, there was a sole agreement on energy cooperation allowing for trade in electricity between the member nations. Even this single agreement was salvaged at the last moment, after Pakistan was persuaded to drop its objections, due to which two other stipulated agreements on road and railway networks could not be concluded. Any agreement on containing terrorism or improving internal security within the member nations was never on the agenda, even though the summit had symbolically opened on the anniversary of 26/11. Modi, of course, occupied centre stage, but beyond a point, hype tends to become counterproductive and does nothing to mitigate the underlying mutual mistrust and suspicion that had characterised the SAARC since its inception.

Ever since the first summit at Dhaka in 1985, tokenism and symbolism have marked the journey of the SAARC all along. For one thing, the SAARC has never been a great integrating force even within the South Asian region. Inheriting widespread poverty and economic backwardness from their common colonial past, SAARC nations indeed have an overarching need to bury their differences and work for the economic uplifting of their people through increased cooperation in trade, connectivity and economic exchanges, if not political integration. The kind of integration that has transformed the socio-economic and political landscape in Europe and many other regions since the last world war remains a distant dream in South Asia. Despite the South Asian Free Trade Area (SAFTA) agreement of 2004 to establish a free-trade zone among the 8 member countries, the goal of achieving zero customs duties on traded goods among SAARC nations by

[35] Originally published in *The Statesman* as "Another Bus Missed in South Asia", 15th December, 2014.

2016 is nowhere in sight. It is not that Pakistan has been the only stumbling block by not granting the 'Most Favoured Nation' status to India; other countries like Bangladesh, Sri Lanka and Nepal are also deeply suspicious of India, the hegemon within this group, and fear Indian goods flooding their markets and stifling their nascent industries. As a result, the total trade within this group does not even account for 5 percent of global trade. Nearly 9,900 km of borders are shared between India and its SAARC neighbours, Bangladesh, Bhutan, Nepal and Pakistan alone, but poor connectivity and lack of infrastructure seriously thwart the chances of better integration.

The existing synergies also remain to be tapped optimally. India has its pharmaceuticals, agricultural products, machinery, iron and steel, software and space technology to help propel the growth of other nations in the region. Bangladesh has jute and textiles, Sri Lanka tea, Bhutan hydro-power potential, the Maldives fish, Afghanistan raw materials and Nepal has a huge amount of potential mountain tourism, but needs infrastructure to realise it. Pakistan at the moment seems to have nothing other than terrorism to trade, but is itself the worst victim of it. These countries can be competitive only by reducing costs through the removal of barriers that restrict the movement of factors of production and trade and by liberalising the flow of technology and investment. The potential is almost infinite–cooperating in infrastructure, education and health care, creating intra-regional energy grids, networks of transport, aviation, shipping and railways spanning different countries, building architectures for mitigating natural disasters all countries are prone to, for harnessing their river potentials for power and irrigation available to others, and for improving security and good governance within each. A credible security architecture could have been erected with the cooperation of all members, side by side with an economic architecture that would have reinforced all members by creating economic opportunities and thus helping to contain terrorism. But security remains fragile, making governments watch helplessly when non-state actors inflict mindless violence on innocent citizens with impunity. One way forward is to ignore Pakistan for the time being and form sub-regional groupings with others, and build supra-regional groupings, like BIMSTEC, bringing East and parts of South Asia together.

SAARC remains the world's second least developed region after sub-Saharan Africa, with per capita income three times below the global average. Despite common cultural and civilisational inheritance and shared geographical congruence, fractious political relationships between member nations have dissipated opportunities for closer alliance and cooperation. The SAARC region that was mostly a single integrated economic region earlier was broken into several nation states, sacrificing trade and connectivity. In the post-colonial era, these nations, thanks to their unimaginative political leadership, became inward rather than outward-looking, closed economies. Reforms are yet to start on most countries opening their mind to new ideas and their economies to new opportunities. Naturally the group has not moved much beyond the tokenism of a SAARC satellite and the symbolism of a SAARC University.

Together, SAARC nations can form an important block in international fora, and the voice of 25 percent of the world's total population living within 4 percent of the world's geographical area cannot be ignored easily. There is hardly any likelihood of anything like this happening anytime soon. But despite its dysfunctional nature, it has attracted nine observers–including the European Union (EU), USA, Australia, Japan and China, which indicates its strategic geopolitical importance in today’s world. China is demanding an enlarged role in SAARC which is being opposed by India. Perhaps India ought to consider that these 2 nations together, till the 1820s, used to command 49 percent of global GDP, as economist Angus Maddison documented in his book, *The World Economy*, before colonialism drained away their resources. It is in their mutual interest to ignore their differences and come together, and see each other as collaborators rather than competitors.

The SAARC leaders can take lessons from international organisations on how the benefits of coming together by burying the acrimony of the past far outweigh the choice of staying apart, especially in today’s technology-driven, connected and flat world. That borders can be turned into bridges rather than barriers has been most convincingly demonstrated by the European Union (EU), which has its origins in the Treaty of Paris in 1951, forming the European Coal and Steel Community to integrate coal and steel industries of the seven original participating members, including Germany and France who were just beginning to recover from the ruins of a World War they had fought so bitterly against each other. As the then French Foreign Minister, Robert Schuman, famously said, “The pooling of coal and steel production will change the destinies of those regions which have long been devoted to the manufacture of munitions war, of which they have been the most constant victims.”

The political thinker Ernst Haas in his 1958 book, *The Uniting of Europe*, pointed out that regional integration moves forward on the basis of processes he calls ‘spillovers’ which can be functional, political, or cultivated. Functional spillover implies that integration in one functional area would necessarily lead to integration in other areas. Political spillover results from political pressures by trans-national interest groups demanding more integration. Spillover can also be cultivated by supranational institutions advocating more integration. The European Union has seen all the above 3 processes working together, moving from economic cooperation to common market and common currency to political union. Given Europe's history of centuries of bloody conflicts, this was a remarkable achievement, a fact recognised by the Nobel Peace Prize awarded to the European Union in 2012.

In 1986, the Single European Act laid the foundation for internal markets allowing free movement of goods, services, capital and people, and mandated the EU members to speak in one voice in international fora. The Treaty on European Union, or Maastricht Treaty, of 1992 then created the EU's Monetary Union and initiated Europe's Common Foreign and Security Policy. It also obligated all member states to defend the interests of the EU. The position of High Representative for Foreign Affairs and Security Policy was created by the Lisbon Treaty in 2009, to coordinate the preferences and priorities of EU member states in international fora.

After the end of the Cold War, Eastern European nations also integrated into the European Union, and today it is a vibrant 28 member body. Integration has helped the nations face the challenges thrown by the global financial crisis of 2008-09, taking the union further forward by instituting new agreements for ensuring fiscal and monetary stability. Today, it is the largest global trading block commanding 15 percent of global trade on goods and 22.5 percent of global trade in services, and has 20 percent of the world's GDP and a strong common currency, the Euro, which, though still young, is a major reserve currency in central banks around the globe. It operates like a single unified country, with similar policies, democratic political systems, borderless travel, employment and trade. Common approaches have been adopted to face common problems and challenges thrown by crisis, of which there are many, with unemployment exceeding 10 percent, in some member nations like Greece, Spain, Portugal and Ireland, which the EU has confronted successfully and held together.

Like the EU, past discords have not deterred other countries to take pragmatic steps overlooking and ultimately overcoming the initial mistrust in the interest of mutual benefits. Russia and China had fought three Sino-Russian wars till 1929, and experienced a 7-month long bitter border standoff as late as 1969. All this conflict did not prevent the rivals coming together in the Shanghai Cooperation Organisation (SCO), established in the mid-1990s, that includes some breakaway Soviet countries as well. Accounting for a quarter of the world's population, its charter emphasises trust, regional stability and economic, social and cultural integration amongst its members. The SCO focuses specifically on countering the "three evils" of terrorism, separatism, and extremism, as well as combating the illicit narcotics trade, arms trafficking, and illegal migration, problems that afflict all the member countries. It has erected a regional anti-terrorism structure in Tashkent, Uzbekistan, ensuring coordinated military, security and intelligence sharing activities, something the SAARC has not been able even to think of. India is keen to become a member of the SCO, but its entry is opposed by China.

There are others, like the Asia-Pacific Economic Cooperation (APEC), a forum for 21 member Pacific Rim economies that seeks to promote free trade, investment and economic cooperation throughout the Asia-Pacific region, established in 1989, or the 8 member Arctic Council formed in 1996, where countries with diverse interests and often with a conflictual past have grouped together for common interest and prospered together in terms of welfare of their people.

SAARC countries have a lot of common problems, poverty, slow growth, unemployment, cross-border terrorism, etc. and together they can combat these evils much better than individually. India, which accounts for three quarters of its population and two-thirds of its area, has the highest stake in it. But it, along with other nations, has missed yet another opportunity to transform SAARC into a dynamic forum.

6. END OF JOBS[36]

(Robots are increasingly taking away human jobs and it is not simply the low-skill, low-wage routine and manual jobs. Even non-routine jobs requiring superior cognitive skills are being taken over by robots which can now learn by themselves. Our education system needs to be geared up to meet this challenge that is increasingly threatening the jobs for our youth.)

A friend who was an office head once told me a poignant story about his steno when a vendor had come to his office to demonstrate the use of speech recognition software that would allow a note to be dictated directly to the computer. After the vendor had left, the steno asked him, "Sir, does that mean my services are no longer needed?" Stenographers are no longer recruited in any office.

In 2014, writing software called Quill was developed by an American Company that could convert numerical data into a written story, accomplishing within seconds what took experienced analysts weeks of synthesis and analysis of huge volumes of financial data. In 2014, the Associated Press began publishing a large number of articles about US corporate earnings, most of which were written not by humans but by robot journalists. These are increasingly getting better, sharper, and more analytical.

All work can be divided into 4r types: routine jobs that require the same task repeated over and over again as opposed to non-routine jobs, and cognitive jobs that require the use of brains as opposed to manual jobs that mostly requires the use of our bodies. Routine labour stagnated way back in 1990, having been replaced by technology, and many manual jobs followed suit. In the 21st century cognitive and non-routine jobs are being automated at an increasing pace, with exponential progress in developing robots that can learn by themselves. The future world will be one in which machines can perform all four types of jobs at a fraction of the cost of human labour. It is creating the spectre of a jobless growth for our youth. In a 2013 study on the impact of computerisation upon jobs, Oxford scholars Carl Frey and Michael Osborne found that algorithms for big data had started to penetrate higher cognitive domains like pattern recognition and to substitute labour in

---

36 Originally published in *The Statesman*, 23rd February, 2017.

a wide range of non-routine cognitive tasks. Computers have already started replacing jobs in easy-to-automate areas like transportation, logistics, production, services, sales, and construction. Harder domains will also be captured during the next wave of computerisation, putting at stake jobs in management, science, engineering, and even arts. They predicted that nearly half of all American jobs will be lost to automation by 2033. It will probably be faster.

Advanced robots are now being produced with enhanced features, mobility and dexterity, allowing them to perform a much broader range of tasks requiring superior cognitive skills. Demands for industrial robots are increasing exponentially–their worldwide sales in 2015 touched 225,000, 27 percent higher than in 2014. This is sending shockwaves across industries and occupations, impacting wages and educational requirements for jobs.

The periodic slump in the demand for skilled labour is nothing new in human history. In the 19th century, manufacturing technologies substituted for skilled labour through simplification of tasks by introducing the electricity-driven, partly-automated assembly-line production system. As a result, real wages stagnated while output per worker expanded due to increased efficiency. In response, the educational system became highly specialised, imparting complex skill-sets that, aided by the phenomenal expansion of transportation networks and the consequent increase in market size for the products, increased productivity manifolds, which in turn led to a rise in real wages and improvement in the living standards in industrial societies after the middle of the 19th century.

The computer and internet revolutions of the twentieth century again dented middle-income jobs, requiring higher levels of education for recruits and giving an unprecedented spurt to innovation and creativity. Productivity increased with the replacement of labour by technology in some industries, attracting more companies to enter those industries and in turn forcing more automation, job-contraction and lowering of wages. Industries that could not be automated shifted to low cost low wage countries, like Bangladesh and Vietnam. But alas, tasks that were hitherto considered non-susceptible to computerisation are now increasingly being taken over by the computers, e.g., textiles and footwear. German sportswear firm Adidas opened its first automated factory last year and showed the robot-made Futurecraft shoes. As Nicholas Carr, author of *The Glass Cage: Automation and Us* said, "Jobs that used to be very complex, idiosyncratic and interesting start to look more like computer operator jobs, just putting in data and interpreting screen readouts." Computerisation is no longer confined to low-skill and low-wage occupations as it once used to be.

The emerging portends are truly ominous. Truck driving is a popular job in the USA, it is easily available, pays decently and has so far remained immune to automation. But no longer; Google, Uber and Tesla are working on self-driving vehicles; once operational, it will immediately send 3.5 million drivers and 5.2 million additional personnel out of jobs. Uber is already testing self-driving cars on the roads of San Francisco and as is Google (Self-Driving Cars now known as Waymo, way to mobility). The ultimate goal is to replace all human drivers with robots threatening millions of drivers' jobs.

If this is not scary enough, consider the following: the e-commerce giant Amazon now has 30,000 fulfilment robots working in its warehouses worldwide. It expects to replace all employees who perform repetitive tasks with machines in not-too-distant a future. The Shanghai-based Cambridge Industries Group, one of China's leading suppliers of telecoms equipment is replacing two-thirds of its 3,000-strong human workforce with robots, eventually creating energy efficient 'dark factories' where robots would work in darkness to save power. Hardware store Lowe's just deployed a series of autonomous retail service robots called 'Lowebots' at 11 stores in the San Francisco Bay area; these multilingual robots are performing customer service and inventory management functions. Pizza Hut has just opened a concept store in Shanghai with robot waiters, which welcome customers, show them to their seats, take orders and serve drinks. Walmart is testing warehouse drones that fly around its distribution centres monitoring inventory levels and flagging up low stock or missing items. Many of the world's major companies spanning practically all sectors, like Nestle, SNCF, Foxconn, Marriott Hotels, ING, DHL, Nissan, Fidelity Investments and Zara, are transferring the bulk of their workloads to robots.

In January 2016, the World Economic Forum brought out a report on "The Future of Jobs". It predicted that the 4th Industrial Revolution, brought about by artificial intelligence and machine-learning, robotics, nanotechnology, 3-D printing, genetics and biotechnology, will cause widespread disruption to business models and labour markets over the next 5 years, with enormous changes in the skillset requirement in the new age, costing a net loss of 5 million jobs in 15 of the world's largest economies, including Australia, Brazil, China, France, Germany, India, Italy, Japan, Mexico, South Africa, Turkey, UK and USA, plus the ASEAN and GCC groups, which together account for 65 percent of the global workforce. These are conservative predictions and the disruptions caused will vary widely across industries. It is only in this context that economists are arguing for decoupling income from work for providing a universal basic income to all to immunise the human workers against the negative effects of automation. Switzerland, Finland, the Netherlands, and Canada and even India are toying with this idea, the costs and benefits of which are right now being assessed.

As technology continues invading the labour market, education and businesses must get ready for upskilling, reskilling and collaborating rather than talent hunting. Tools made us human, and the tools we now have, artificial intelligence and computers, are the most powerful tools ever invented. In our networked age, innovation, adaptability and speed would be essential for survival, to equip our youth with a new set of cognitive skills combined with creative and social intelligence to work alongside robots. Mere cognitive skills are not enough in the robot economy. As Geoff Colvin asserts in his book, *Humans Are Underrated*, the new age of industry needs empathy, and people who can understand what the client or customer really feels and wants, which requires social skills and creativity which robots don't have, not as yet. And that requires new curricula and pedagogy for our schools, colleges and universities, something we are not yet ready for. We may be the fastest growing economy, but the growth is going to be jobless as it has been in recent years, and governments can't do much. In the days to come, the clamour for reservation in government and private sector jobs is only going to be louder and more contagious, not only from Patels, Jats, Marathas and Ahoms, but from all communities, backward or forward alike.

Our educators and policy makers – do they ever listen to Bob Dylan?

"Yes, how many times can a man turn his head/Pretending he just doesn't see?/The answer my friend is blowin' in the wind /The answer is blowin' in the wind."

7. DEMONETISED LIVING[37]

(Technology has reduced our cost of living substantially and is opening up the possibility of a cost-free life for us in this planet ensuring both quality and quantity of the goods and services that we need for healthy and sustainable living.)

India has just been through a rough patch wrought by the demonetisation of high value currency notes amounting to about 86 percent of the total value of notes in circulation, and worth about ₹15 lakh crore. The measure, claimed as a 'surgical strike on black money' by the government, attracted widespread opprobrium from the so-called liberal literati. The measure was opposed and derided almost universally by leftist academicians, self-proclaimed experts, opposition politicians as well as economists of many hues including those famously described as "Harvard trained economists". They demonised the step as a "historic blunder" and its driver as a heartless, Tughlaqesque despot insensitive to the unspeakable suffering it had caused to common people. But the measure apparently did not alienate the people, on the contrary, it rather seemed to have gained their approval. While everybody cried that the entire cash-driven informal sector was finished by this thoughtless step and predicted the imminent collapse of the Indian economy, nothing like that happened; even a state like UP where the economy was largely dependent on the informal sector voted to power, by an overwhelming majority, the party that demonetised the high denomination notes on November 8th, 2016.

That was demonetisation at a gross level. Peter Diamandis, a Harvard-MIT trained engineer and founder of the Singularity University, talked of "rapid demonetisation of the cost of living itself" within the next 20 years, opening up ever cheaper means to satisfy our basic needs. In the face of robots increasingly taking away our jobs, this sounds too good to be true. But Diamandis has shown that powered by innovations in "exponentially accelerating technologies" like network sensors, artificial intelligence, robotics, synthetic biology and 3D printing, the costs of humanity's basic requirements, like housing, transportation, food, healthcare, entertainment, clothing and education on which an average Indian spends 90 percent of his

---

[37] Originally published in *The Statesman*, 6th April, 2017.

income, will continue to fall exponentially, eventually becoming nil. It will radically alter the way humans have lived and worked all along on this planet since the dawn of civilisation.

In the book *Abundance: The Future is Better than you Think* written jointly with the science journalist Steven Kotler in 2012, Diamandis showed how products and services worth $900,000 (₹6 crore) if we were to purchase these between 1969 and 1989, like a video conferencing facility, GPS, video player, digital voice recorder or a 5 megapixel camera, have already become demonetised, and which today carry zero cost, thanks to our smartphone of ₹5000 in which all these features come free. The smartphone has even obviated the need for a free press. So even if your child is not getting a job, rest assured, because his basic needs will be taken care of almost free of cost. Progress in exponentially growing technologies will enable us to make the next 2 decades more productive in terms of benefits to humanity than the last 2 centuries. The divide between the privileged and the commoner which has all along thwarted humanity's progress would then be a thing of the past, and abundance will be within everybody's reach. It is all about technology and innovation, which managed well, can turn scarcity into abundance.

Technology has indeed solved many of our problems and drastically reduced the costs associated with those. Remember the depressing memories of the PL-480 days during the mid-sixties, when, after 2 successive years of savage drought, and lacking any foreign exchange to buy food in the world market, we were forced to import American wheat under the most humiliating terms? If today we are able to feed our billion plus population and then export the surplus food-grains, it is only thanks to green, blue, white and yellow revolutions brought in by technology.

As Diamandis points out, thanks to the use of exponential technology, many of our basic needs have already become practically demonetised, for example, photography, music and entertainment, access to information and research, telephone or video calls etc., and many more are in the offing. Once Uber launches its fully autonomous services, transportation and insurance costs will plummet, and the automotive market worth a trillion dollars will become effectively demonetised. Price of food globally has been on a downward spiral since the last century, having already dropped by more than 50 percent since 1960, and with the use of vertical farming that eliminates the need for fertilisers and pesticides, advances in genetic engineering of food products and with better management of transportation, storage and handling that today accounts for 70 percent of total food costs, hunger could be effectively eliminated from the world. The increasing world population and growth in income will continue to exert pressure for increased and more sustainable agricultural production to feed the planet. A report on "Food Security in a World of Natural Resource Scarcity: The Role of Agricultural Technologies" released in 2014 by the International Food Policy Research Institute (IFPRI), Washington D.C., estimated that improved agricultural technologies could increase the yield of crops globally by as much as 67 percent and cut food prices nearly by 50 percent by 2050.

Housing today is costly only because of location, but once we are able to operate from any place, and access all essential services that we need, there would be no need to seek a preferred location in a city. We can then live anywhere, work from our homes or drive to the nearest workplace in autonomous cars, and it matters little even if the journey is taking a long time, because the time can be productively utilised thanks to the improved connectivity. Our workplace may even be a virtual office and we may no longer need to commute even - just plug to our virtual workspace, and telecommute. It would be the same with energy, the driver of technology and civilisations. The poorest countries on our planet, fortunately, are the sunniest and the cost of solar power is plummeting radically. With advances in technology, energy will continue to demonetise ever faster.

Healthcare remains a stubborn area, but advances in robotics are already opening the possibility that in the near future, robots will take over surgery, exercising a precision far beyond the capability of the most experienced of human surgeons. With increasing deployment of robot-surgeons, the cost will reduce drastically. As regards prognosis of diseases, the price of genomic sequencing is dropping fast, and the more accurate our sequencing becomes, the easier it would be to arrive at the correct diagnosis. The cost of medicines will also come down as we learn to use 3-D printing for manufacturing medicines with our home-based 3-D printing machines.

Access to good education has always drawn the dividing line between the elites and downtrodden, the rich and the poor. But even education has already been substantially demonetised. Information and knowledge are freely available on the internet, and with free Massive Open Online Courses like Coursera, Khan Academy, and online availability of high-quality instructions from Harvard, MIT, Stanford, IITs, etc. available to anyone with an internet connection, much of the problem of access has already been solved. It will of course still take several decades in a country like India, but it would be far easier to impart internet-based quality instruction than reform our decrepit public school system which is in complete disarray toady. Education will be liberated from the tyranny of universities and schools, with the child of a billionaire and the child of a commoner having access to the same education in the foreseeable future. That would be the perfect democratisation, liberalisation and globalisation of education.

Diamandis and Kotler co-authored another book *Bold: How to Go Big, Create Wealth and Impact the World* in which they identified the 6 phases of exponential technologies: Digitalisation, or introduction of digital technology; Deception, during which technologies advance quickly, often below the radar; Disruption, which disrupts established industries; Demonetisation, eliminating the need to buy something, like digital photography abolishing the need to buy films; Dematerialisation, when physical tools are replaced by digital apps; and Democratisation, when access becomes universal as costs decrease.

In a lecture delivered at the World Economic Forum at Davös in 2015, Diamandis gave an example of the power of exponential technologies. In 2010, the average speed of a $1000 computer was 100 billion calculations per second. In 2023, it would become 10,000 times as much, which is the speed at which our brain computes. In 25 years, a $1000 computer is likely to have the computational power of the entire human race, leading to unprecedented democratisation of knowledge.

But the revolution may also cause disruption, if we cannot manage it well. An example is Kodak, which in 1996 was a $28 billion company with 140,000 employees. It had invented the digital camera in 1976, but failed to see its potential. In 2012 it went bankrupt, disrupted by its own invention in the same year that another digital imaging company, Instagram, with only 13 employees, was acquired by Facebook for more than $1 billion. A similar story is that of HMT in India which was a market leader in wrist watches, but failed to see the potential of quartz watches, an opportunity that others grabbed and pushed HMT out of the market altogether. These disruptions will cause turmoil in the short term, but eventually everything will settle into a demonetised equilibrium in which humanity, if it so chooses, can live peacefully and harmoniously, without scarcity and without conflict.

SECTION 5

THE CHURNING OF SOCIETY

1. Cultural Revolution – A Putrid Experience in India
2. Leave Religion Alone
3. Keep Religion out of Education
4. Triple *Talaq*
5. Triple *Talaq* to Uniform Civil Code: Towards Liberation
6. Constitutionality of Ecclesiasticism
7. A Uniform Civil Code Welcome
8. Flutter in the Wind

1. Cultural Revolution – A Putrid Experience in India[38]

(A civilised society thrives on differences and disagreements. A uniform set of values and norms is an oxymoron in a diversified country such as India, where the value for one is non-value for another, and what is sacred for one is profane for another. Norms and standards are valid only in relation to the social milieu in which they apply. In forcing uniform values, these nationalist brigades are trying to bring the Chinese Cultural Revolution to India.)

Carl Jung, the famous Swiss psychoanalyst of the 20th century, once recounted an interesting case of a woman who was known for her stupid prejudices and stubborn resistance to reasoned argument. One night she had dreamt of attending an important social function, where she was greeted by the hostess with the words, "How nice that you could come. All your friends are here and they are waiting for you." The hostess then led her to a door and the dreamer stepped out... into the cowshed. Jung remarked that the dream language was simple enough to be understood even by a complete blockhead, and though the woman would not admit as much initially, the message was eventually driven home and after a while she corrected her behaviour.

The cow is an apt metaphor for the enthusiastic and growing army of *gau-rakshaks* and evangelic anti-beef-protesters who with impunity are targeting anybody who has anything to do with the harmless bovine. But the message is not being conveyed to our leaders. In the process, the script of development and good governance, on which the present government was voted so overwhelmingly to power, has started going awry.

The government was voted to power on the promise of development. It was expected to end the phase of policy paralysis that had characterised the last years of the previous regime, the end of the plethora of scams and corruption scandals, the shameless exhibition of crony capitalism and wastage of national resources and forfeiture of the promise of a vibrant, rapidly-growing economy for which there was abundant scope. The promise of

[38] Originally published in *The Statesman*, 24th April, 2016.

development meant a return of the vanishing jobs for our children, addressing the inequality and inequity that have stymied our society while strengthening the edifice of our nation built on the twin pillars of democracy and secularism. It also meant promoting harmony between different religions and caste groups and ushering in growth and hope for the future. Unfortunately, none of this seems to be happening right now, and the script of development seems to have stopped running.

Soon after the government was voted to power, things had seemed to be on course. Hope returned, growth accelerated, the Sensex bounced back, crucial issues that had been neglected–*Swachh Bharat, Jan Dhan, Beti-Padao Beti Bachao*–were addressed, the anachronism of centralised planning was discarded, and a rustic, robust spirit was overwhelming. An energetic Prime Minister immediately started engaging with our neighbours and the international community at large, immensely improving our relations. Auctions of coal and the telecom spectrum, conducted in a transparent manner, yielded rich dividend. But the hope turned out to be short-lived.

Before long, certain elements that had sinister designs to hijack the growth story and sabotage the script of development had virtually taken over. They have tried to turn the clock back to the medieval era. A clueless government helplessly watched in despair, not knowing how to react or deal with these characters.

First, it was the beef issue which sprang out of nowhere, so suddenly and with so much vehemence that the country was taken by surprise. It was the time for elections in Bihar and the election scenario became a cauldron of beef, identity and caste. BJP lost quite predictably, and a dynasty was brought back to power, forgetting and forgiving its many past misdeeds. Then there was the unfortunate suicide of a Dalit student at Hyderabad Central University, who was driven to despair by an insensitive administration. Almost immediately the anti-national debate erupted at JNU, further blurring the script of development. The latest victim of this unfortunate trend is the NIT Srinagar.

The Indian nation is certainly not so brittle and fragile as to start disintegrating over a few slogans, howsoever high-decibel or 'anti-national' these outpourings might have been, even if they were raised by a few radical students in one of our best institutions. Neither will the Indian federation, which has survived several challenges and mutinies, crack up if some students start demanding *azadi*. Not all students may be mature enough to realise what *azadi* means. Logical analysis is the prerogative of the human mind, which, however, seems to be guided rather by instinct in most situations. A mature state is expected to respond to such aberrations in a mature manner, but unfortunately such maturity was nowhere on display. Instead, all sides overreacted beyond all measure to an incident that qualifies to be termed as trivial, bringing the matter to an incendiary flashpoint.

The administration's overreaction was brazenly evident in the arrest of students who needed counselling rather than imprisoning. The media in a way forced the government to react the way it did; it abandoned all semblance of morality, responsibility and ethics while flaming and fanning the raw passions of youth. The respected professors who are supposed to mentor students, and whose advice is heeded by them, did not show the wisdom that was expected of them. On the contrary, they provoked the administration and fuelled the rebellion among the students. While responsible ministers made irresponsible statements vitiating the atmosphere further, political parties jumped into the fray, not losing the opportunity to show their solidarity with the students and derive political capital.

Such duplicitous hypocrites are ever so concerned over the cause of higher education, but none of them has ever uttered a word against the crumbling infrastructure at JNU, Jadavpur, Allahabad or Patna universities. The striking features are the faculty vacancies in our public universities, the decline in standards, and the increasing unemployability of students.

Distractions and entertainment are never found wanting or waning in India, and the latest to come up is the slogan *Bharatmata Ki Jai.* Jung had talked about archetypes or collective thoughts that create myths and religions and philosophies that influence and sometimes characterise nations. We are witnessing a different set of archetypes which are not the product of society's collective thoughts, but are promoted by religious zealots, fundamentalist Hindus and hyper-nationalists who are not much different in substance from the terrorists of the Islamic State who want the entirety of humanity to be ruled by their version of the Sharia. These elements are projecting *Bharatmata* as the new archetype for the nation expecting everyone to line up before her image and take a test in nationalism and patriotism by raising the slogan. These who fail the test either by remaining silent or by not displaying enough lung-power and enthusiasm in shouting the slogan will be pilloried, branded anti-national, and driven out of India. These vicious elements are planning a collective levelling of the individual by forcing everyone to adjust to norms defined by them.

A sane and civilised society thrives on differences and disagreements. A uniform set of values and norms is an oxymoron in a diversified country such as India, where the value for one is non-value for another, and what is sacred for one is profane for another. Norms and standards are valid only in relation to the social milieu in which they apply. In forcing uniform values, these nationalist brigades are trying to bring the Chinese Cultural Revolution to India. Stretched to its logical conclusion, the Indian variant of the Cultural Revolution could mean the branding of 'anti-nationals' and their public humiliation, forced confessions and self-denouncements, public beatings and the tyranny of the lumpen that the government shows little or no willingness to control.

Goethe's Faust asserted that in the beginning, there was only the deed. Thought came much later. Sanity will be the last to come, if at all. *Bharatmata* can wait indefinitely and she will.

2. LEAVE RELIGION ALONE[39]

(Religion should not be dragged into every debate concerning the conduct of public affairs or administration of public policy in the country. It serves no purpose except igniting passion not based on logic and rationality.)

> *"They knew that to put God in the constitution was to put man out... [...]They intended to found and frame a government for man and for man alone. They wished to preserve the individuality of all to prevent the few from governing the many and the many from persecuting and destroying the few."*
> —Robert G. Ingersoll, *Individuality*

Clashes between religion and secular society have been pretty commonplace all over the world. A secular state does not promote the cause of religion nor allow ecclesiastical authorities to exercise public authority. While a secular state does not wish the demise of any religion, it treats religion as something personal to the individual and not to be used as a determinant of public policy. The dominant values of a society may spring from religious roots, but secularisation of society replaces religious mores with secular ethics, which hold as sacrosanct the freedom of religion and the dignity and rights of an individual which also includes his right not to believe in religion. A secular state does not concern itself with the good or bad of religion, its only interest being that religion is not to be mixed with the affairs of the state. A non-secular society, in contrast, does not allow its people to ignore religion; religion forms a part, often being a determinant, of its public policy.

The Constitution of India declares our nation as secular, but our practices thoroughly belie that claim. We drag religion and its illegitimate child, casteism, into every public debate, from politics to terrorism and into every domain of public policy, from the imparting of education to the delivery of justice. No discourse or policy issue today can be settled in India without bringing religion or caste into it–be it framing the syllabus of our state-run institutions or making appointments to various positions, from ministers to heads of reputed institutions. Political parties that solely depend on religious or caste-based vote banks for their growth and survival are the ones that

---

[39] Originally published on www.ourstories.org, as "Should India Ban Head Scarves?", 25th August, 2016.

loudly and brazenly proclaim themselves as secular. We see the re-politicisation of religion with the concomitant de-secularisation of society all around all the time; these processes manifest themselves in various forms in public life. The latest instance of this was witnessed in the recent retest of the All India Pre-Medical Test (AIPMT) conducted by CBSE on 25th July, which was followed by lots of high-voltage drama and tohubohu.

To recap the events leading to it, the AIPMT examination was initially held on 3rd May, in which more than 6 lakh students had appeared. It was marred by reports of large scale cheating by students, who smuggled various gadgets into the examination hall like Bluetooth devices and SIM cards, some of these stitched onto their clothing. The test was cancelled by orders of the Hon'ble Supreme Court, which also ordered a retest on 25th July. For this retest, CBSE took no chances and issued a strict dress code making it difficult for students to hide any chits or gadgets. The code, which many found bizarre, barred students from wearing full-sleeved shirts or metallic items like hairpins and hairbands. It mandated all students to wear open shoes and half-sleeved clothes without big buttons and prohibited headscarves. These restrictions, especially the one barring headscarves, were perceived as a violation of religious freedom by some Islamic organisations. Three Muslim students and a little-known organisation called the Students' Islamic Organisation of India took the matter to the Kerala High Court, which allowed the girls to wear the hijab during the retest.

Buoyed by this order, they now took it to the Supreme Court for granting a similar relaxation to all Muslim girls–seeking permission for them to wear full-sleeved dress with hijab. The Supreme Court was not in the least amused by the antics of flaunting religious beliefs to seek immunity from the requirements of examination prescribed universally for all students. It firmly rejected the petitioners' contention by saying: "The CBSE has come out with a dress code for the sake of keeping the examination fair and proper. It is a matter of 3 hours. You observe the dress code mandated by the CBSE for 3 hours and then wear the scarf as long as you want." It advised them to go and appear in the test and not to waste time in the court, asserting that no disrespect will be shown to religion by appearing at the test without a headscarf. To the argument that students were ready to come to the examination centre well before the scheduled time to subject themselves to a thorough check, the Court asked: "If all the students come dressed similarly, how would the invigilator examine their religion and determine whether they were entitled to claim relaxation in dress code?" In the face of such tough questioning, the counsel of the petitioners had himself sought and obtained the Court's permission to withdraw the petition. The Court rightly stressed that, "Faith is something different from wearing some kind of cloth".

It is not unusual for the state to impose dress codes even in the most liberal of countries for cogent reasons. The first school dress code law was established in 1969 by the US Supreme Court in the case of *Tinker vs. Des Moines Independent School District*, when high school students wore black armbands in school protesting against the Vietnam War. In a far-reaching decision, the Court ruled that schools may limit student expression like enforcing dress codes if there was a legitimate concern that such expression would be disruptive to the learning environment or violated the rights of others. Countries like France, Belgium, Canada and China have banned headscarves; even Islamic countries like Syria, Tunisia and Turkey had banned it for many years together.

On 25th July, while girls from all communities abided by the dress-code, a 20 year-old Muslim student in Lucknow opted out as she did not want to take off her abaya. A 19 year-old Catholic nun in Thiruvananthapuram also opted out after refusing to remove her veil and the Cross attached to it, when the Mother Superior of her religious order disapproved of this. It was the girls' personal choice which they exercised and there was nothing wrong or objectionable in this; some Sikh students also had to leave their articles of faith–like 'kirpans' and 'karas'–outside, to be allowed entry into the exam hall. Most other societies would have ignored such trivialisation of religion, but in the secular country that we live in, these incidents became a major governance issue, providing opportunity to the clergy as well as the laity to jump into the fray.

The Cardinal of a Catholic church in Kerala held the incident as disturbing and raised questions regarding the rights of a citizen, wondering what was being targeted—religious symbols or exam malpractices? The president of a Gurdwara management committee said they would challenge the decision of a school not to allow a baptised Sikh student without 'kara' and 'kirpan' into the exam hall. The Court verdict had expectedly angered the Islamic clergy. A Muslim organisation asserted that wearing headscarves was the fundamental right of Muslim girls, while the president of a foundation held that it was 'a gross interference in the personal affairs of Muslims'. Muslim intellectuals also chipped in; a university professor thundered that it was 'like asking them *(the girls)* to strip', while a vice chancellor affirmed that religious questions are best left to religion and that the 'court shouldn't play clergy'.

As spring inevitably follows winter, political parties were not to squander such an opportunity to play up religious sentiments to extract maximum political mileage in such an impassioned scenario. The ruling congress and its major coalition partner the Indian Union Muslim League (IUML) in Kerala now entered the arena. The Kerala PCC President said the decision of the authorities not to allow the nun to write the examination was 'unfortunate' and ‘against the Constitutional right given to citizens’, urging the government to take steps to avoid moves ‘that would hurt the sentiments of the faithful’. Echoing similar sentiments, the IUML National Secretary said that the Supreme Court decision on the 'hijab' that involved issues of faith was not right. No one bothered to remember the underlying ethos of a secular nation that faith should not be mixed with affairs of the state, which includes the conduct of an examination for entry to medical education in the country.

In a secular nation, there exists a clear distinction between religion, politics and law. While the reasonableness of the dress code can, of course, be questioned, it is too far-fetched to suggest that it was devised with a particular religion or denomination in mind. There is need for people of faith to recognise that there cannot always be straightjacketed ‘either-or’ situations in such matters. In any case, administrative requirements in a secular society are essentially religion-neutral; it is unfair to expect the needs of different religions to be reckoned while determining such requirements.

Citizens of a secular state should know where to draw the boundary. The line between bigotry and logic is too thick to be ignored except for those whose vision has been rendered short-sighted by religion or reasons of political expediency. Liberties guaranteed in the Constitution are not absolute; they also often collide with each other. The right to freedom of religion does not supersede other fundamental rights. Like all fundamental rights in our Constitution, religious freedom too is subject to reasonable restrictions imposed by the state. A secular nation is under no obligation to respect the norms or commandments of religion, just as it does not have the liberty to violate such norms without reason. There is need to balance any liberty with the outcomes the restriction placed upon it is intended to beget to a society. To quote Sir Thomas Moore, “No man shall be blamed for reasoning in the maintenance of his own religion.”

3. Keep Religion out of Education[40]

(Secular education should be free from religious content.)

A colleague recently returning from a visit to Tajikistan, a predominantly Muslim country with 96 percent of its estimated 8 million population practising Islam, had something very interesting to report–that Tajik law specifically prohibits, under penalty of hefty fines, children below 18 years of age from attending mosques or places of religious worship. Under the so-called "Parental Responsibility Law", parents are made responsible to ensure that underage children do not attend public religious activities with the exception of funerals; neither can they attend Hajj. Law does not prohibit parents from teaching religious beliefs to their own children in the privacy of their homes, provided the child expresses a desire to learn, but restricts home-schooling of children outside the immediate family. Law enforcement officials routinely round up children found attending mosques–the declared policy of the government being that children should be studying in schools rather than worshipping in the mosques till they are mature enough to judge by themselves.

Tajikistan's constitution provides for freedom of religion. However, religious activities are tightly controlled by the government which closely monitors the activities of religious institutions to keep them from espousing and disseminating extremist tendencies, and from turning overtly political. There is no official state religion in Tajikistan. The government controls religious activities through the Committee on Religious Affairs (CRA) and the Ministry of Education. Tajik law prescribes criminal penalties for violating restrictions on sending Tajik citizens abroad for religious education, preaching and teaching of religious doctrines and establishing ties with religious groups abroad without CRA consent. I confirmed the facts from the International Religious Freedom Report for 2013 prepared by the US Commission on International Religious Freedom.

The law of the Republic of Tajikistan "On Religion and Religious Organisations" requires compulsory registration by all mosques and religious communities to ensure that religious groups act in accordance with

---

[40] Originally published in *The Statesman*, 17th July, 2015.

the law, failing which their places of worship may be forced to close and members penalised. Imams preaching in a mosque require 'attestations' by the CRA on their knowledge of Islamic teachings and religious principles, failing which they could be dismissed. To counter religious indoctrination, the government issues high-school textbooks on the history of Islam for teaching in public schools. The law also regulates registration, size, and location of mosques, limiting the number of mosques that may be registered within a given population area. Madrassas are required to impart secular education along with religious teaching in accordance with government prescribed curricula and standards, and are inspected and monitored strictly by the government, with any violation forcing closure.

The landlocked country of Tajikistan, surrounded by China, Kyrgyzstan, Uzbekistan and Afghanistan, was a part of the erstwhile USSR as the Tajik Soviet Socialist Republic. It declared independence in 1991 after the disintegration of the Soviet Union and became the Republic of Tajikistan. Its independence was followed by turmoil degenerating into prolonged civil war and internecine conflicts, worsening its already precarious economic situation and making the country ever more dependent on foreign aid. A comprehensive peace agreement brokered by the United Nations ended the civil war in 1997, and peace returned after years of strife, following which the warring groups started entering the political arena. Sporadic attacks engineered by determined Islamic fundamentalists nevertheless continued, disrupting life and commerce. Islamists opposed to the ceasefire that had reinforced the democratic nature of the republic of Tajikistan then joined the Islamic Movement of Uzbekistan, a terrorist organisation formed in the late 1990s that draws membership from ethnic Uzbeks, Kyrgyz, Tajiks, Chechens and Uighurs. Funded mainly by migrant Uzbeks, in particular Saudi Arabia's 300,000 strong Uzbek diaspora and other Islamist and sympathetic foundations throughout the Arab world, it allied with Al-Qaeda with the stated goal of uniting Central Asia as an Islamic state ruled universally by the Sharia, much like what ISIS is striving after. The Islamic terrorism in Tajikistan is thus a trans-national phenomenon, inspired from across borders, with implications in many neighbouring countries. Drawing a parallel with our situation may thus not be too far-fetched, though the contours and dimensions may be vastly different.

Terrorism and fundamentalism do not breed in a vacuum. The making of a terrorist needs years of indoctrination and radicalisation. A combination of poverty and illiteracy–usually these two go together–with religion delivers a deadly cocktail for fundamentalism to thrive. The hold of religion on the poor and uneducated usually being stronger, religion acts as a powerful catalyst to the ideological mobilisation of the poor. Children are especially vulnerable to this kind of indoctrination, because irrationality thrives best when the mind lacks maturity and can easily be filled with toxic thoughts. It is therefore extremely important to prevent indoctrination when the mind is not mature enough to distinguish between dogma and logic, and is susceptible to trust the Ulema or the priest when they interpret religious texts according to their own and often misplaced understanding. It is in this context that the tight religious restrictions imposed by the state in Tajikistan may be considered. Unless monitored, the mind-space of poor children can easily become fertile breeding grounds for hatred and terrorism.

Religion has the potency to be turned into a most noxious instrument for radicalisation, unless society monitors it. A radicalised mind seeks justice in violence; it does not detest violence. The defining features of fundamentalists' ideal of an Islamic Caliphate that ISIS, the Taliban, Al Shabab or Boko Haram are trying to establish include enslavement of women, denial of freedom of thought or expression and complete intolerance of a different belief system or faith; in short, revival of a theocratic governance system steeped in the medieval times which is obviously an anathema to Muslims in India as elsewhere. Their justifications of violence are even more comical.

After the cold-blooded massacre of schoolchildren in Peshawar by a suicide squad of the Tehreek-e-Taliban-i-Pakistan, it released a photo of the murderers taken against the backdrop of a banner proclaiming the core tenet of Islam: "La ilaha illa-llah, Muhammadun rasulullah" "(There is no god but God and Muhammad is his messenger)". The very next day, seeking to justify the slaughtering of children, it quoted a Hadith that a boy with pubic hair was no longer a child!

After every massacre inflicted by terrorists, we hear impassioned condemnation of such violence by Islamic clerics and leaders, asserting that the perpetrators of such terror are not true Muslims. Where then do they get their Islam from? Understandably, no religious text preaches violence–violence is inflicted by individual perpetrators, regardless of their religious affiliations. The point is who fills their minds with such hatred and xenophobia? Part of the answer may come from how we school our young.

In West Bengal, most Muslim children including a sizeable number of poor non-Muslims in rural areas attend Madrasas in the absence of an adequate network of affordable schools. There are High Madrasas that follow the prescribed syllabus formulated by the West Bengal Madrasah Board, which has no religious content; the Left Front Government took initiative to align their syllabus with that of the state board. There are also Senior Madrasas where Islamic theology is taught along with some modern subjects. As Nilanjana Gupta in her book *Reading with Allah: Madrasas in West Bengal* (Routledge, 2010) points out, these are in a pathetic state, and can address neither the secular nor the theological needs of the community. But both these are recognised by the Madrasa Board, unlike the 3rd type, the Khariji Madrasas, which are mostly residential. They do not take any assistance from the government. The education is primarily theological–based on the Quran and Hadith.

Instruction is imparted in Arabic so that the Holy Book can be studied in its original form. Graduates from these Madrasas generally find employment in mosques as Ulemas, Imams and Moulavis. To the rural poor, the Madrasas are a godsend as they provide free education, board and lodging to their children. Gupta points out that while some of these may have incorporated secular content in their instructions, many inculcate an insular mentality among their students. There is no quality control on the ability of instructors who can easily vitiate vulnerable young minds. Such Madrasas exist not only in India, but also in Bangladesh and Pakistan where they often morph into factories for producing fundamentalists. Should the government exercise no control over their syllabus and instructions to ensure that they are not teaching B for Banduk, J for Jihad and S for Shahadat (martyrdom)? We also do not know if radical Hindu outfits are running similar schools.

The guiding philosophy of a secular nation does not support the view that religious education is the only education that one needs in life. The intellectual straight-jacketing of socio-religious discourses has not allowed open debate on this question for fear of possible reprisals, as witnessed in Pakistan and Bangladesh. Radical Islamic movements today aim at substituting the legal constitutional structure in countries by Sharia laws to be enforced through the agency of Islamic State. Inoculation of educational curriculum from religious content may be a worthy step towards strengthening our defence against such a medieval onslaught on liberties. It is to be understood that radical elements, irrespective of religious denominations, are products of identical mutations.

4. Triple *Talaq*[41]

(A medieval practice like triple talaq and its proponent Mullahs have no place in a modern, democratic and secular society like India's.)

"Power does not corrupt. Fear corrupts...perhaps the fear of a loss of power", John Steinbeck famously said. That the fear of loss of power may not only corrupt one's morality and judgement, but also blur the distinction between sanity and insanity in the minds of otherwise normal and distinguished individuals was in ample evidence in the way the All India Muslim Personal Law Board (AIMPLB) defended the practice of triple *talaq* in an affidavit submitted to the Supreme Court (SC) last month, by stating that women were lesser mortals than men. In response to a petition challenging polygamy and triple *talaq* by a Muslim woman named Shayara Bano and by some Muslim Women's Organisations urging the apex court to declare triple *talaq* and polygamy unconstitutional, they came up with this gem, "Shariah grants right to divorce to husbands because men have greater power of decision making. They are more likely to control emotions and not take hasty decisions."

If it was not for the seriousness of the matter, one would dismiss this as a joke, albeit one in extremely poor taste. But the complete abandonment of reason by these powerful men who constitute the AIMPLB and–supported by the Mullahs, the gatekeepers to Allah's kingdom–rule the Muslim society and its womenfolk, did not cease here. While asserting that the practice of triple *talaq* as part of Islam was protected by the fundamental right to religion that was beyond the adjudication of SC, the AIMPLB also vigorously defended polygamy, which allows a Muslim man to have 4 wives, as being necessary to 'curb illicit sex' and to 'protect women'. "Concern for women… lies at the core of the provision for polygamy", they declared in their compassion for women. In saying "polygamy meets social and moral needs and the provision for it stems from concern and sympathy for women", it redefined morality. In avowing that "[a]n unlawful mistress is more harmful for the social fabric than a lawful second wife", it

---

[41] Originally published in *The Statesman*, 18th October, 2016.

appropriated unto itself the wisdom and ultimate authority to decide what is good and bad for Muslim society.

These learned gentlemen, who reek of a misogynist medieval mindset that is completely out of sync with the values and beliefs of a modern society, need to be shown their place in secular and democratic India ruled not by Shariah, but by the Constitution. I am not sure if in echoing these sentiments they are truthfully reflecting the position of their scripture either. As Karen Armstrong says in her authoritative and extensively researched *Islam – A Short History*, "The Quran gave women rights of inheritance and divorce centuries before western women were accorded this status…there is nothing in the Quran that requires the veiling of all women...These customs were adopted some three or four generations after the Prophet's death…The Quran makes men and women partners before God, with identical duties and responsibilities."

The Muslim Personal Law (Shariat) Application Act, 1937, allows Indian Muslims to be governed by the Shariat. The absence of codification has legally allowed community leaders to hold the practices as sacrosanct, thereby subjecting Muslim women in India to arbitrary triple *talaqs* by weird methods, through postcards, telegrams, emails or SMS, which were always upheld by the Mullahs. Similarly, the argument of AIMPLB that the purpose of polygamy is to prevent women from leading a spinster's life is bizarre, given the sex ratio of 951 females per 1,000 males among Indian Muslims.

Personal laws of Muslims, like the Hindus, flowed from patriarchy, misogyny and subordination of the marginalised sections of society. These were put in place to protect entrenched interests when religion lost its vitality and intellectual appeal and gave way to meaningless rituals. These laws have to be reformed to meet the changing dynamics of an evolving and vibrant society. Hindu society has done so to empower their women and so have many Muslim societies, though much more remains to be done. Triple *talaq* has been banned in more than 20 Muslim countries, including Pakistan, Bangladesh, Afghanistan and Iran. Polygamy is similarly prohibited in many Muslim countries like Turkey, Azerbaijan or Tunisia. The ethos of a democratic society is clearly against these theocratic practices the AIMPLB would like to enforce for Indian Muslims.

Unfortunately not many prominent Muslim voices have been heard against these abhorrent practices in India, the reasons for which can only be the fear of retaliation–which does not exclude physical violence–by violent orthodox elements within the community that blindly follow the dictates of its powerful clergy. That clergy, lacking in modern liberal education, derives their power from the poverty, ignorance, and the economic and educational backwardness of large sections of the community. Governments in the past have always shied away from taking on this clergy, for fear of losing Muslim votes and left the hapless Muslim women to the whims of their Mullahs. The fact that some Muslim women have now approached the judiciary proves a weakening of their overwhelming hold, which is why they are reacting so loudly–and so miserably.

In 1985, in the Shah Bano case, when the Supreme Court had ruled that a divorced Muslim woman was entitled to fair maintenance far above what was granted under the Muslim Personal Law, the same AIMPLB and the Mullahs had threatened that the judgment was tantamount to interference in their religion and blackmailed the Rajiv Gandhi Government into capitulation. They forced it to enact the Muslim Women (Protection of Rights on Divorce) Act, 1986, that annulled the judgment. An opportunity that could have been a milestone in Muslim women's search for justice was thus surrendered for petty vote bank considerations. India did not have a dearth of liberal Muslim intellectuals even then, but not many voices of protest were heard against the injustice perpetrated to Muslim women. The government meekly withdrew and abdicated its responsibility to uphold the constitutional right to equality.

This time, however, the government has put up a spirited defence, and dissociated the issue from that of the Uniform Civil Code. In its response to the affidavit, it clearly stated its position that "gender equality and the dignity of women are not negotiable". If Islamic states could reform Muslim personal laws, these certainly could not be considered an integral part of the practice of Islam. Arguing that “No undesirable practice can be elevated to the status of an essential religious practice,” it said, “any practice that leaves women socially, financially or emotionally vulnerable or subject to the whims and caprice of menfolk is incompatible with the letter and spirit of Articles 14 and 15 of the Constitution”. Further, Muslim women, merely by virtue of their religion, cannot be relegated to a status more vulnerable than women belonging to other religious faiths.

But the fundamental question is whether in a secular democracy, religion alone can be a reason to deny the equal status and dignity available to women under the Constitution. Article 25 of the Constitution guarantees all citizens the right to practice and profess a religion of their choice. But liberties guaranteed in the Constitution are not absolute, and the right to freedom of religion does not supersede other fundamental rights. Like all fundamental rights in our Constitution, religious freedom too is subject to reasonable restrictions imposed by the state. A secular nation is under no obligation to respect the norms or commandments of any religion, just as it does not have the liberty to violate such norms without reason. Further, Article 13 states that any law impinging on fundamental rights shall be void, and the practices of triple *talaq* and polygamy should therefore be declared illegal, since they violate the fundamental right to equality.

As expected, the AIMPLB and the Mullahs from Darul Uloom Deoband, Barelvi and Jamiat Ulema-e-Hind are up in arms against the centre's position which will render them virtually powerless. In the coming days, they can be expected to work out a religious hysteria to retain their coercive power and vice-like grip over the community. India has one billion Hindus and 180 million Muslims who, save a few hardcore Hindutvawallas, Mullahs and of course the AIMPLB members, believe in the idea of a secular, liberal and progressive India in which religion plays no role except for matters of personal faith and worship. Hopefully, they will together counter any move to convert this country into a theocracy. Hopefully they will redeem themselves by not letting the mistake of 1986 be repeated. Mullahs may hear this message loud and clear.

(Afterword: In a landmark judgment delivered in August 2017, the Supreme Court declared triple talaq unconstitutional. However, the reasoning used by the Hon'ble Justices attracted widespread criticism. Please refer to the essay "Constitutionality of Ecclesiasticism" later in this section.)

5. TRIPLE *TALAQ* TO UNIFORM CIVIL CODE: TOWARDS LIBERATION[42]

(Triple talaq practised in whatever form will remain discriminatory for Muslim women. The only way to resolve the contradictions that will arise from retaining triple talaq in any form will be to replace it with a uniform civil code for the entire country.)

I

The discord over triple *talaq* and rights that Muslim women have been fighting for has now boiled down to a single point: whether 3 *talaqs* uttered in a single sitting should be treated as a single *talaq*. This has been the thrust of arguments so far proffered before the Supreme Court, and it appears that settled justice will be done and will be seen to have been done by all parties. The learned judges of course know the best, but the questions concerning the equality of Muslim women in respect of marital rights and discriminatory marital practices against them appear already to have receded into a distant background. Whether that is also an issue the Hon'ble judges will consider while deciding on the core issue of the validity of triple *talaq* is not known. But since fundamental rights integral to the basic structure of the Constitution are involved here, it can be expected that the wisdom of the Court would encompass the whole set of all linked issues and not be limited merely to a part of it. The petitioning Muslim women and Muslim women's organisations are fighting for their rights of gender equality while those opposing them are contesting to deny them these rights under the pretext of protecting their so-called religious freedom.

The Constitution Bench of the Court that is adjudicating the issue has five judges from five different faiths–four from minority communities and only one from the majority community, which was probably done to ward off the possible criticism of imposition of majority view on a minority community, given the sensitiveness of the matter and also to limit the scope of whipping up religious passions by a determined clergy, aided by an unruly media,

---

[42]Originally published in *The Statesman* as "Towards Liberation", 21st & 22nd May, 2016.

especially an electronic one. The Bench had initially taken a stand to delink the questions of *nikah-halala* and polygamy from its purview, and to limit itself only to examine whether triple *talaq* is fundamental to Islam. However, immediately afterwards, they had to reverse their stand and clarify that they had not closed the window to scrutinise the 2 linked and contentious issues of polygamy and *nikah-halala*, and that the decision on triple *talaq* may or may not have a bearing on these other two issues. They made it clear that they had kept the *nikah-halala* and polygamy outside their radar only for want of adequate time during the current 6-day-long hearing. It reinforces the belief that the Court would not allow its judgment to be constrained and would deal with the matter holistically in all its aspects for the sake of justice.

From the way the arguments have been going so far, nobody seems to have been able to demonstrate convincingly why triple *talaq* should be considered as fundamental to religion, especially since many Islamic countries have prohibited the practice. Nobody can doubt that the belief in the oneness of God is a fundamental tenet of Islam, but can triple *talaq* be considered equally fundamental? Or is there a hierarchy of fundamental elements in Islam? Where would triple *talaq* fit then, since it is not mentioned in the Holy Quran, and especially when divorce itself has been described as 'sinful' and "*abghaz-ul-mubahat indallah*"–most detestable in the sight of God–as pointed out by Tahir Mahmood, a former member of the Law Commission and a scholar?

The argument has now veered to the question whether the 3 *talaqs* uttered on 3 separate occasions each spaced a month apart to facilitate efforts for reconciliation would serve the needs of justice, even without curtailing the husband's unilateral right to seek divorce. This argument is bogus and militates directly against the fundamental constitutional rights to equality and freedom, as enshrined in Articles 13, 14, 15 and 21. A practice, like triple *talaq* under Muslim personal law, even without having a legislative origin, has acquired the force of law through custom and usage which contradicts the fundamental rights guaranteed by the Constitution. Such a practice should automatically be rendered null and void under Article 13 of the Constitution, as affirmed by several existing court judgments. Further, the right to freedom of religion guaranteed under Article 25 is not an absolute right, like all other fundamental rights; this is also subject to reasonable restrictions. By no stretch of the imagination, can this right to freedom of religion be said to supersede any other fundamental rights including the rights to equality and freedom. Personal laws cannot have the same standing as fundamental rights; if the exercise of triple *talaq* as per

"The Muslim Personal Law (Shariat) Application Act, 1937" violated fundamental rights guaranteed under the Constitution, then it is not the fundamental right that should be compromised for the sake of personal law of a religious community, but the personal law, practice or custom in question must be abolished. Also, as the Attorney General has pointed out, the right to freedom of religion operates within the precincts of religious establishments, while fundamental rights operate everywhere without any boundary.

The learned lawyer, the veteran Congress MP Mr Kapil Sibal, engaged by the defendants, the All India Muslim Personal Law Board (AIMPLB), has proffered some impossible and ludicrous arguments in trying to defend the indefensible–"Triple *talaq* has been there since 637. Who are we to say that this is un-Islamic? Muslims have been practicing it for the last 1400 years. It is a matter of faith. Hence, there was no question of constitutional morality and equity." By that logic, all customs, howsoever monstrous and repugnant they might be, could be justified, including many of the abhorrent practices which have since been abolished by law, like sati, untouchability and caste discrimination. Indeed, the list of now-extinct social and religious practices which reigned for a long time and are universally condemned today would be endless. If we did not dump these abhorrent practices to the dustbin of history, human society would not have progressed much beyond its primitive stages, and remained stranded in a time-warp, where clearly the AIMPLB, an enterprise of the mullahs who have vested themselves with absolute powers over the community as guardians of Muslim personal law, wants the Indian Muslims to languish so that they can exercise their powers to control it according to their whims and fancies, interpreting religious laws according to their convenience and protecting the vested interests of the mullahs who still have an overwhelming sway over the community.

The AIMPLB, a body that believes that males have more superior judgment and decision-making powers than females and expressly stated so in its affidavit before the Supreme Court, had earlier carried on a systematic misinformation campaign in favour of triple *talaq*. In response to a March 2015 survey by the Bharatiya Muslim Mahila Andolan (BMMA), one of the petitioners in the instant case, in which 97 percent of female respondents had said they were opposed to triple *talaq*, polygamy and *nikah-halala*, the AIMPLB conducted a countrywide signature campaign to garner support for triple *talaq*, taking advantage of the congregational nature of worshippers in mosques where an Imam can exhort them to act in any particular manner and claimed an overwhelming support by the majority of Muslim women. Finally, it announced 'social boycott' of those misusing the provisions of marriage annulment under Islamic law. If anyone is in need of a social boycott, it is this body of clerics who are steeped in medieval times and a medieval mindset. As Mr Julio Ribeiro pointed out in a recent article, these clerics have appropriated all the powers and benefits given to the minority community by successive governments, while the rest of the community has continued to wallow in poverty, illiteracy and deprivation.

Sensing the direction of the wind, it has now changed tack. In a desperate attempt to protect their monopoly, it is now advocating that the *nikah-nama* which is a contract for marriage between consenting adults can have clauses for invoking triple *talaq* by both husband and wife. Apart from the question of how many *Qajis* in the country would abide by this diktat, it also brings out the tenuousness of their argument about triple *talaq* being fundamental to Islam.

II

Even the analogy of Muslim majority countries which have abolished triple *talaq* might not be valid and appropriate in the Indian situation, in view of the fundamental rights to equality before law (Article 14), right against discrimination on grounds of religion, race, caste or sex (Article 15), and right to life and personal liberty (Article 21) guaranteed in our Constitution. But we may still draw some very useful lessons.

The objective of equality and gender justice are perhaps best served by the Tunisian law, the Tunisian Code of Personal Status, 1956, under which a husband cannot unilaterally divorce his wife through verbal pronouncements; he has to first consult a judge and convince him. Marriage and divorce are controlled by the state, and all divorce proceedings must occur before a judge, with a court-directed effort at reconciliation being mandatory. Each party has the right to ask for divorce, but each has to convince the judge about the reasons thereof. The judge can order a compensation to be paid by either the husband or the wife, depending on which party has been harmed by the other. Iraq was one of the first Arab countries to replace Shariah Courts with government-run Personal Status Courts in 1959. According to Iraq's Personal Status Law, three verbal or gestural repudiations pronounced at once will count as only one divorce, but both husband and wife can ask for separation which is to be decided by the court. Sri Lanka, a Buddhist nation, has also enacted a law for the minority Muslims that allows divorce through *talaq* by the husband only, after notifying a Muslim judge (*Qadi*) and after 30 days to allow for reconciliation attempts by relatives and elders.

In Pakistan, the husband must pronounce *talaq* in 3 successive menstrual cycles, not in a single sitting. Most Muslim nations, including Bangladesh, Jordan, Egypt, Indonesia, United Arab Emirates and Qatar have adopted a similar law on triple *talaq*, which is based on the interpretation of the 13th century Egyptian scholar Ibn Taimmiyah. In Pakistan, the husband must first give notice to a government appointed council that will attempt reconciliation before the divorce becomes valid. The wife does not have the power to seek separation, but can remarry her ex-husband after divorce.

By allowing a similar system, the harshness of the existing practice in India can surely be reduced and some sections of the clergy can perhaps be brought around, but that will fall short of the needs for gender justice and fundamental rights. It is to be realised that *talaq* is inherently discriminatory against women and denies them not only their rights, but also their dignity. Again, Tahir Mahmood in his book *Introduction to Islamic Law* co-authored with Saif Mahmood had quoted the Deobandi theologian Ashraf Ali Thanvi (1863-1943): "A man pronounces a revocable talaq. He reconciles and resumes cohabitation. A few years later under some provocation he pronounces a revocable talaq once again. On recovering from provocation he again resumes cohabitation. Now two talaqs are over. Thereafter whenever he pronounces a talaq, it will be counted as the 3rd talaq, which will dissolve the marriage forthwith." The right is absolute for men, and women will always be at the receiving end, whether they receive the 3 talaqs in a single or 3 separate sittings.

The inescapable inference is, logically only a uniform civil code, as mandated in Article 44 of the Constitution under Directive Principles of State Policy, which states that the state shall endeavour to secure for the citizens a uniform civil code throughout the territory of India, can resolve all the contradictions that will arise from the substitution of the present system with any other system that derives its sustenance and sanctity primarily from religion. A commendable example is Turkey, which under Mustafa Kemal Ataturk adopted the Swiss Civil Code in 1926, discarding the Islamic laws governing divorce and marriage. The code was revised in 1980, but still remains insulated from religious footprints. We have to bite the bullet and recognise unapologetically that religion here is the root of the problem. As long as we shall give primacy to religious considerations in matters of marriage, women will continue to suffer from inequality and discrimination, and the Ostrich-like mentality of the AIMPLB will continue to rule the roost. In fact, that is how it came into existence in the first place, by exploiting the persecution complex among members of the minority community.

In the early 1970s, Mrs Indira Gandhi was attempting to control the dominance of the Sharia Law of 1937 applicable to the Indian Muslims, and the then law minister Mr H. R. Gokhale introduced the Adoption Bill in Parliament declaring it as "the first step towards a Uniform Civil Code". This predictably sparked an outcry among the Muslim clergy who started whipping up religious passions against what it called the government's attempt to "subvert Shariah law applicable to Indian Muslims through parallel legislation". The first meeting of several Muslim organisations to 'save the Shariah' was convened at Deoband at the initiative of Hazrat Maulana Syed Shah Minnatullah Rahmani and others, followed by a convention at Mumbai in December, 1972, which unanimously decided to create the AIMPLB. It was finally set up in April 1973, and ever since, it has consistently asserted that Sharia is beyond the reach and scope of India's courts of law, including the Supreme Court, as in its opinion, secular courts do not have the authority to either interpret or apply Sharia, which is based on the Quran and the Hadith, which are above any man-made law.

In its self-appointed role as the sole arbiter of Muslim destiny in secular, democratic India, the AIMPLB may have taken upon itself the onerous task of saving the minority of Indian Muslims from the persecution of majority Indian Hindus. The point is, once you remove the words 'Muslims' and 'Hindus', only Indians remain–with no majority or minority–but equal in every respect before law (today they are guided by different sets of laws) enjoying equal rights and privileges under the Constitution. That can happen once the Shariah is no longer allowed to control the lives of Indian Muslims, and their freedom to worship and follow their religious practices is left to individuals, as in most religions. The AIMPLB cannot allow it to happen, since it then loses its *raison-d'etre.* In no other religion and perhaps in no other country, least of all in any democracy, are the clergy, or the mullahs, allowed by the state to wield so much power.

At independence, the plight of Hindu women was no different to the plight of Muslim women today; in many respects, it was worse. They suffered from various discriminations and inequalities, in marriage, divorce, inheritance, widow remarriage, abortion, dowry and job opportunities. However, legal reforms initiated in 1955 and 1956 had removed most of these inequalities in respect of Hindu, Sikh and Parsi women. Of course, legislation alone cannot be effective in addressing gender disparity in an agrarian society, in which women are ignorant of their rights and continue to suffer from deeply entrenched patriarchal practices and mindsets. Traditional beliefs shaped by religion still limit the growth and liberty of women from all religions in rural

India. But a beginning at least has been made for other communities, while for Muslim women, time has stood still.

Shah Bano's case has been bad enough; it has been an indelible blot on our secular credentials and loud and vain proclamations about equality. Let us try to redeem ourselves this one last time. Let us not shy away from demanding a uniform civil code for all. BJP with its raw electoral power can bring this about. Then there will be no need to enact a separate law for Muslim divorce, in case the Honourable Court annuls triple *talaq* not only as something that is not integral to the practice of Islam, but also as something that violates the Indian Constitution. And BJP will still have an assured vote bank of most of the 84 million Muslim women living in India.

(Afterword: The Supreme Court declared triple talaq unconstitutional, but the logic was based on Islamic Personal Law; see the next article.)

6. Constitutionality of Ecclesiasticism[43]

(In pronouncing their judgment on triple talaq, the Hon'ble judges of the Supreme Court ought to have depended on the Constitution rather than religion. It makes a travesty of justice that religious arguments have been given primacy over constitutional rights, even though the judgment was right.)

In pronouncing their judgment on triple *talaq*, which has been universally hailed as a landmark judgment for striking down a 1400-year old abhorrent practice of Islam prevalent in our country, the Hon'ble judges of the Supreme Court (SC) ought to have carried their inscrutable logic one step further. The majority judgment in the case held triple *talaq* unconstitutional, but the majority of the judges in the inter-faith bench agreed in their wisdom that the personal laws of any religion were not justiciable and enjoyed the same status as fundamental rights which are integral to the basic structure of our Constitution. Even the majority judgment was based not primarily on questions of constitutional morality and rights to equality or protection against gender discrimination as guaranteed by the Constitution, but on the interpretation of Muslim Personal Law as understood by the learned judges. With due respect to their erudition, it must be said that the argument has not been carried to its logical conclusion. Just as the personal laws of all religions have suddenly been elevated almost to the status of fundamental rights, the Hon'ble judges ought to have amended the preamble to our Constitution as well, by deleting the word 'secular' from it, for, under this judgment, India might be well on its way to cease to be one. The state has finally and formally been merged with religion. Let us sing the dirge of our dear 'secular' state, which is already in an advanced state of decay.

The judges had taken nearly 3 months to decide on a question that frankly required not much debate if it had to be judged by the constitutionality of the practice alone, and after so much pondering finally sacrificed constitutionalism at the altar of religious bigotry. The learned CJI, after a 272-page long discourse, had opined that triple talaq was an "essential religious practice" of Islam followed by the Hanafi School of Sunni Muslims for 1400 years and enjoys the protection of Article 25 dealing with

---

[43] Originally published in *The Statesman*, 10th September, 2017.

freedom of religion, an opinion Justice Nazeer also endorsed. They held that the practice, condemned universally as unjust and awful except by the mullahs and members of the AIMPLB, is lawful, and does not violate Articles 14, 15 and 21. In a chilling statement, they affirmed that as part of personal law, the appalling practice of triple *talaq* has a stature of the fundamental rights not to be interfered with by any court, and then curiously decreed that the government should bring in a law–"Unfortunately, the Union seeks in our hands, what truly falls in its own." They said that reforming personal law was within the domain of the government, and gave examples of sati, devdasi and polygamy of the Hindu personal laws which were abolished by separate acts before codifying the personal law for the Hindus. The logic is rather enigmatic, because if a personal law is given the stature of a fundamental right beyond the jurisdiction of any court, how could then a law be framed to change the fundamental nature of that right?

Justice Kurien, who shared the majority view, cited the SC judgment in the Shamim Ara Case (2002) in which the SC had ruled that triple *talaq* lacked legal sanctity unless pronounced in a step-by-step compliance with the true Islamic procedure, again using religious laws to test the constitutionality of a practice. Tripe *talaq* has been held unconstitutional by him not on constitutional grounds, but ironically, on ecclesiastical grounds because the practice in his opinion was not integral to Islam. It seems that henceforth judicial officers will have to inculcate expertise not only in the Constitution and the civil and criminal laws of the land, but also in scriptures belonging to different religions to test whether a practice in question is 'integral' to a religion.

Justice Nariman said the practice was arbitrary and violated Article 14 on equality before law and hence unconstitutional–a view also endorsed by Justice Lalit, but the arguments used by them again derived heavily from Islamic jurisprudence. They cited that Islam divides all human action into 5 groups according to the degree of obedience required: (1) Fard, i.e. whatever is commanded in Koran, *Hadis* or *ijmaa*, and Wajib, which are obligatory, (2) Masnun, Mandub or Mustahab, which are recommendatory; (3) Jaiz or Mubah, which are permissible, and to which religion is indifferent; (4) Makruh, which are unworthy and undesirable; and finally, (5) Haram, which are forbidden. Instant triple talaq, they said, falls in the 3rd at best, or, more likely, in the 4th group. Since instant triple *talaq* is neither obligatory nor recommended, and is rather sinful or undesirable, it cannot meet the test of essentiality of a practice to a religion, and is therefore not protected by Article 25. Elaborating further, they said, "Given the fact that triple talaq is instant and irrevocable, it is obvious that any attempt at reconciliation between the husband and wife by two arbiters from their families, which is essential to save the marital tie, cannot ever take place…It is clear that this form of talaq is manifestly arbitrary in the sense that the marital tie can be broken capriciously and whimsically by a Muslim man without any attempt at reconciliation so as to save it." Being arbitrary, it is unconstitutional and ultra vires to Article 14 on the right to equality, which includes the right against arbitrariness. They also referred to the Muslim Personal Law (Shariat) Application Act, 1937, which sanctified the practice, ruling that since all laws that violate the fundamental rights are automatically void under Article 13 of the Constitution, Section 2 of the Act is void "insofar as it seeks to recognise and enforce triple talaq".

The weighty argument ignores the discrimination, ignominy and injustice that Muslim women face on a daily basis, to prove which religious discourse was completely unnecessary–knowledge of constitution alone should have been enough. The Act of 1937 is an obscurantist legacy from the colonial era that surrendered to the mullahs the jurisdiction on marriage, divorce, succession and maintenance, and could have been struck down simply on the grounds of discrimination and arbitrariness. It does not require any ecclesiastical scholarship to conclude that triple *talaq* is abhorrent, discriminatory and unfair to women. The judgment has indeed set a dangerous precedent that for resolving complex issues emanating from the religious practices of any community, judges now shall have to decipher the meanings of religious and canonical texts and interpret them, the ridiculous nature of which is apparent from the fact that the judges in this case had conducted their own inquiries into essentially theological issues related to Islamic laws and practices, and came up with differing interpretations. Letting what should be decided on pure constitutional logic be determined on the basis of religious arguments is making a mockery of the constitutional ethos and principles the judges are under oath to uphold.

In this case, while the majority view held triple *talaq* as unconstitutional, the majority view did not give supremacy to the Constitution over religious beliefs and practices. The majority of the inter-faith bench rather drew inspiration from religion to arrive at the conclusion. One would have expected that constitutional arguments would prevail over religious arguments as befits a democratic society, reinforcing a clear separation between religion and the State that is fundamental to a secular society. The court may have reached the right conclusion, but it did so following a convoluted logic which does nobody proud and goes against the values not only of our constitution, but also of a modern, liberal, secular society. It will further embolden the dark obscurantist forces in all religions to assert their views and silence the rational voices. On the 70th anniversary of our independence, it is a sad commentary on our democracy that religious rights are still given precedence over women's fundamental rights of equality before law and equal protection of the law. None of the judges from five different faiths–one wishes there was a woman amongst them–found it outrageous enough to outlaw not only *talaq-e-biddat* but all other forms of *talaq*, which are inherently discriminatory and empowers only Muslim males to pronounce *talaq*, whether in a single or in multiple sittings.

In the S. R. Bommai case (1994), the Supreme Court observed, "If the Constitution requires the state to be secular in thought and action, the same requirement attaches to political parties as well. The Constitution does not recognise, it does not permit, mixing religion with state power. Both must be kept apart." The centrality of this logic should have guided the Hon'ble judges also to keep the Constitution and religion apart. Sadly, another opportunity has been missed to assert the secular nature of our state.

7. A Uniform Civil Code Welcome[44]

(How long will the country have to wait for a Uniform Civil Code that will free marriage, divorce, inheritance, etc., from religion?)

Even after the Supreme Court judgment on the triple talaq case, inequality and discrimination against Muslim women are unlikely to disappear. The judgment dealt with only one form of divorce, *talaq-i-biddat*, which is only one of the forms of divorce obtainable through *talaq*. After the Supreme Court judgment on triple *talaq*, the debate on personal laws and the need for a Uniform Civil Code (UCC) have again occupied the centre-stage.

Under Islamic law, a husband may divorce his wife by merely pronouncing the word *talaq*. No reason needs to be stated, and the pronouncement alone is sufficient. Apart from *talaq*, the other modes of divorce are *ila*, and *zihar* which differ from *talaq* only in form. A wife does not have the right to divorce her husband–she can do so only when the husband has delegated such a right to her or under a mutual agreement, as in khula or mubarat. The Dissolution of Muslim Marriages Act 1939 gave Muslim women the right to seek and get divorce legally on certain specified grounds–like the husband's inability to perform his marital obligations, imprisonment, adultery, impotency and cruelty toward his wife. It is not known how many Muslim women have actually benefited from the provisions of this act, but arguably, very few from the lower strata of Muslim society, over which the Mullahs exercise a vicelike grip, would be aware of it.

Under Muslim law, a husband can divorce his wife through *talaq*, *ila*, and *zihar*. *Talaq* literally means setting free, apparently from the bondage of marriage, but actually it pushes a woman into an existence of lifelong misery without justice. It was strange that in a modernising India, this abhorrent practice that gave absolute arbitrary power to a Muslim husband to divorce his wife literally at his whim was not only practiced, but enjoyed the unstinted support of the Mullahs. It came in two forms: *talaq-i-biddat* and *talaq-i-sunnat*, which again came in 2 forms: *talaq-i-ahasan* and *talaq-i-hasan*. The *ahasan talaq* consists of a single pronouncement of *talaq* made during *tuhr* (a period of purity between two menstruations), followed by

---

[44] Originally published in *The Statesman*, 1st October, 2017.

abstinence during the *iddat* period of 3 months, before the expiry of which the divorce can revoked. In *hasan talaq*, the husband is required to pronounce *talaq* 3 times during three successive *tuhrs*. After the last pronouncement, the *talaq* becomes final and the marriage is dissolved irrevocably.

Besides *talaq*, a Muslim husband can repudiate his marriage by 2 other methods, *ila* and *zihar*. In *ila*, the husband takes an oath not to have sexual intercourse with his wife and abstains from sexual intercourse for 4 months, at the expiry of which the marriage dissolves irrevocably. In *zihar*, the husband treats his wife like a woman with whom marriage is prohibited, like mother or sister, and does not cohabit with her for a period of 4 months after which the marriage stands dissolved.

The divorce by wife under Muslim law can be obtained either through *talaq-i-tafweez*, or legally through the Dissolution of Muslim Marriages Act 1939. In *talaq-i-tafweez*, the husband can delegate this power (of pronouncing divorce) to his wife or any other person with or without conditions. This form of delegated divorce may be stipulated in prenuptial agreements.

The last form of divorce under Muslim law is by mutual agreement, it takes 3 forms: *khula*, *mubarat* and *lian*. In both *khula* and *mubarat*, the wife has to part with her rights to her husband's property. Here again the woman is at the receiving end; she has to seek freedom by paying compensation to the husband out of her property, usually the *mahr* that was paid by the groom at the time of marriage. In *mubarat*, either party may propose to give up all mutual rights and obligations, while in *lian*, if the husband levels charges of adultery against his wife without witness under oath to Allah, and the wife counters these allegations as false, also under similar oaths, then the marriage is dissolved by mutual consent.

Thus, it is seen that except in case of divorce through mutual consent, the Muslim personal law gives arbitrary power to men and discriminates against women. It is argued that once the Muslim personal law is codified like the Hindu personal law, much of this arbitrariness would disappear, and for this the Bharatiya Muslim Mahila Andolan, a party to the triple *talaq* case, wanted codification of Muslim personal law. Garbage of theological abstruseness which has accumulated over centuries also needs clearing. But it needs to be understood that the majority religion is easier to reform anywhere, as governments would not like to be seen as imposing the majoritarian will on minorities in trying to reform their personal laws. Further law alone cannot bring in social change, it comes gradually and incrementally. The Hindu personal law was codified in the 1950s by Parliament, but it could not erase the gender gap between Hindu men and women. The Hindu Succession Act was enacted by Parliament only in 2005 to regulate interstate or unwilled succession among Hindus, Buddhists, Jains, and Sikhs and giving women equal rights to property as men. Christian divorce rights were made gender neutral only in 2001. But Muslim personal law has not been codified by Parliament, except through the Shariat Act of 1937 and the Muslim Women (Protection of Rights of Divorce) Act of 1986, enacted in the aftermath of the Shah Bano judgment of the Supreme Court that is a blot on our democracy and a shameless example to kowtowing to the Mullahs. Judges still rely on Islamic jurisprudence for resolving disputes related to Islamic practices.

The discrimination against women will not be removed only by codification, just as it has not been done so for Hindu women. To remove gender discrimination and to bring in transparent justice with equality as promised in Article 14, a Uniform Civil Code (UCC) is imperative. In my article in these columns, "Towards Liberation – II, May 22, 2017", I had argued that only a uniform civil code, as mandated in Article 44 of the Constitution under Directive Principles of State Policy, can resolve the contradictions that will otherwise arise from any system that derives its sanctity from religion. In today's political climate, in which even national parties vie with each other to woo voters on the basis of religion and castes and indulge in selective secularism, consensus on a UCC would be well-nigh impossible. It is imperative that a single-party majority government must show the courage and conviction to carry it forward and not be swayed by vote bank politics. That is the only way to truly unify India, and close the divides created by religion.

In the Constituent Assembly debates, Dr Ambedkar forcefully argued for the adoption of a Civil Code against those who stood for upholding personal laws of religion and Shariat: "I personally do not understand why religion should be given this vast, expansive jurisdiction, so as to cover the whole of life and to prevent the legislature from encroaching upon that field. After all, what are we having this liberty for? We are having this liberty in order to reform our social system, which is so full of inequities, discriminations and other things, which conflict with our fundamental rights." However, in those uncertain strife-torn post-partition days, the Constituent Assembly did not force it. Instead, it included it as desirable under the Directive Principles, to be made mandatory once the time is ripe.

Seven decades hence, has the time still not arrived to enact a UCC for the entire country, covering all religions and all communities uniformly and removing all traces of religion from our marriage, succession, inheritance and divorce in a fair and just way? Throughout the 7 decades, we have ignored and forgotten the individual citizen–the fulcrum in a democracy that is built on the foundation of individual adult franchise–and instead perfected the art of pampering to groups and subgroups on the basis of religion, i.e. Hindus and Muslims, majority and minority, castes and sub-castes, while treating and cultivating them as vote-banks. The demands of these groups have been given precedence over the rights of the individual. That is why in the recent Supreme Court judgment, no judge talked about the abhorrence and unfairness of the practice to the individual woman and instead drew their arguments and conclusions from the personal laws of the minority group they belong to. It is time to restore the forgotten dignity and rights of the individual through the UCC and abolish, once and for all, the intrusion of religion and the clergy into our personal lives, to redeem the ideals of our founding fathers.

8. Flutter in the Wind[45]

(The VIP culture in our country that flows directly from a feudal mindset is hard to shed. The ruling elites known more for bending rather than following the rules will never sacrifice their ill-designed privileges.)

Old habits die hard, and so does the deeply ingrained feudal mindset of our rulers that inculcates in them the feeling that they are and shall always remain more equal than all others, no matter if the country they live in happens to be a democracy that promises equal rights and liberties to every citizen. So they are not likely to easily give up one of their numerous privileges: use of a symbol of power to flaunt. It was first the ubiquitous red beacon, which then mutated into the blue beacon and now it has metamorphosed into a flag, of different sizes and shapes. A mere tokenism like the central government's order prohibiting use of all kinds of beacons by ministers and bureaucrats was not expected to make any serious dent into the entrenched feudal mindset of our rulers, but one was sadly mistaken in believing that the rulers and rule makers will at least show the courteousness to follow rules. One forgot that they are known more for bending the rules to suit their needs–in this case, their lust for clinging to the vestiges of some imagined power whose charm ad relevance are fast disappearing in a modernising India that is gradually shedding its medieval appendages.

The beacons in red, yellow, blue, amber and white signified the various shades of our VIP culture and our sacred feudal inheritance. At the sight of these propitious lights, traffic gets cleared instantly while all others are made to wait, toll plaza barriers are lifted automatically with no fees charged and duty officers smartly stand up and salute the cars carrying the holy agents of our *Mai Baap Sarkar*. But then a thoughtless central order has spelled the ultimate doom for these fabulous privileges enjoyed since eternity by the mighty and powerful in this land of the ordinary and the untouchables.

From May 1st, the centre has banned the use of beacons on cars used by VIPs: ministers, politicians, bureaucrats and all other dignitaries. The ban does not exempt even the country's highest dignitaries–President, Prime

[45] Originally published in *The Statesman*, 24th June, 2017.

Minister and Chief Justice. Only ambulances and vehicles of emergency and security services, those of the fire, police and army are allowed to use beacons for reasons no one questions. But the *lal-batti* culture, equated with being a status symbol ever since the colonial rulers introduced it, was sought to be ended once and for all, even though no one expected the colonial mind that has nurtured and flaunted it to be reformed overnight.

Rule 108 of the Central Motor Vehicles Rules, 1989, that gave the states the power to decide who should be allowed to display red and blue beacons has been amended, removing Clauses 1(iii), 2, 3, 5 and 6 (vide *Gazette* notification dated 1st May 2017) and the states now have no power to amend these rules to reintroduce the omnipresent beacons widely despised by everyone other than their users (beneficiaries?). But West Bengal has now found a unique and ingenious way to beat the centre's beacon ban for government vehicles. Bengal seems yet to retain some residue of its once-famed brainpower, even though it is now counted among the laggard states in India in terms of educational standards, economic prosperity and political violence, factors that are driving its remaining talent fast towards greener southern pastures of the country. The West Bengal government has just notified a scheme under which senior officials of the Indian Administrative Service, who represent the government at various levels, can use different types of flags on their official vehicles.

As per the "flag scheme", 3 types of flags (rectangular, swallow-tailed and triangular) have been notified depending on the rank of the official for use on the bonnet of their designated vehicles. While the rectangular, 10”X6”, navy blue coloured flags will be used by the Chief Secretary, addl. chief secretaries and principal secretaries, the secretaries will be allowed to use swallow-tailed flags. The Divisional Commissioner can use only a rectangular flag, while commissioners can use only a triangular flag. Not to leave out the districts, the District Magistrates have been allowed to use triangular flags. The Personnel and Administrative Department’s notification justifies the scheme using a queer logic, "[i]n view of the significant rise in the level of interaction with various international and national level authorities, it is felt that a flag for use on vehicles being used by senior officials of the state government shall convey a greater sense of the government's intent and enable smoother interactions without compromising protocol."

Even before the ban came into effect, the West Bengal Chief Minister was not known to use any beacon or even a pilot vehicle, like many union and state ministers, among them CMs of Delhi, Uttar Pradesh and Punjab,

Arvind Kejriwal Yogi Adityanath and Captain Amarinder Singh, and union ministers Venkaiah Naidu and Kiren Rijiju. While most ministers and officials in the union and the states have gracefully abided by the decision, some have stubbornly refused. There are many instances of vehicles of VIPs, officials and unauthorised persons defying the ban in West Bengal, Bihar, Karnataka, and other places, including even lower-level politicians and officials, on the pretext that such a ban could pose challenges in case of law and order problems and for enforcement (which is any case not affected by the ban).

Kolkata's Shahi Imam Maulana Barkati had earlier defied the orders, saying the beacon has been there for "hundreds of years" and accusing the RSS for trying to convert India into a Hindu Rashtra, which was apparently being facilitated by removal of the beacon. He was, however, persuaded to remove it later. In Karnataka, the Minister for Food and Civil Supplies refused to remove the red beacon, questioning how such a move would help poor people and remove their hunger, implying that by flaunting the beacon he was actually helping their cause. The West Bengal PWD Minister Arup Biswas and Chairman of Siliguri Jalpaiguri Development Authority were seen using the beacon long after the ban had come into effect, while the Bihar Transport Commissioner R. K. Mishra said that the ban on beacon lights would not be enforced in Bihar till the central government had 'resolved' objections raised by the state against the already amended rule 108. Clearly, the Transport Commissioner did not care for the transport laws of the country. But VIPs in our country are always a law unto themselves, as demonstrated clearly by the recent unruly behaviour of Shiv Sena MP Ravindra Gaikwad and TDP MP Diwakar Reddy.

Let alone removing a powerful symbol of power, the ban is unlikely to be followed in a country where concepts of public service, civic sense, decency, civilised behaviour and democracy have all acquired perverted meanings, as all attempts to do away with such symbols of depravity had failed earlier. The ban has come 3 years after the Supreme Court called the widespread use of red lights "reflective of the Raj mentality and the antithesis of the concept of a Republic." On December 10th, 2013, the Court ruled (in Abhay Singh vs. State of Uttar Pradesh and Others) that vehicles fitted with red beacons will be allowed only for high dignitaries, directing all authorities to enforce these regulations within a month. Nothing really happened. The initial list of 5 dignitaries was expanded to 12 and then to 27 while state officials and politicians merrily continued to flout all rules.

An American academic on his first visit to India a few years ago with whom I was travelling on the streets of Kolkata during the peak morning office hours was watching with keen interest the passing ambassador cars flashing red beacons, their windows screened with white lace curtains. I was amused by his remark that he had heard of the famed Indian *Jugaad*, but never known that ambulances could be innovated and recreated in such an exciting manner. I had to explain to him that these were not ambulances run by hospitals for ordinary patients, but ambulances run by the state machinery for people sick with a sense of power they did not possess. While actual power continued to drift away from their inept hands, they have been clinging to the symbols ever harder. They will never let go of these.

SECTION 6

TUMULT IN THE STATES

1. Article of Discord
2. Asymmetric Solution for Kashmir
3. A Populist Waiver
4. A Dynasty Returns to Rule Bihar
5. Special Category Status Will Remain a Chimera for Andhra

1. ARTICLE OF DISCORD[46]

(Article 35A of the Indian Constitution is a contentious article, but any decision by the Supreme Court to strike it down may open up a Pandora's box.)

In any book on the Constitution of India, one is unlikely to find Article 35A except, maybe, in the appendix. This is because the article did not enter the Constitution through the Constituent Assembly nor via the usual route of Constitutional Amendments as defined in Article 368, but through the unusual mechanism of a Presidential Order, using the provisions of Article 370 which gave special status and a constitution to the state of Jammu & Kashmir (J&K), the only state in India to have its own separate constitution.

Article 35 is the last article in Part III of our Constitution dealing with fundamental rights, and deals with legislations to give effect to these rights. Article 35A defines and regulates the rights and privileges of the permanent residents of J&K while insulating these from the purview of fundamental rights as applicable to Indian citizens elsewhere. It states that only the permanent residents of the state shall enjoy the rights to seek employment under the state government, acquire immovable property within the state, and to get government scholarships and aid. Normally, every citizen of India enjoys these rights everywhere within the country.

Restrictions on the purchase of land by outsiders in J&K date back to 1846, when the British handed over Kashmir to the Dogra kings after the First Anglo Sikh War. A subsequent order of Maharaja Hari Singh and notification I-L/ 84 issued in 1927 restricted the rights to acquire land only to the permanent residents. Post-independence, the Instrument of Accession signed by the Maharaja in October 1947 gave the Indian Parliament the authority to enact laws in relation to J&K only in respect of three subjects: foreign affairs, defence and communication. A subsequent agreement between Nehru and Sheikh Abdullah in 1952 known as the Delhi Agreement extended the fundamental rights of the Indian Constitution to J&K and recognised the state's citizens as Indian citizens while giving the state legislature the power to define and regulate the rights and privileges of

[46] Originally published in *The Statesman*, 31st August, 2017.

the permanent residents, which was the genesis of Article 35A. The Delhi Agreement also extended the powers of the Supreme Court to J&K. The Constituent Assembly in which Sheikh Abdullah was a member had adopted Article 370 in 1949, which mandated that for extending the provisions of the Indian Constitution to J&K in respect of subjects in the union and concurrent lists, the state government's prior concurrence would be required along with incorporation of such provisions in the state's own constitution after their adoption by the Constituent Assembly of Jammu & Kashmir, and that such an extension would be affected through presidential orders. These provisions of Article 370 broadly define the contours of autonomy of J&K and its special status.

Following the Delhi Agreement, a Presidential Order called "The Constitution (Application to Jammu and Kashmir) Order, 1954" was issued by the President of India, extending Indian citizenship to the residents of J&K, and simultaneously inserting Article 35A into the Indian Constitution, thereby enabling the state to define and protect the privileges of its permanent residents. Article 35A was thus an asymmetrical provision, like Articles 370 or 371, which was added to the Constitution without any discussion in parliament. It derived its legitimacy from Article 370, which was also used for incorporating Sections 6, 8 and 9 in the J&K Constitution adopted by the Constituent Assembly of the State on 17th November 1956. Section 6 defines a permanent resident of the state as one who was ordinarily resident in the state for no less than ten years prior to 14th May 1954, or a returnee migrant who had migrated to Pakistan after 1st March 1947 but returned later under any law of the state. Section 8 gives the state the right to define permanent residents, while Section 9 empowers it to alter this definition.

Article 35A was challenged earlier in 2014 by a Delhi-based NGO, 'We the Citizens', on the grounds that it violated Article 368, and also Article 14 which guarantees equality before law, by denying Indian citizens outside J&K any right to own land or vote. The J&K Government had filed a counter-affidavit asking for the plea to be dismissed. Appearing for the central government, Attorney General K. K. Venugopal had told the Court that given the "sensitive" nature of the issue, the centre wanted a "larger debate on it". He also asked for the matter to be referred to a larger bench, given the constitutional issues involved. But it rang alarm bells across the entire valley and raised a storm of protests from various quarters ever since a Supreme Court advocate, Ms. Charu Wali Khanna, a Kashmiri Pandit married and settled in Delhi, had challenged the article before the Supreme Court. Ms. Khanna wanted to build a house in J&K, but found that her marriage to a non-Kashmiri had made her a 'non-permanent resident' in her home state, automatically depriving her of the rights to acquire immovable property, seek employment or aid from the state by virtue of Article 35A and also disenfranchised her in her own state.

The article, read with the aforementioned sections of the J&K Constitution, is discriminatory between male and female permanent residents. If a Kashmiri man marries a non-permanent resident, his children would enjoy the right to his property, but the children of a Kashmiri woman who is a permanent resident but marries a non-Kashmiri would lose such right over her ancestral property, as per a 1965-ruling of the J&K High Court. Though overturned by a full bench of the same High Court in 2002, the judgment left the status of children of such women unclear. It was on this ground that Ms. Khanna challenged the article before the Supreme Court. But there are other sections in the Constitution of J&K that are also equally discriminatory between permanent and non-permanent citizens, like Sections 51 and 140 which respectively empower only a permanent resident to contest legislative seats or even vote in elections to state legislature. Those opposing Article 35A say that it was inserted just to maintain the predominance of Muslims in the valley permanently.

Political parties in the valley warned of a severe backlash in case it is scrapped. Chief Minister Mehbooba Mufti warned that “no one will be left in the state to hold the national flag”, while National Conference leader Farooq Abdullah said that questioning the validity of Article 35A–"an article of faith"–would be as good as challenging the accession of J&K, warning of an agitation “far stronger” than the Amarnath land row of 2008.

But the real reason behind the inflamed passions is the fear of a demographic change, once the right to settlement within the state is allowed to outsiders. It may be mentioned that such restrictions on fundamental rights of Indian citizens are not unique to J&K alone, they are also applicable in the other so-called “Special Category States of India”, by virtue of Article 371-A as well as the 5th and 6th Schedules to the Constitution of India. This has not caused much of a problem in those states, and the fear for inundation of the valley by outsiders may be rather unfounded, despite the BJP election manifesto for the J&K assembly elections promising “land at cheap rates for establishment of Sainik colonies in major towns” for retired soldiers. But a revisit to this article also opens up the possibility for closer scrutiny of Article 370 which was added to the Constitution of India only as a “Temporary Provision with respect to the State of Jammu & Kashmir”. But as I have explained in my book *Special Category States of India* (OUP, 2016), the original Article 370 has been diluted and eroded so much that scrapping it altogether would not make any real difference to the autonomy of the state whose financial interests are protected by its special category status conferred in 1969. In fact, the only autonomy left is article 35A. But other issues might be raised as well.

One of the issues would be the validity of all the constitutional orders issued by the President. As pointed out by Muzameel Zaleel, the Constitution Order of 1954 has been amended 41 times since, and through these amendments, 94 out of 97 entries in the Union List, and 260 of the 395 articles of the Indian Constitution, have been extended to the state. The legality of these orders may come under scrutiny in case Article 35A is struck down by the Supreme Court.

The issues involved are indeed tricky and contentious, and may raise questions over asymmetrical arrangements in place in other parts of the country as well. Hopefully the Supreme Court would give due consideration to all relevant issues; nevertheless, the centre would have to tread with caution and prudence, and weigh all options objectively while ignoring jingoism on both sides.

(Afterword: The Supreme Court Judgment on Article 35A is still awaited.)

2. ASYMMETRIC SOLUTION FOR KASHMIR[47]

(It is time to address the Kashmir problem by drawing lessons from other asymmetric federations and discarding conventional solutions which are no longer working.)

I

Once again, Kashmir is under siege. Violence has been convulsing the unfortunate state since July 8th, when the 22-year-old charismatic separatist leader Burhan Muzaffar Wani was killed by the security forces. In the violent protests that ensued, and in the response of the security forces, scores have died and thousands injured, half of them being security personnel. This time, the all too familiar script of containing violence with force and simultaneously engaging in dialogues with the stakeholders including separatist leaders is no longer working. The unrest shows no sign of abating and the state government seems to be bereft of all ideas about how to bring peace back to the troubled state. Maybe it is time to think of options and to experiment with some out-of-the-box solutions, by drawing lessons from how similar situations have been handled by other countries in the world.

The history of Kashmir's accession is too well known to merit any repetition. After the Constituent Assembly of J&K ratified the accession of the state to India in 1956, the government of India's stand remained unchanged that Kashmir's accession to India was a settled fact and a plebiscite was no longer an option. Article 370 of the Constitution, adopted by the Indian Constitution Assembly in 1949, promised a special status and internal autonomy for J&K while limiting the Indian Parliament's jurisdiction only to defence, foreign affairs and communication. The Union of India could not make laws with respect to the state without its concurrence. But "Article 370 - Temporary provisions with respect to the State of Jammu and Kashmir" was meant to serve only as a temporary measure till Kashmir was finally integrated into the Indian Union. The Delhi Agreement signed in July 1952 between the Indian government and Sheikh Abdullah much diluted the article, by extending provisions of the Indian Constitution to the state in respect of fundamental rights, jurisdiction of the Supreme Court of India

[47] Originally published in *The Statesman*, 7th and 8th September, 2016.

and emergency provisions under Article 356 and also empowering parliament to make laws for the state. The special category status awarded to the state later in 1969 addressed some of the developmental bottlenecks faced by it, but the promises held out by Article 370 were never fulfilled. The promises were of guaranteeing an asymmetric status within the federation to integrate the state, dissimilar to other Indian states in many respects, into the Indian federation.

Many federations have learnt to accommodate diverse socio-economic, ethno-religious and cultural-linguistic differences between their constituent units, especially in large federations where differences between the constituent units are serious enough to breed and nurture the seeds of future potential conflicts. All federal systems have to provide for independence, autonomy and self-determination of their constituent units within a broader political union. While in symmetric federalism no distinction is made between the constituent units in terms of their powers or autonomy within the federation, in asymmetric federal systems different sub-national entities are given differential constitutional status with differential powers, with some entities enjoying higher degrees of autonomy than others.

The Indian Constitution's makers were aware of the many divergent tendencies that existed within a new born 'majoritarian' nation, and consciously decided to accommodate these fissiparous tendencies in a harmonious manner through Article 370 for Jammu and Kashmir and Article 371, beside Schedules V and VI of the Constitution in respect of the north eastern states and certain other areas. Asymmetric powers embodied in these instruments were envisaged to accommodate the conflicting demands of language, religion, caste and tribe in our north eastern states. Similar powers have been institutionalised in many other countries.

No large society in the world is wholly integrated or wholly diversified. All societies fall somewhere in the wide spectrum between these two extremities. Similarly, all federal countries thrive on the basis of a compromise between the union on the one hand and autonomy and independence of all constituent subunits on the other, combining, as Edward Freeman has said, "the advantages of the large state–peace, order and general well-being–with those of the small state–the full development and autonomy of the individual citizen".

As Luis Moreno and César Colino pointed out, of the 65 countries in the world exhibiting substantial diversity, meaning where ethno-cultural, linguistic or religious minorities account for more than 5 percent of the population, only 15 have federal systems. Some of these countries have devised different institutional arrangements through legal, political and constitutional processes, political participation, fiscal federalism or other institutional means to deal with their own configurations of diversities arising from economic disparity, migration, religion, language, culture or ethno-national identities. The oft-quoted examples are Belgium, Canada and Spain.

Belgium is a small country in Western Europe inhabited by a little over 10 million people; 58 percent of the population are Dutch speakers who live in the northern part of the country in Flanders. About 32 percent are French speakers who live in Wallonia in the south. The remaining 10 percent of German speaking Belgians live in the Brussels capital region. Though territorially, Belgium is divided into three regions, linguistically it is divided into 3 communities, Dutch, French and German, as seen above. Each of the regions and communities has its own parliament and executive, with their constitutionally-assigned powers. The executive and legislative powers are also divided evenly among the 3 regions and communities.

Both houses of the national parliament are divided into linguistic groups. The 71-member Senate has 41 members from the Dutch, 29 from the French and 1 member from the German-speaking communities. In the lower house, there are 150 representatives who are elected from the respective political parties through proportional representation. Thus, there is no scope for over- or under-representation by any linguistic group, which holds the diverse groups together within a coherent federation.

Unlike Belgium, Canada is a large federation with a population of 35 million, divided into two major linguistic groups: 59 percent Anglophone and 23 percent francophone of whom 80 percent live in Québec. Canada is often described as a bi-national federation, with the predominantly French-speaking Québec seeking constitutional recognition 'as a distinct society or nation', or aspiring to become an independent country while retaining its economic and political association with the rest of Canada.

Political tension between the British and French immigrants is a historical legacy dating back to the 18th century, when French and British immigrants came together to settle in Canada. Québec became home to the largely Catholic French settlers, while the largely Protestant English settled in Ontario. They were like 'two nations warring in the bosom of a single state' separating in 1840 and then coming together again in 1867 in a confederation of 'equal partnership', with both having rights to their language and religion guaranteed by the Constitution Act of 1867, which recognised the 'unique character' of Québec, permitting the Quebecers to practice their own civil law as distinguished from the common law system prevailing in the rest of Canada, in striking similarity to our article 370. The Canadian Constitution ensures that the Canadian Parliament is bilingual, that each province is sufficiently represented, its provincial autonomy being fully protected.

There has been a consistent struggle between centralising and decentralising tendencies in Canadian society throughout its history. During the 1960s and 1970s, the Québec nationalist movement was intensified by the separatist political party, Parti Québécois, which sought independence for the Québec 'nation'. Besides its language and culture, Québec has retained exclusive authority employment and immigration issues within its borders, issues that are prerogatives of the federal government in all other provinces, a script that may be tried in Kashmir when everything else seems to be failing.

The asymmetry in the Canadian federation actually goes much deeper than the issues of autonomy and rights. It addresses the fundamental question whether two distinct societies or nations can co-exist within a federation with an option to exit. It was a question of whether Québec can be constitutionally recognised as a distinct society within Canada with the right to secede. In a landmark judgment, the Canadian Supreme Court, while ruling that such a right did not exist under the Constitution, asserted that if Québec decides to secede on the basis of a 'clear question' and 'majority vote', then the other federal partners would have the constitutional obligation to 'negotiate a new pact', making Canada one of the few countries to recognise the right of secession by a constituent unit. In a subsequent development, through a simple motion in the House of Commons in 2006, the federal government recognised Québec as a distinct society and assured that it would not support any constitutional change without the support of Québec and other regions of Canada. It resolved that Québec, at least sociologically, constitutes a 'nation' within Canada.

Canadians have so far failed to resolve their differences, but that has not prevented them from holding together as a strong, multi-national, multi-cultural federation committed to the constitutional principles of federalism, democracy, rule of law and respect for minority rights. The Canadian experiment is an example of a fine balance between unity and diversity, symmetry and asymmetry and of peaceful and democratic management of multiple diversities through negotiation, accommodation and renegotiation.

II

Complex societies that display remarkable heterogeneity are often the products of their complex histories. Spain is a multinational state–a 'nation of nations' or to some, a 'plurinational state'–with a long and complex history, during which it has experimented with republicanism, dictatorship, democracy and had to contend with anarchy, violence, civil war and periods of prolonged political instability. It was a dictatorship under General Francisco Franco till his death in 1975. In 1978 when its present constitution came into force, Spain became an Autonomic State–*Estado de las Autonomias*–comprising 17 Autonomous Communities (AC) through an extensive asymmetric decentralisation of 'competences'–i.e. powers and responsibilities.

Spain has a multilingual population which is widely divergent–economically, territorially, demographically, ethnically as well as culturally. A strong Castilian majority exists with a number of minority nationalities– Catalonia, Galicia and the Basque Country–each with its distinctive history, culture and language. The four largest ACs– Andalusia, Catalonia, Madrid and Valencia–share among themselves about 58 percent of the national population of 46 million, and nearly 60 percent of Spain's GDP. Catalonia and the Basque Country, regions that have histories dating back several centuries, regard themselves more as 'historical nations', and demand recognition as such. In many ways Kashmir resembles the Basque Country which is similarly isolated in the Pyrenean mountains and is inaccessible with limited economic potential. This seclusion marginalised it to resist assimilation into Christianity and the Spanish mainstream for a long time.

A homogenous administrative and legislative standard is applied to governance in all 17 ACs: each AC has a legislative assembly. However, as regards financial autonomy, 2 ACs, Navarre and the Basque Country, have additional competencies not enjoyed by the other ACs–they can collect some of the state taxes like income tax and pay to the state for the services they receive from it, while the other communities follow a uniform tax regime based on collection by the state and their redistribution and devolution to ACs.

Distributing legislative competences between the centre and the ACs is rather complicated and ambiguous. As Wilfried Swenden pointed out, such complexity arises from the lack of agreement on where the Spanish state should be heading: a federal, a regionalised or unitary decentralised state? The Spanish Constitution lays down separate lists of competences for the federal centre and ACs, much like the 7th Schedule of the Indian Constitution. Further, each of the regions also has a 'Statute of Autonomy' that must contain certain competences within the framework of the Constitution, which can be expanded by amending the Constitution; ACs can even encroach upon 'exclusively Central' competences. This opens a road for bilateral negotiations between the state and the ACs, and some ACs may wrest more powers from the state than others.

The Spanish Constitution does not recognise the right of self-determination by Spain's nationalities or regions. However, both Basque and Catalan Parliaments have already voted for recognition of the right to self-determination for their ACs. Permitting a referendum is the exclusive prerogative of the Spanish Parliament and hence a referendum by an AC would be invalid without its consent. In June 2008, the Basque Parliament passed a law for conducting a referendum, which was contested by the central government before the Constitutional Court which confirmed the unconstitutionality of this law. The Basque government consequently abandoned the idea of holding this referendum. A similar thing happened with Catalonia. The rejection of their demands has incited nationalistic sentiments in both the regions, but Spain is still holding together as a strong, unified nation.

Nearer home also, there is a federation, Malaysia, whose constitutional mechanism has quite a few similarities with India's and which also exhibits a high degree of diversity. Malaysia is a union of 30.5 million people living in 13 states, 11 in peninsular Malaysia and 2 in the northern part of Borneo–Sabah and Sarawak, separated by 640kms from the peninsula by the South China Sea. Malay and other indigenous people, called *Bumiputeras* (Sons of the Soil), together constitute nearly 62 percent of its population; among the rest, 23 percent are Chinese and 7 percent are Indians, besides 8 percent non-citizen immigrants. Islam is the official religion, though the Constitution gives fundamental right to all citizens to profess, practice and propagate their own religions. Muslims constitute just above 60 percent of the population and Buddhists 19 percent. Like India, Malaysia is multi-ethnic, multi-racial, multi-lingual and multi-cultural.

Malaysia was formed in 1963 by the merger of the independent Federation of Malaya and the formerly British colonies of Singapore, Sabah and Sarawak. Singapore was a part of Malaysia until 1965, but the political and ethnic tensions between the ethnic Malays of Malaysia and the largely ethnic Chinese population of Singapore ultimately led to the secession of Singapore from the federation in 1965 and its emergence as an independent sovereign country under Lee Kuan Yew, after the Malaysian Parliament voted to expel it from the federation.

Malaysian society has perpetual tensions between the *Bumiputeras* and non-Malays largely based in peninsular Malaysia, between fundamental Islamists and moderate Muslims and also among the *Bumiputeras*–between Muslims based largely in the peninsula and non-Muslim natives of Sarawak and Sabah. The communal nature of these conflicts has close parallels in India. Malaysia addresses these conflicts by granting significant autonomy to Malays and indigenous peoples of Sabah and Sarawak, much in excess of the autonomy exercised by the other 11 states. The Constitution of Malaysia, like India's, provides for positive discrimination by safeguarding the special position of the Malays and natives of Sabah and Sarawak and the legitimate interests of other communities, by protecting and promoting their interests in the four main areas of reservation: land, quotas for admission into certain sectors of federal public service, the issuing of licences and permits for the operation of certain businesses and the provision of educational assistance.

Malaysia is a highly centralised federation where powers are strongly concentrated in the central government rather than being evenly distributed between the centre and the states, much like in India. Taxation is almost an exclusive monopoly of the federal government, but Sabah and Sarawak are allowed to make laws for imposing taxes; they are also exempted from the provisions of Article 76 that allows the federal government to encroach upon state subjects as enumerated in the State List. While the right to secede from the federation is denied, there are constitutional safeguards, known as the Twenty Points, for Sabah and Sarawak for their participation in the federation. These include that Islam's status as the official religion is not applicable to Sarawak and Sabah, besides granting them exclusive immigration control and special powers for raising revenues. No specific safeguard granted under the Twenty Points can also be amended by the federal government without the concurrence of Sabah and Sarawak state governments.

The Malay Federation gained independence from the British in 1957, and special privileges and rights of these communities emerged from its imperial legacy as they had enjoyed these rights also under the British administration. The Independent Constitutional Commission appointed in 1956 prior to the independence of the Federation of Malaya, while deciding to continue with these privileges, recommended that with the gradual integration of these communities into a common nationality, the need for these special preferences would gradually disappear, and, 'in due course the present preferences should be reduced and should ultimately cease so that there should then be no discrimination between races or communities'. Their constitution finally rejected their stipulation of a time limit of 15 years for this purpose, and made the Head of State responsible for activating a periodic review of any proposals.

In heterogeneous societies, as in these countries, the extent of diversities and differences determined the level of asymmetry necessary to establish the equilibrium for dissipating discontent and conflicts. More accommodation does not necessarily mean weakening of the federation to the point of disintegration. It may actually contribute to assimilation and stability within the democratic structure and within the limits defined by the rule of law. In a centralised federation like India, this stability can be reinforced only if the process is guided not by considerations of political expediency, but by national interests established though consensus among the centre and states and also among the political parties and all other stakeholders. This can happen when all the stakeholders rise above their narrow, parochial and short-term visions. Sadly, this consensus is yet to emerge for the beautiful state of Jammu & Kashmir which has been pulverised by repeated cycles of violence and terrorism. It is time to experiment with an unconventional solution like the ones discussed.

3. A POPULIST WAIVER[48]

(Loan waivers are inefficient answers to farmers' problems, even though the recent UP loan waiver was announced in fulfilment of an election promise. But freebies promised in elections present a far more serious problem.)

In one of the first acts of his newly elected government, replicating Congress-style populism, the UP Chief Minister Yogi Adityanath has announced a waiver of a loan up to ₹1 lakh for about 85 lakh small and marginal farmers in UP covering more than 90 percent of the state's farming community. This will cost the UP exchequer a whopping ₹36,729 crore, coming close to the ₹52000 crore farm-loan waiver scheme announced by the then UPA Finance, Minister Mr Chidambaram, in the 2008 budget, ahead of the 2009 general elections that returned the UPA to power. The UP government will have to finance this through market loans, putting in serious jeopardy its fiscal deficit limit of 3 percent of GDP set by the FRBM Act which it has already breached. Of course, Adityanath was only fulfilling BJP's election promise, and he cannot perhaps be faulted on this. But both the election promise and the loan waiver raise several disturbing questions, and the nation needs to ponder seriously over these questions.

Whether the scheme will relieve the woes of the farmers is an altogether different matter, given the pathetic record of the state in delivery. Despite the energy the new CM seems to have infused into UP's decrepit administrative apparatus, he has to deal with the same dysfunctional bureaucracy that has failed the state for so long. It will be foolhardy to expect that the delivery system will transform itself overnight into an efficient one.

Governance is all about efficient and effective delivery, which calls for careful planning and monitoring. Most government schemes suffer universally from wastefulness, leakages, financial misappropriations, and institutionalisation of corruption, which together render the outcomes of such schemes poor and sub-optimal. The 2008 UPA loan waiver scheme was audited by the CAG, whose report revealed many serious lapses and deficiencies in delivery. Out of 3.73 crore farmers who were given debt

---

[48] Originally published in *The Statesman*, 5th May, 2017.

relief, the CAG had test-checked some 90000 cases, and more than 20,000 (22 percent of checked cases) revealed serious lapses. Thousands of ineligible farmers received benefits of the waiver while deserving farmers were left out; benefits were irregularly extended to microfinance institutions and banks in violation of the guidelines. Tampering of records was widespread. In fact, the BJP itself had then demanded a CBI inquiry at that time, terming this as “a big fraud committed on the nation” involving a “huge scam of ₹10000 crore.” The outcome is unlikely to be different this time also.

Further, NSSO data shows that less than half of the small and marginal farmers in UP were actually indebted to banks, while the majority of farmers were indebted to informal or non-institutional sources like local money lenders, traders, or bigger farmers; they will not get any benefits under the scheme. The smaller the land holding of a farmer, the less likely he is to get a bank-loan. Among farmers with less than one acre of land, just 28 percent have outstanding bank loans; the remaining 72 percent owe money to non-formal creditors, mainly money lenders. Thus, the intended relief to small and marginal farmers remains in doubt.

As regards the economic fallout of the waiver, one needs to remember that UP’s debt burden is next only to West Bengal and Punjab, with its outstanding liability amounting to over 32 percent of its GSDP in 2014-15, in which alone it raised ₹35,520 crore, compared to ₹14,900 crore in the previous year. The fiscal deficit had exceeded the FRBM limit by 0.33 percent as a result, and interest payment amounted to ₹18865 crore, or 11 percent of revenue expenditure. With this additional ₹36,000 to be raised in 2017-18, its debt burden and interest liability will increase alarmingly. Servicing this debt will squeeze availability of funds, with most of the borrowed funds going towards repayment of the existing loans, and very little accruing to the state for use in development. The consequences on development of the impoverished state would be disastrous.

This is not to argue that distressed farmers should not be provided succour when they need it the most, but the mode of providing such succour needs to be carefully thought through. It distorts the loan discipline and encourages wilful default, as the RBI Governor had already pointed out. It actively promotes a culture of irresponsibility. The banking system, already reeling under unmanageable NPAs, takes a further beating while the wilful defaulters stand to benefit. There are many other ways of providing assistance to affected farmers.

Further, this may signal the beginning of a much more serious contagion which is likely to spread like a cancer in our body-politic. As Ashok Gulati and Siraj Hussain pointed out, in Punjab, Congress's manifesto promised a similar step. Madras High Court has suggested farm loan waivers to the Tamil Nadu government. Maharashtra, Karnataka and Kerala, which are suffering from drought, will follow suit. With state elections due in several states before the 2019 Lok Sabha elections–in Gujarat, Himachal Pradesh, Rajasthan, Madhya Pradesh, Karnataka, Chhattisgarh and four north eastern states–it could only be a matter of time before such waivers become an all-India norm, to be financed through state budgets, throwing any semblance of fiscal and financial discipline to the winds. FRBMs which had rescued the states from the brink of the disaster of falling irrevocably into a debt trap might as well be scrapped.

History has proved time and again that bad economics is not good politics. But then it harps on the question of political parties promising freebies–ranging from colour TVs, laptops and mixer-grinders to free electricity, and water or loan waivers in their election manifestos–which is the root of the problem. Political parties have appropriated for themselves the blanket authority to dole out national resources under the garb of democracy.

In the case of S. Subramaniam Balaji *vs*. Government of Tamil Nadu (2013), the Supreme Court observed, that "the reality cannot be ruled out that distribution of freebies of any kind undoubtedly influences all people. It shakes the root of free and fair elections to a large degree." However, since distribution of freebies or other promises made in an election manifesto cannot be construed as a 'corrupt practice' under Section 123 of the Representation of the People Act, 1951, the Supreme Court directed the Election Commission to frame appropriate guidelines in this regard.

All political parties predictably reacted to this judgment, because it hurt their common interest by limiting their authority to dole out national resources for petty electoral gains. They argued that political parties, being committed to the constitutional goal of a welfare state, were within their rights to frame their election manifestos highlighting the way they would serve the voters if voted to power, and hence the promises were neither meant to act as bribes nor to influence the voters unduly.

Article 324 of the Constitution gives the Election Commission unfettered powers to superintend, direct and control the election process which implies monitoring activities of political parties including promises made in their manifestos for conducting free and fair elections. In accordance with the

Supreme Court directive, the Commission introduced in its Model Code of Conduct the following 'Guidelines on Election Manifestos':

- "The Election Manifesto shall not contain any promises that go against the ideals and principles enshrined in the Constitution."
- Due to India being conceived as a welfare state under the Directive Principles of the Constitution, "There can be no bar on the state adopting welfare measures. But, political parties must refrain from making promises that undermine the purity of the election process or aim to exert undue influence on the voters."
- "There must be transparency with respect to the promises and how the parties aim to implement their promises. The promises must also be credible. Wherever freebies are offered, parties must broadly state how they plan to gather the funds and finances to fulfil such promises."

The wording of the guidelines thus leaves the field wide open for political parties to make any promises including freebies to the voters which goes against the spirit of the Supreme Court ruling. Apparently, the Commission had succumbed to the pressure of the political parties, forgetting that in a mature democracy, a political party only owes good and corruption-free governance and nothing else to the electorate. It also undermines the fact that the relief offered by the freebies like loan waivers or subsidised power etc. is only temporary and ignores the solution to the larger problems of scarcity, input costs and capacity, which have to be addressed effectively, over a longer time-period, using the same national resources.

In view of the spate of impending elections, the Election Commission may be well-advised to revise its guidelines in respect of freebies to bring in a semblance of discipline and responsibility in the election process. It owes this to the country and it might be its lasting legacy.

(Since then other states like Punjab, Maharashtra and Rajasthan have announced loan waivers. Please see "Death of Austerity" in Section 2).

4. A Dynasty Returns to Rule Bihar[49]

(Return of the Lalu dynasty in Bihar may have reinforced the trend of dynastic democracy in India.)

With the resounding defeat of the NDA in Bihar elections, the outraged feelings of secular liberals of our country have at last been assuaged. The talk of growing intolerance has disappeared almost overnight, and no more awards are being returned by the eminent recipients of various national awards. Just as the motor-mouths in the BPJ have stopped issuing daily vitriolic statements condemning the slaughterers of *gau-mata* and their perceived sympathisers, the fervour of others in a matching tit-for-tat demonstration of the consumption of her meat in public also seems to have evaporated, reminding one of the *Rubaiyat-I-Omar-Khayyam*: 'I came like water and like wind I go.' We all can now breathe a great sigh of relief; India is no longer intolerant and communal. It has again become a benevolent, vibrant and secular democracy as it has always sought to be. As Mr Jay Panda, an MP from Odisha, wrote, perceptions do matter and it was no coincidence that the narrative of rising intolerance always seemed to peak around the elections, steered mostly by the non-vernacular media that is a safe sanctuary for our elites and liberals, despite the fact that on an average, 2 communal incidents had occurred per day during 2011-13 before the NDA had come to power.

Intolerance has perhaps been embedded in the Indian psyche since the beginning of time; what was the caste system but intolerance against humanity itself, against the very notion that all men are born equal? Many commentators have pointed out that one had never heard so much talk about intolerance during the countless communal riots that had happened in this country since independence, during the Sikh riots in 1984, Babri Masjid in 1992 or Godhra and Gujrat in 2002, even if we ignore the imposition of emergency of 1977, and all that had followed in its wake including the compulsory sterilisation of Muslims, as a temporary aberration. No awardees returned their national awards and the TV channels, few as they were then–never aired endless debates about the danger posed by rising intolerance. We can probably rest assured and comforted that till the time

[49] Originally published in *The Statesman*, 24th November, 2015.

the next elections come up in Assam, West Bengal, Kerala and Tamil Nadu next year, and in UP in 2017, not much will be heard about intolerance, consumption of beef, or the increasing communalisation of our socio-cultural fabric. Perhaps there will be no more return of awards too. Bihar elections have restored the equilibrium in our democracy that was seriously under threat of being sabotaged, but the saboteurs have now been silenced and India can rejoice in the wisdom Bihar has so convincingly exercised.

It is well-known that among all land vertebrates, the ostrich has the largest eye. Its eyes are, in fact, bigger than its brain; they provide fantastic eyesight but the undersized brain does not necessarily facilitate good judgment. Ostriches bury their heads in sand when scared of something they do not want to see. No wonder many of our political leaders astoundingly exhibit some of these remarkable traits, and so do many of our liberal secular intellectuals, including the wise men and women who frequently grace our adored TV channels that propagate the truth and nothing but the truth on a 24/7 footing. While they will seize every opportunity to denigrate the Congress leadership and its dynastic roots in the hoarsest of voices, they did not raise even a dim cacophony when Mr Lalu Prasad Yadav hoisted 2 of his sons–both first-time MLAs–to preside over the fate of the people of Bihar for the next 5 years: one, a 26-year-old school-dropout, as the Deputy Chief Minister, putting him in charge of some crucial portfolios and the other, an intermediate-pass 27-year old lad, as a Cabinet Minister with 3 important portfolios. People cannot miss uncanny similarities in circumstances, when he had to hoist his wife Rabri Devi onto the throne of Bihar in 1997, being under intense pressure to quit in the aftermath of the fodder scam. Both his sons, like his wife, are absolute greenhorns with little experience of politics, governance, administration or statecraft.

Lalu was the real emperor behind the throne then, and remained the undisputed controller of the destiny of Bihar for one and half decades, even though he was not on the throne for half the time. Assuredly, he will become so even now, despite being unable to contest any election due to his conviction and sentencing in the fodder scam cases. In addition to the crucial portfolios of roads and building construction, Tejaswi has been given the portfolios of welfare of other backward castes and extreme backward castes. Tej Pratap has been entrusted with the crucial portfolios of health, minor irrigation and environment and forests. Together, these 6 ministries accounted for ₹18,000 crore of expenditure out of a total ₹132,593 crore in the revised estimates of 2014-15 for Bihar. Lalu's two sons will now command ministries which make up about 15 percent of the budget of Bihar, for augmenting the resources of which Mr Nitish Kumar has steadfastly been demanding the special category status for the state.

With Mr Abdul Bari Siddiqui, also from RJD, getting the important finance portfolio, although without the plum part dealing with commercial taxes, which goes to Bijendra Pasad Yadav of JD(U), Lalu will be the real controller of Bihar's purses. He will become the undisputed commander of Bihar's caste-infested political landscape too. Both the parties have 12 ministries each, with the collateral beneficiary Congress getting the remaining 5 including the important portfolios of education and animal husbandry, but RJD has now succeeded in bagging the additional important portfolios of transport, cooperatives, labour, tourism, mining, disaster management and Department of Youth, Art and Culture, apart from the Ministry of Minority Welfare.

Minorities, OBCs and EBCs are of vital political importance to RJD for expanding and consolidating its base in the state. This will clearly go against the long-term interests of JD (U) which has managed to keep only the Department for Welfare of SCs and STs with it. That Lalu's nominees are in charge of all ministries and departments dealing with the interests of minorities, OBCs and EBCs, is not a mere coincidence, given their importance in a state where elections are by and large still determined by caste equations. Any overenthusiasm displayed by either party in respect of minority welfare is likely to bring the two allies into direct conflicts of interests. One can expect there will be close competition in expanding the distribution of doles to SCs/ STs and other minorities/ OBCs/ EBCs by the 2 ministries represented by these two parties, once bitter foes but now tied together in a unique marriage of convenience. The ministries allotted to RJD together account for about 20 percent of the total expenditure budget of the Bihar government, but with the finance ministry safely secured, Lalu will firmly be in the saddle, reigning the finances in and out as he desires, dispensing favour and disfavour as he likes. Apparently to allay the fears of return of the Jungle Raj which had prevailed under the previous Lalu-Rabri dispensation, Mr Nitish Kumar has kept the home portfolio with himself, and for good reason–to ward off Lalu's influence in deciding the transfers and postings of police personnel to manipulate the law and order machinery. But there should be no doubt as to who the real the mover and shaker behind the government is.

The equations between the 2 parties were made abundantly clear during the oath taking ceremony itself; after Nitish Kumar, the next JD(U) member to take oath was Bijendra Pasad Yadav at number 5, after the 2 sons of Lalu and Mr Siddiqui. It was not only flaunting the superior numerical strength of Lalu's 80 against Nitish's 71, but also a reminder of the coming of age of 'Yadav Raj'–every 4th member in the newly elected Bihar assembly is now a Yadav. As the Patna edition of a national daily came out with the headline "In Lalu Raj, Nitish wears a crown with RJD thorns." The thorn is likely to be more than a mere irritant in the days to come.

The fight back and subsequent rise of Mr Lalu Prasad Yadav has been nothing short of a miracle. Like the proverbial phoenix, he has risen from the ashes and his persona now looms larger than life over the political horizons of Bihar. But his figure will from now on be flanked by his sons too, who have been initiated into politics without any education, experience or training. Of course, they are not the first of their kinds, and certainly will not be the last in the strange political culture practiced in this country.

In a democracy, one does not question the wisdom and prudence of people's choice. It needs no reminding that it was an absolute 'Upper Caste Raj' in Bihar before Lalu took over in 1989, and that 'Jungle Raj' under Lalu was, in a way, a retribution for the unspeakable atrocities inflicted by the Upper Caste Raj on the lower castes and Dalits. If Biharis have now decided again to be ruled by Bihar's first family and voted with their castes, they must have good reasons for that.

There are few ways of entering politics in India: through family, through money and muscle-power and through hard work from the grassroots. As Patrick French has shown, as many as 156 MPs in the 15th Lok Sabha were hereditary MPs, who came to politics only by virtue of their families. Bihar's destiny is inseparable from India's, and may the Great Dispenser of India's Destiny install more such dynasties to redefine democracy, *a-la* Indian style. May our secular and liberal thinkers wallow in the glory of our dynastic democracy and live barricaded lives in intellectual hallucination pontificating before the TVs.

(Afterword: In July 2017, Nitish Kumar broke his alliance with Lalu's RJD, reeling under a barrage of charges related to various land scams involving Lalu's family members which have systematically surfaced during the past few months. Corruption was raising its ugly head in Bihar again, and criminals were again starting to have a free run under Lalu's protection and encouragement, and it was severely denting the clean image of Nitish Kumar. Unable to continue associating with the scam-tainted family, Nitish submitted his resignation to the Governor bringing to an end the JD(U)-

RJD government. With the support of BJP, he returned to power immediately.)

5. SPECIAL CATEGORY STATUS WILL REMAIN A CHIMERA FOR ANDHRA[50]

(Despite demands by Chief Minister Chandrababu Naidu, the residuary state of Andhra Pradesh is unlikely to get special category status anytime soon.)

In February 2016, Prime Minister Narendra Modi assured the Andhra Pradesh Chief Minister Chandrababu Naidu to consider conferring the special category status to his state. Apart from the special category status, Mr Naidu has been demanding a special package for the residuary state of Andhra Pradesh after it was carved out from the erstwhile composite state in June 2014, and an additional ₹16,078 crore to bridge the budget deficit arising from the bifurcation of the state. It may be recalled that Special Category Status allows a state to avail central funding at liberal terms for centrally sponsored schemes (90 percent grant) apart from various tax sops and incentives to industries.

The erstwhile composite state of Andhra Pradesh was divided with effect from 2nd June 2014, by the Andhra Pradesh Reorganisation Act, 2014. Of the 23 districts of undivided Andhra Pradesh, 9 districts in the coastal region and 4 districts in the backward Rayalaseema region remained with the residual state of Andhra Pradesh, while the remaining 10 districts including the most prosperous Hyderabad district with the capital city of Hyderabad and the contiguous Ranga Reddy district, also equally prosperous, went to Telangana. As per the act, the total liabilities of the undivided state were to be shared by the two successor states in the ratio of their population, i.e. 58:42.

The division left the residual state of Andhra Pradesh much poorer. As per the 2012-13 accounts, the residuary Andhra Pradesh with its own revenue of ₹11,627 crore and expenditure of ₹60,750 crore inherited a total liability of ₹90,910 crore, while Telengana with a revenue of ₹56,476 crore and expenditure of ₹42,376 crore inherited a debt liability of ₹65,832 crore only. But the asymmetry in the whole arrangement becomes striking, once we consider that the combined revenues of the two prosperous districts of

[50] Originally published in *The Statesman* as "Andhra Revenues", 16th June, 2016.

Telangana, Hyderabad and Ranga Reddy, came to ₹51478 crore, or 91 percent of the total revenues of Telangana and these two districts together accounted for expenditure of ₹23,302 crore or 48 percent of the total expenditure of Telangana during 2012-13. It was anticipated that this would lead to increased impoverishment of Andhra Pradesh as its own revenue would be too inadequate to meet even 1/5th of its expenditure requirements. The huge debt inherited in addition would impose a further heavy repayment burden on the poor state, and consequently stymie its growth with gaping fiscal deficits. Given the need to establish a new capital at Amaravathi, according a special category status giving it access to liberal central aid at least for the first few years thus seemed imperative.

The latest accounts of the government for the first completed year 2014-15 after its formation, placed in the legislature last month, however, has allayed these apprehensions to some extent. The state's revenue did drop from ₹1.10 lakh crore in 2013-14 when it was undivided to ₹90,672 crore in the full year 2014-15, while its expenditure went up from ₹1.10 lakh crore to ₹1.14 crore. This left a revenue deficit of ₹24,194 crore and a fiscal deficit of ₹31,716 crore for 2014-15, in which the contributions of the last 10 months of the state's existence as a residuary state were respectively ₹13,777 crore for the revenue deficit and ₹20,745 crore for the fiscal deficit. In contrast, Telangana had a revenue surplus of ₹369 crore but a fiscal deficit of only ₹9,410 crore for these 10 months. Of course, the higher revenue deficit and hence the higher fiscal deficit of Andhra were partly the state's own creation; in fulfilling its election promises, it waived the agricultural loans of farmers to the extent of ₹7,070 crore and increased the amounts under the Indiramma Old Age and Disabled Pension Scheme to ₹3,344 crore, which together accounted for 76 percent of its revenue deficit of ₹13,777 crore. The previous year, the composite state had a revenue surplus of ₹344 crore and a fiscal deficit of ₹18,041 crore.

Revenue of a state comes partly from its own resources and partly from central transfers that include the state's share in the divisible pool of union taxes, besides central grants. As a result of the bifurcation, during the ten months of its existence as a residuary state, Andhra's own revenues, tax plus non-tax combined, from its 13 districts amounted to ₹38,038 crore. The central transfers, including the state's share in the divisible pool and central grants, amounted to ₹27,657 crore, bringing the total revenue to ₹65,695 crore during the period, against which the revenue expenditure was ₹7,9471 crore, leaving a deficit of ₹13,777 crore in the revenue account, even with the election-promised sops. In contrast, the total own revenues from Telangana's 10 districts were almost the same as Andhra's (₹35735 crore), which means the loss of Hyderabad and Ranga Reddy districts did not affect Andhra's revenue position as drastically as anticipated–in fact the total revenue receipts of Andhra exceeded that of Telangana by over ₹14,600 crore, though it was because of the central transfers, in which Telangana's share was only ₹15,306 crore compared to Andhra's ₹27,658 crore. Andhra commands a larger share in central transfers, partly due to its higher population which has 25 percent weightage in the divisible pool transfers.

Instead of total expenditure, per-capita developmental expenditure is a better and more reliable proxy for actual expenditure spent on development. Andhra, with 2011-population of 4.9 crore, had a per capita developmental revenue expenditure of ₹12,226, and per capita capital outlay of ₹1,331, making up the total per capita developmental expenditure of ₹13,557. In contrast, Telangana with population of ₹3.52 crore had a per capita developmental revenue expenditure of ₹10,340 and per capita capital outlay of ₹2,379, making up a total of ₹12,719, which was lower than that of Andhra.

Going by the above financial results of the state, it thus seems improbable that Andhra Pradesh is getting special category status anytime soon. While replying to the debate on the Andhra Pradesh Reorganisation Bill in Parliament during the last days of UPA-II, the then Prime Minister Manmohan Singh assured that the resource gap likely to arise in the successor state of Andhra Pradesh in the very first year would be compensated in the regular Union Budget of 2014-15. The new government, apart from flagging the issue to the Niti Aayog, which apparently had submitted its report, has not yet taken any concrete step so far on this promise. Special category status could have helped in attracting industries into the state by creating a congenial ecosystem for industrial growth through tax incentives. As of now, industries seem more interested in setting or expanding their units in Hyderabad which is in Telangana rather than in Amaravathi, which is not yet ready. In fact, readying it would need massive capital investments and resources, which the state lacks presently. It is to be seen if Chandrababu Naidu will succeed in getting at least some assistance from the centre towards this end.

SECTION 7

THE WORLD AROUND

1. The Eclipse of Spring
2. The End of the Oil Age
3. The Catalonian Conundrum
4. The Breaking of the Berlin Wall and Making of a New World
5. The South China Sea Dispute
6. Drift in Bangladesh
7. China's Market Crash
8. The Death of a Prisoner
9. The Future of Artificial Intelligence
10. Immortality is My Name

1. THE ECLIPSE OF SPRING[51]

(Five years after the Arab Spring, most countries in the Arab world are in ferment again. Has the Arab Spring been eclipsed, or is it gathering strength again?)

On 17th December 2010, in the dusty town of Sidi Bouzeid in central Tunisia, a police woman by the name Faida Hamdy confiscated the vegetable cart of a street vendor, slapped him and spat on his face. In despair, that young man, Mohammed Bouazizi, set fire to himself. His death on January 4th, 2011, sparked widespread protests that ultimately overthrew the dictator President Zine El Abidine Ben Ali after 23 years of rule, who had to flee to Saudi Arabia with his family in the spring of 2011. The world watched with a mixture of joy and disbelief as thousands of people danced and celebrated their new-found freedom as these images were beamed live to TV screens across the world. On that day–24th January 2011–fear had died in Tunisia. The Jasmine Revolution, named after Tunisia's national flower, then triggered a series of similar protests in Egypt, Yemen, Bahrain, Libya, Syria and Morocco, sending ripples of fear throughout the entire Arab world which, with a few remarkable exceptions, were ruled by autocratic Sultans and Sheikhs, to whom words like democracy or human rights, especially women's rights, were anathema. This spring of discontent in the Arab world became known as the Arab Spring.

In Egypt, the first street protests erupted Cairo's Tahrir Square on 25th January, 2011. Three days later, President Hosni Mubarak's police marksmen shot dead hundreds of people in Cairo and Alexandria, and Tahrir Square became a symbol of the protests. It galvanised an entire nation in an ultimate do or die struggle against decades of poverty, oppression, tyranny and denial of human rights. After 18 days of demonstrations and more than 800 deaths, Mubarak was finally overthrown. That day, around sunset, in Tahrir Square, thousands of people danced and recited poetry, to celebrate the end of his three decade long dictatorial rule.

In February 2011, protests erupted against the rule of Colonel Muammar Gaddafi, which subsequently turned into an 8-month long civil war,

---

[51] Originally published in *The Statesman*, 14th July, 2016.

ultimately snowballing into an international war in which rebel forces were supported by NATO air attacks. The war ended with the death of the hated dictator in October 2011. In February 2012, President Ali Abdullah Saleh in Yemen was forced out of power. In Morocco, more than 37,000 people marched in nationwide protests demanding political reforms and democracy in February 2011, forcing King Mohammed VI to cede some of his powers to a newly elected government in the parliamentary elections held in January 2012. The spread of the contagion seemed unstoppable. In Syria, protests against President Bashar al-Assad that began in March 2011 have turned into a complex, intractable and prolonged bloody war. Thousands of Syrians are dead, thousands more have fled the country seeking refuge elsewhere, and hundreds have died on their perilous journey to safety on the European shores. The Syrian conflict has created the largest refugee crisis of the 21st century.

Now after 5 years, the Arab world is in ferment again. Syria, Iraq, Libya and Yemen are tottering on the verge of collapse, while militant terror and repression stalk the region, taking their daily toll. The movement for democracy has now morphed into a struggle between Islam and liberal forces on the one hand, and between Sunnis and Shias within Islam itself on the other. Iraq and Libya are being torn asunder in endless bloodletting between nationalists, Islamists, Shias, Sunnis, tribes and plain old thugs–all deeply entangled in a conflict that shows no sign of abating. Al-Qaeda and Islamic State roam free in much of Syria, Iraq, Yemen and Lebanon. Just as the Islamic identity has been badly shaken by its encounter with the Western world, the West is struggling hard to come to terms with Islam. The space vacated by the democratic movements in the Arab world has already been occupied by radicalised adherents of Islam, whose appeal, strangely no longer seem confined only to the deprived and marginalised sections of the community. Failure of the Arab Spring seems to have sparked and unleashed the fury of a resurgent Islam, whose appeal is proving to be especially strong among the Muslim immigrants in Europe.

In Tunis, protests started in the central avenue Habib Bourguiba. The main public square called the November 7th Square, now renamed Mohammad Bouazizi Square, was the place where protesters converged in thousands, demanding democracy and justice. Visiting the tranquil and beautiful square around a fountain, I reflected on the turmoil that had convulsed the country and gave a rebirth to another nation. Tunisia probably remains the sole success story in a region that has been unable to shake off the burden of the past. It has successfully sailed through two general elections since then, with a coalition led by the moderate Islamist party, Ennahda, winning the first.

Under its governance, the country drew up its constitution that guarantees basic fundamental rights and freedoms including rights to freedom of movement, opinion, expression and assembly, including the rights to form association and political parties, and guaranteed "equality of opportunities between women and men to have access to all levels of responsibility and in all domains", making Tunisia one of the few countries in the Arab world to do so. The transition to democracy has fundamentally changed the country. The public are now free to debate on contentious issues which are considered taboo in the Arab world, ranging from religion, political orders, rule of law, reform, gay rights, artistic expression, the meaning of revolution and, of course, on democratic polity, and they do so with gusto. Ennahda was defeated by an alliance of secular parties led by the liberal Nidaa Tounes party in elections held in October 2014. After 5 years though, the currents of discontent and frustration are again surfacing due to high unemployment and inadequacy of economic policy reforms, belying the hope of better life for the youth who had massively participated in the protests five years ago. But democracy is now deeply embedded in the psyche of the country.

In contrast, in Egypt, the revolution devoured its own children. After the overthrow of Mubarak, the Muslim Brotherhood, one of the world's oldest and most influential Islamic movements that also became the face of political Islam, was elected to power in the elections held in late 2011, and its leader Mohamed Morsi became the country's first democratically elected President. He tried to force an Islamist constitution by decree, granted himself unlimited powers and cracked down on dissent, triggering nationwide protests. In July 2013, the unpopular government was toppled in a coup led by the army chief Abdel Fatah al-Sisi who outlawed the Muslim Brotherhood as a terrorist organisation, herded its members into jail, including President Morsi, who was subsequently convicted on corruption and spying charges and sentenced to prison and death. In one of the harshest crackdowns on dissent, more than a thousand protesters, mostly supporters of the Brotherhood, were killed across Egypt. Sisi elected himself as President in May 2014, and Egypt is back to military dictatorship again, with thousands jailed, brutalised and dead. This has only reinforced the indispensability of the military as the only reliable source of establishing political order and stability in that country.

The voice of the liberals that had supported the overthrow of Muhammad Morsi has fallen silent. As *The Economist* has commented, "tarnished by this history, riven by infighting and lacking broad appeal, the liberals now appear helpless to check Egypt's slide back to authoritarianism." The violence unleashed by the regime has ensured that another Arab revolution of the kind that sparked the protests on 25th January 2011 does not spring in Egypt again. As a result, Egypt has now become a rich recruiting ground for the Islamic State's merchants of death. Restoring past Islamic glory now seems to be more appealing to the youth than restoring democracy. Most Egyptians seem to have reconciled themselves to the new reality, and protests are becoming infrequent, even though the economy is weakening and unemployment rising. The country today is in dire financial straits, with more than 80 percent of its budget going to debt service, subsidies and wages, leaving very little to spend on education and other activities that build the future of a country. The cry for bread, freedom and justice that had sparked the revolution five years ago now seems infinitely far away.

In downtown Cairo, Tahrir Square, once the revolution's beating heart and healing symbol, is busy and vibrant as usual. It was hard to believe that hundreds of thousands of protesters had occupied the square in that tumultuous January of 2011. A little further away, in one corner of the square stands the majestic Egyptian Museum that houses the ancient glory of one of the mightiest empires the world has ever seen. Sitting around it on a summer afternoon, I reflected whether time, space and history had become warped inside that small square. More than five years ago, the Arab Spring was born in the act of the self-immolation of a vegetable peddler. Most of the countries which were then swept by the spring winds of change seemed to have been caught again in the vortex of a spiral of violence and are reverting into a past they are trying hard to forget. Through revolution and counter-revolution, they have sailed from the heights of elation to the depths of despair. Is the Arab Spring finally dead? Or is it gathering strength, unseen, within human hearts that are too resilient to accept defeat, and will suddenly unleash a gale of irresistible force that will overthrow the old order and usher in a world where justice and freedom will finally prevail? What would be its price in terms of human lives?

2. THE END OF THE OIL AGE[52]

(The Oil Age is ending, signalling the beginning of a new era in human civilisation.)

The Princeton Professor Harold James in a recent article pointed out that just as the price of oil acts as a thermometer to the health of the world economy, it can also act as a barometer for measuring the intensity of approaching geopolitical storms. Probably it is acting as a barometer of something much more significant. The death throes of oil may be covering the birth pangs of a new age being ushered in upon our planet. It is probably signalling not only a change in our energy consumption patterns, but along with it, changes in the character of our socio-political institutions and institutional processes also.

Professor James indicated that a rising oil price acts as a brake on growth and led to global recessions in 1973, 1979, and 2000, while economic slowdown in turn leads to falling oil prices, like it did after 2008, when oil prices plummeted in anticipation of economic stagnation, only to recover from the strong growth in demand from the emerging markets. With the slowdown in all emerging economies except India's, the current drop in oil prices was not unexpected.

The plunge in the price of a barrel of crude oil from nearly \$150 in June 2008 to only \$30 now has badly shaken not only the world's energy and commodity markets, but also the major oil economies like Russia, Saudi Arabia, Venezuela, Nigeria, Iraq and other Gulf countries, which are predictably in turmoil. With Iran joining the fray after the lifting of sanctions imposed on it, the price is expected to plummet further. Sinking oil prices have presaged not only financial instability, but also social and political instability. The Russian economy has been thrown into a deep recession, as oil and gas account for 70 percent of its export earnings and half its budget. Russia loses about \$2 billion in revenue for every drop of \$1 in oil prices,

[52]Originally published in *The Statesman* as "From the Death Throes of Oil…", , 7th March, 2016.

and the Russian rouble sunk to its lowest point ever, despite a steep hike in the interest rate to protect its troubled status.

Low oil prices are not just squeezing Saudi Arabia's domestic budget for 2016, imposing austerity measures unheard of in the country and drastically cutting subsidies for water, electricity and petroleum, Saudi Arabia is also contemplating to impose income tax for the first time. Nigeria, Africa's top oil producer, finances about 75 percent of its budget from sale of its crude oil, and unemployment has soared in the country to 9.9 percent in the 3rd quarter of 2015. Venezuela, where inflation has soared to a surreal level of 720 percent, loses about $700 million annually for each $1 drop in oil prices, and that means less financing for health, education and housing which both brought Hugo Chávez to power and kept his successor Maduro there till now. Iraq has been experiencing enough bloodbath and turmoil from its ceaseless spiral of internecine violence, but it is now poised precariously. In the cash-strapped country, dependent on oil for 95 percent of its budget, falling oil-prices led to huge public debt eroding the government's capacity to pay its security forces which are fighting not only internal turmoil but also the sinister Islamic State, and both will now become harder.

On the other hand, plummeting oil prices may have helped stabilise the fragile Eurozone countries and also contain India's fiscal and current account deficits. But overall it appears to be causing income redistribution, from the rich oil exporters to middle and low-income importers, which may still spur an acceleration in overall global growth. For predictable reasons, neither the OPEC countries nor Russia are willing to cut production for fear that they will lose their market shares permanently to the US and other countries.

But there is a more serious threat to our fossil fuel–coal and oil–based society from concerns of climate and environment. At the 21st Conference of Parties (COP21) attended by 196 countries in Paris last December, the world recognised the dangers and agreed unanimously to curb the emission of greenhouse gases. Next to power plants, oil and gas are the most prolific emitters of these gases. The world economy will now have to restructure itself in response to this agreement, leading to the use of cleaner sources of energy, through higher investment and technological innovation in renewables. It will also upend the geopolitical landscape very seriously, sparking political instability and greater demands for freedom and democracy in oil-producing countries.

Thomas Friedman, in his book *Hot, Flat and Crowded*, noted a strong and interesting correlation between the price of oil and the pace of freedom and democracy. Between 1979 and 1995, as oil prices continued to fall, democratic movements around the world gathered strength and momentum, especially since the fall of the Berlin Wall in 1989. In 1993 Nigeria privatised its first oilfield, and in 1997, Iran called for a dialogue between civilisations, displaying a rare openness. The same Iran, in 2005, when oil had reached $70 a barrel, elected Mahmoud Ahmadinejad, who called the Holocaust a myth and demanded the destruction of Israel. The 2016-Iran has already elected a moderate parliament. Saudi Arabia is relaxing some of its draconian religious, especially anti-women, laws. This is not difficult to explain. Weakening oil prices undermines the authoritarian regimes that control the major oil-producer nations, in which oil revenues have corrupted the political system. As prices fall, the tyrants who have ruled these countries with iron fists are automatically destabilised and forced to let loose their vice-like grip on power.

Energy is the driver of civilisations, and progress of civilisation has been synonymous with higher use of energy. Jeremy Rifkin in his 1980-book *Entropy: A New World View* suggested that the nature of our civilisations is conditioned by the kind of energy that we use. The demand for more energy reduces the period between each new energy watershed. It took millions of years to exhaust the environment that supported the hunter-gatherer societies to make the transition to agricultural civilisations, but it only took a few thousand years to make the next transition to an industrial society. Coal power triggered the First Industrial Revolution in Europe between 1750 and 1850, centred around factory-based manufacturing, starting with the mechanisation of the textile industry. The Second Industrial Revolution that took place between 1870 and 1914, based on an advent of assembly-line manufacturing technology, was powered by electricity, mostly coal-based, and ushered in the era of mass-production, beginning with the automobile industry. Automation of manufacturing heralded the Third Industrial Revolution, based on electronics and information technology in the 1970s, powered again by fossil-fuel-based electricity. At each stage, as old processes were weeded out by newer technologies, large scale disruption and tumult were experienced along with radical economic and societal changes, and people who failed to adapt perished. But the energy base of non-renewable fossil fuels remained unchanged. Now as our store of fossil fuels is running out, the entire economic superstructure built upon it is beginning to crumble. The Great Depression of the 1930s, the oil crisis of 1971, sub-prime crisis of 2008 and the consequent global economic meltdown were not mere accidents, but manifestations of this process, not its cause but effects. There is not enough of the old energy left to mend all the cracks that have appeared in our energy superstructure. Transition to a new energy base is imperative, probably within a generation, before we become hostages to obsolete technologies.

Before coal, wood was the major source of energy. The pressure of an expanding population meant more land needed to be cultivated for food, which could only be claimed from the blanket of thick forest covering the continents. By the middle of the 14th century, the population had outstripped the energy sources, and an energy-watershed was reached. The clearing of forests reduced the available wood supply, and society had to shift to coal. But it was not as simple as replacing one form of energy with another. The changeover necessitated radical uprooting of an entirely wood-based existence. Steam engines were designed to facilitate the mining and movement of coal. The need for transporting coal to different locations led to the invention of railroads and steam locomotives which laid the basis for the industrial era. It also ended the community and kinship-based agricultural existence. Towns were built around mining centres. Joint families gave way to nuclear families, who moved to these centres. Dealing with machines needed specialisation; hence the education system became specialisation-based. Any changeover in the energy base necessarily leads to socio-economic and political changes. Communism and socialism were offshoots of this changeover.

Social and economic institutions, like machinery, are transformers of energy. They facilitate the flow of energy through cultures as designers and coordinators of new technologies. Any transformation of energy into products and services and exchange of energy between various groups creates disorder. As technologies multiply, these disorders mount, impeding the energy flow and reordering the system, which enlarges institutions. Being forced to absorb the rising social and economic disorders, they swell and sometimes burst. Our caste-based social and economic orders today are bursting at the seams, seriously upsetting the societal equilibrium. When these institutions become so large and complex that they require more energy to maintain themselves than they can deliver–when instead of facilitating the flow of energy through society, they become a drag upon it–then they start disintegrating. We are today witnessing unmistakable signs of such disintegration all around us.

Today a fourth industrial revolution is staring at us as we are reaching the new energy-watershed. As Klaus Schwab says in his book *The Fourth Industrial Revolution*, this is going to be fundamentally different, characterised by a fusion of technologies that blurs the lines between our physical, digital, and biological worlds, impacting all disciplines, economies and industries. The resulting disruptions offer both great promise and equally great peril. As billions of people get connected to digital networks, putting their energies together, it may dramatically improve the efficiency of organisations, help regenerate the natural environment and undo the enormous damages caused by previous industrial revolutions. The peril is that society may not be able to adapt easily to the new technologies that will be powered not by fossil fuels, but by renewables, or a combination of these. The measurement of the flow of energy that characterises the industrial age will be replaced by examining the flow of interconnected phenomena. The external world will be examined not as a series of isolated causal relationships, but as a web of interrelations for movement and change. It will be a much more holistic and harmonising transformation of our world into an intricately interconnected entity encompassing the entirety of humanity, where nation states will slowly lose their appeal and fade away. In the death throes of the oil age, we can hear the faint signals of the coming age.

3. THE CATALONIAN CONUNDRUM[53]

(Negotiation in the true spirit of give and take is the only way out of the Catalonian crisis in Spain.)

I

The images beamed live across the world last week looked more like scenes from a movie rather than real life scenes playing out in the heart of a modern bustling European city. Hundreds of thousands of furious citizens, their fists raised in anger, literally taking over Barcelona's streets, riot police in frightening black gear and helmets, their faces covered with black masks, firing rubber bullets into uncontrollable crowds and mercilessly beating people with truncheons, men, women and elderly alike –these gruesome images are unlikely to fade away from the memory anytime soon. They remind us of the complex, tempestuous, and often violent history one thought Spain had left behind. The Spanish police unleashed this terror on unarmed citizens of the far north-eastern province of Catalonia who were casting their votes in a referendum the Constitutional Court and the central government had stubbornly refused to recognise. The referendum was to decide whether the wealthy Catalonia should proclaim independence from Spain. As the government tried its utmost to shut down the vote, it sent riot police to break into polling stations and confiscate ballot boxes, as Catalans shouted "Out with the occupying forces!" and sang the anthem of Catalonia. More than 900 people got injured in clashes with the police, while King Felipe IV, in a rare TV appearance, accused Catalan leaders of shattering democratic principles and dividing society by disrespecting "the powers of the state", and putting "at risk the economy of Catalonia and even of Spain", and for their "unacceptable disloyalty".

Separatist sentiments and protests are not confined to Jammu & Kashmir alone. *The Independent* last week published a map showing separatist movements with secessionist tendencies all over Europe, from Provence in France to Bavaria in Germany and Corsica in Italy, in Scotland, Crimea, and elsewhere. They will likely draw inspiration and momentum from Catalonia. The European Commission is naturally wary, and has called for

---

[53] Originally published in *The Statesman*, 13th & 14th October, 2017.

"unity and stability" in the fourth largest Eurozone country. Spain's federal model and right to self-determination have already created a divide across the political parties and given rise to demands for constitutional reforms to make Spain into a "plurinational state".

The referendum that threw the country into its worst constitutional crisis in decades has been rejected by the federal government as illegal and unconstitutional. Spain's Constitutional Court ordered a suspension of the vote, which, irrespective of the outcome, will have no legality. Though only a minority (40 percent) of Catalonia's population was expected to vote in the referendum, the brutal crackdown has angered all Catalonians who rose in protest in a scale unprecedented in its turbulent history. The Catalan President Carles Puigdemont has already announced that 90 percent of almost 2.3 million voters voted "Yes" to secede from Spain and he might as well proceed to declare independence.

Complex societies are the products of their complex histories, and Spain has one of the most complex societies among European nations, often described as 'a federation all but in name' –a federation without federalism. Spain was a dictatorship under General Francisco Franco from 1939 until his death in 1975. The present Constitution of Spain came into force in 1978, when Spain became an Autonomic State *–Estado de las Autonomias–* comprising 17 Autonomous Communities (AC) that enjoy varying degrees of autonomy through an extensive decentralisation of powers and responsibilities which are called 'competences'. It was a constitutionally constructed 'shared rule', based on a concept of a 'sub-state *nacionalidad'* that was shaped by historical realities as well as identity politics to keep the federation somehow together.

During its long history, Spain has been a dominant colonial power in Europe, along with Britain and France. Like France, it has experimented with republicanism, dictatorship, democracy and had to contend with anarchy, violence, civil war and periods of prolonged political instability. It has a multilingual population which is widely divergent–economically, territorially, demographically, ethnically as well as culturally. A strong Castilian majority exists with a number of minority nationalities–Catalonia, Galicia and the Basque Country–each with its distinctive history, culture and language. The four largest ACs –Andalusia, Catalonia, Madrid and Valencia–share among themselves about 58 percent of the national population of 46 million, and nearly 60 percent of Spain's GDP. Catalonia and the Basque Country are regions with histories dating back several centuries to the middle ages and regard themselves as 'historical nations' more than a part of Spain, and demand recognition as such. In particular, Catalonia has a population of 7.5 million; it accounts for 6.3 percent of Spain's territory and 16 percent of its population. It is the richest AC of Spain, and contributes almost 19 percent to Spain's GDP. It is also one of Spain's most highly indebted regions, with an accumulated debt of 75.4 billion euros, constituting 35 percent of its GDP. Barcelona, the second largest city of Spain, is the vibrant capital of Catalonia where most of its population lives; it is also its major economic hub. Incidentally, Catalonia also contributes a number of players to Spain's national football team.

The secessionist sentiments have been fuelled in recent times by Catalonia's resentment that it pays much more to the federal government in Madrid in taxes than it receives from the federal budget through investments and transfers–in 2014, it paid about 10 billion euros–about 5 percent of its GDP–more than it received from the federal government. Catalonia's share in federal investments has also systematically declined from 16 percent in 2003 to only 9.5 percent in the 2015 budget. Spain's economic collapse at the height of the Eurozone crisis and the consequent austerity measures also stoked separatist sentiments, with many Catalans blaming Madrid for the economic morass. But the underlying reasons for its secessionism go far deeper into history.

Catalonia's history dates back to the 9th century to the time of Charlemagne, but Catalonia has been part of Spain ever since the Kingdom of Spain came into existence in the 15th century, when King Ferdinand of Catalonia's neighbouring kingdom Aragon had married Queen Isabella of Castile and united their territories. But Catalonia never bowed completely to the authority of Madrid, it revolted repeatedly against the House of Habsburgs. After the discovery of America, Catalonia's importance increased with the growth of transatlantic navigation and trade. The 19th century industrialisation of Spain was pioneered by Catalonia, simultaneously with a cultural renaissance that saw the revival of the Catalan language and culture and a renewed sense of a national identity leading to demands for the right to self-determination. It was then that the seeds of secession were sown in the Catalan soil.

In 1931, Spain became a republic and Catalonia got a regional government with substantial autonomy, which lasted till the civil war broke out in 1936. Catalonia became a key Republican stronghold, but fell finally to Gen. Francisco Franco's right-wing forces in 1939. Under Franco's ruthless dictatorship, its autonomy was revoked, and both Catalan language and nationalism were ruthlessly suppressed. Thousands of Catalan activists were put to death or forced into exile. The memory of Franco's repression still fires the fierce football rivalry between FC Barcelona and Real Madrid, Spain's top football clubs.

The autonomy could be restored only after Franco's death in 1975. Under the new king, Juan Carlos, in 1978, a new democratic Spanish Constitution was adopted that recognised the existence of distinct "national communities" within Spain which displayed remarkable diversity and asymmetry, in terms of history, language, culture and economic development. While asserting the 'indissoluble unity of the Spanish nation', the Constitution recognised multiple nationalities and their right to self-govern. But all the regions were not treated in an identical manner; Spain became an asymmetric federation based on uneven distribution of power and autonomy between different regions, some 'with common historic, cultural and economic characteristics', some 'insular territories' and some 'provinces with a historic regional status'. To enjoy autonomy, a region needed first to become an Autonomous Community (Comunidad Autónoma) and adopt a "Statute of Autonomy" that defined the contours of its autonomy, following a prescribed procedure that includes a referendum. In 1979, Catalonia was given a Statute of Autonomy and was recognised as a 'nationality', with Catalan as its official language along with Spanish (Castilian). Catalonia and the Basque Country were deemed as 'historical nationalities', and described as such in their respective Statutes of Autonomy.

II

Section 2 of the Spanish Constitution, read with Section 143, guarantees the fundamental rights of Autonomous Communities (AC) to self-governance, while Section 151 outlines the procedures for implementation of this right by laying down two major routes to regional autonomy: a fast track route for 'historic regions' that already have their Statutes of Autonomy (the Basque Country, Catalonia and Galicia became ACs through this route) and the other is a slow route applicable to other regions which need at least five years following the procedure described in the section. But a homogenous standard is applied to governance in all 17 ACs. Each AC has a legislative assembly, elected directly through proportional representation; the Government Council is headed by a president with legislative and executive powers and each AC has a Supreme Court of Justice under the jurisdiction of Spain's Supreme Court. Castilian is the official language, but Section 3 of the Constitution recognizes the existence of, and accords co-official status to, other Spanish languages in their respective Statutes. However, as regards financial autonomy, 2 ACs, Navarre and the Basque Country, have additional competencies not enjoyed by the other ACs–they can collect some of the state taxes like income tax and pay the state for the services they receive from it, while the other communities follow a uniform tax regime based on collection by the state and their redistribution and devolution to the Communities.

Distributing legislative competencies between the centre and the ACs is rather complicated and ambiguous. Sections 148 and 149 of the Spanish Constitution lay down separate lists of competencies for the centre (the Constitution uses the word "State") and the regions (ACs), much like the 7th Schedule of the Indian Constitution, but what is special is that such allocation of powers and responsibilities remain open to negotiation, and this renders the federal dynamics highly flexible. As the political scientist Wilfred Swenden says, "Such complexity stems in part from the lack of agreement on where the Spanish state should be heading: a federal, a regionalised or unitary decentralised state?" Here a fragile central authority tries to hold together diverse nationalities which are in themselves powerful enough to demand additional competencies to serve their respective interests. The conflicts and clashes of interests which are bound to arise from such an ambiguous arrangement are to be addressed by the Spanish Constitutional Court.

The high degree of asymmetry in its political arrangements was subsequently sought to be reduced through the so-called policy of '*cafe para todos*'– coffee for everyone instead of 'champagne for the *nacionalidades* ', through 2 agreements. The first one called LOAPA (Law for the Harmonisation of the Autonomous Process) was signed between the state and the major national parties in 1981 challenging the preferential status of some ACs even though these were ratified earlier by the Spanish Congress, which naturally brought these ACs, especially Catalonia and the Basque Country, into conflict with the state. The Constitutional Court finally nullified a large number of its provisions as unconstitutional reinforcing the autonomy of the ACs, but the agreement still managed to bring in more uniformity and symmetry in the process. A 2nd agreement, *Pacto Autonomico*, was signed in 1992 by the state with the two largest national parties for removing the asymmetry between the fast-track and slow-track ACs, by equalisation of their competences through an Organic Law that was passed in December 1992 and followed by necessary reforms of the Statutes of the disadvantaged ACs. This allowed major competences in education health and some social services to be transferred to them. The progressive transfer of competences to the ACs enabled the Spanish system to reduce the extensive asymmetry in the original constitutional arrangement.

Demands for renegotiation of the Statutes were subsequently raised by the Basque Country and Catalonia, driven by their nationalistic movements. While the Basque country wanted to be ‘a free state associated with Spain’, a demand that was rejected by the Spanish Congress in 2004, Catalonia demanded recognition as ‘a nation’ and higher levels of competences reflected in its Statute of Autonomy in 2006 which was passed by its legislature. Most of these demands met with the approval of the Spanish Congress and were later ratified in a referendum by Catalan voters. However, Spain’s Constitutional Court ruled in 2010 that parts of Catalonia's revamped statute of autonomy were unconstitutional; it also did not recognise Catalonia as a nation–a ruling that fired up nationalist sentiments in Catalonia demanding independence from Spain. Catalans looked at the judgment as “an act of contempt against the will of the Catalan people expressed by its Parliament and referendum”.

In January 2013, Catalonia's parliament approved a "declaration of sovereignty" through independence from Spain to be ratified by a referendum to be held in late 2014, but in March 2014, the Constitutional Court declared it unconstitutional. But Artur Mas, the then president of Catalonia, still went ahead with the referendum, already made non-binding by the Court, in November 2014. Though the turnout was estimated at around 37 percent (2 million out of total 5.4 million voters), about 80 percent of voters voted for independence. Catalonia of course has the economic means to survive independently, it has a language of its own and it conforms to the definition of a nation in every sense.

In September 2015, separatist parties secured an absolute majority in the regional parliament and in November, they voted for a resolution to support independence, which was again struck down by the Constitutional Court in December. In January 2016, the staunch separatist, Carlos Puigdemont, was chosen as the successor to Mas, who vowed to carry out a binding independence vote. He pushed the legislation authorising another referendum whose results would be binding through the Catalan parliament with a narrow majority. Before the referendum took place, opinion polls had suggested that only 41 percent of Catalans wanted to break away, while the majority still wanted to stay with Spain. The Constitutional Court ruled the proposed referendum as illegal and the federal government under Prime Minister Mr Mariano Rajoy stubbornly opposed it, and tried to prevent it with all its might–using disproportionate force to crack down on those who dared to vote, and to stop the referendum from going ahead. But all he succeeded in doing was to anger most Catalans beyond measure, including many of the 59 percent who were opposed to the referendum and favoured national unity over attempts at self-determination by subnational groups. Clearly, the people who had voted for independence did not represent the majority of Catalans. But now, thanks to Mr Rajoy's heavy-handed techniques, the majority may actually be turning against Spain.

As *The Economist* has commented, a well-run democracy must abide by the rule of law to protect democratic liberties and not to curb the freedom of minorities to express dissent and discontent. Puigdemont may not have a strong case for independence or a claim for majority mandate. But democracy rests on the consent of the governed, and constitutions exist to serve citizens, not the other way around. Rather than upholding the rule of law, Mr Rajoy ended up tarnishing the legitimacy of the Spanish state, and Spain may have to pay a price for it. The case for unity must be won by argument and persuasion, not by the use of brute force and display of coercive state power, which instead of preventing might actually be precipitating a break up of Spain.

Mr Puigdemont seems all set to declare independence, which will obviously be a reckless and irresponsible act that might prompt Mr Rajoy to unleash even more repression but that will only compound the imbroglio. Negotiation is the only way out, and some give and some take should take place, giving Catalans more political and financial autonomy.

If the foundation of belief of an autonomous society is threatened, it may unravel the federation, just as an overabundant use of asymmetrical federalism may result in secession. Multiple identities are natural in large and complex societies. The essence of a cohesive federation is to capture the complexity of society as a whole, to integrate unity with diversity while allowing distinct identities to flourish, and to provide an inbuilt mechanism to deal with the tension and conflicts which are parts of the natural order of things in every society. Only in doing so, a common identity is evolved which does not subsume the individual identities of the constituent units, but helps them blossom further.

(Afterword: The Catalonian drama is still unfolding. The federal government has dismissed the provincial parliament, revoked their autonomy by invoking Article 155 and called for an election in December 21st 2017. Some leaders of the independence movement including ministers of the dismissed government have been jailed under charges of sedition,

rebellion and embezzlement. President Puigdemont and some of his associates have moved to Belgium trying to evade arrest. What result the December election will bring is not known and cannot be predicted.)

4. THE BREAKING OF THE BERLIN WALL AND MAKING OF A NEW WORLD

(The fall of the Berlin Wall a quarter century ago ushered in a new world and a new world order.)

The Berlin Wall fell quarter of a century ago, on November 9th, 1989. It fell when it had to, and in falling, it took along with it the last vestiges of the old world–a world dominated by a rigid command and control structure enforced by a brutal, coercive state–a world wrecked by the misery of divided people and torn by the hostility of a Cold War that brought the possibility of a nuclear conflagration dangerously close to reality.

At the end of the Second World War, in June 1945, the defeated Germany was divided into 4 sectors between Russia and the other three Allied powers, the USA, the UK and France. While the eastern half of the country (East Germany) came under the control of Soviet Russia, the western half (West Germany) came under the allied Western powers. Even though the pre-war capital Berlin was located entirely within the Soviet controlled territory of East Germany, the city was also split into similar sectors. Within a short time, however, living conditions between the two Germanies became vastly different. While West Germany experienced an economic miracle, growing rapidly with the support of the capitalist Western powers and offering a high living standard to its people, East Germany, having been robbed of its assets by the occupation forces of the Soviet Union and then becoming a communist nation controlled by it, continued to languish in poverty. As the economy failed, individual liberties came under increasing restraints in East Germany. The prospect of a better life then started attracting people into West Germany.

The existence of capitalist West Berlin within communist East Germany 'stuck like a bone in the Soviet throat' and in 1948, Soviets blockaded West Berlin in order to starve and drive the western powers out of the city, but the latter supplied their sectors from the air, in what became famously known as the Berlin Airlift which lasted for more than a year. But tensions continued to flare from time to time as the flood of refugees in search of a better life into West Germany continued unabated. As East Germany started imposing restrictions on the movement of people from the eastern to the western part of Germany, the flood became uncontrollable. In July 1961, 30,000 people fled to West Germany and on a single day on August 12, 1961; 2,400 people escaped to West Germany. The very next day, the border was sealed and within just two weeks, East Germany constructed barbed-wire fencing and reinforced it later with a concrete wall which would ultimately become the most hated symbol of the Cold War as the Berlin Wall. The wall divided families, lovers, friends and neighbourhoods. It isolated West Berlin from the rest of Germany and made thousands of easterners lose their jobs in West Berlin. As insanity ruled supreme, a second wall was constructed in 1962. The space in between known as the 'Death Strip'–the strip of soft sand for catching footprints–was kept under strict vigil of vicious dogs, floodlights, trip-wire machineguns and patrolling guards who shot mercilessly at everyone attempting to cross over into West Berlin. An even more formidable wall was built in 1975, complete with 45,000 sections of reinforced concrete cement and 300 watch towers spread across its 125 km of fencing, guarded by 250 dogs, besides round the clock vigil by nearly a thousand guards. Yet people continued to flee, and more than 5,000 people including 600 border guards escaped to their freedom, driving through the Death Strip, jumping across from houses along the border, crawling through sewers or tunnels dug underneath; 171 people laid down their lives while attempting to do so.

But then the Soviet Union began to change in ways the world did not expect. As its economy nosedived with growth reaching almost zero levels, factories became decrepit, agricultural production plummeted and living conditions became abysmal. By the mid-1980s, people were no longer afraid of denouncing the Bolshevik experiment openly. To control public resentment and anger, in March 1985, the ageing leadership had brought in a young, energetic Mikhail Gorbachev as General Secretary of the Communist Party who immediately embarked upon his famous 'Perestroika'–a radical restructuring of the economy along with political reforms introducing liberal democratic freedoms, or 'Glasnost'. It opened the floodgates of pent-up anger and unfulfilled aspiration of the people, shaking the foundation of the Soviet Union to the core that led to the ultimate dismantling and dissolution of the USSR.

Meanwhile, in October 1985 Gorbachev told its Eastern European allies that they must now take responsibility for their affairs without any more support–military or otherwise–from the USSR. While massive protests erupted in Czechoslovakia and East Germany displacing their entrenched Communist leaders, the oppressive Communist regimes in Bulgaria and

Romania crumbled. In Poland, the anti-communist union Solidarity swept to power after the 1989 elections.

The fall of the Berlin Wall came as suddenly as its rise. In 1987, the US President Ronald Reagan visited West Berlin. In a speech in front of the Brandenburg Gate, he exhorted, "Mr Gorbachev, tear down this wall." On November 9th, 1989, the East German government suddenly announced removal of all travel restrictions between East and West Germany. Thousands of people immediately flocked to the checkpoints along the wall, chanting 'Tor auf!'–'Open the gate'–forcing the guards to leave. As celebrations broke out, people began chipping at the wall with hammers and chisels, and with each stroke of the hammer, one piece of the ultimate state tyranny symbolised by economic and political oppression, denial of individual freedom and suppression of democratic rights irrevocably fell apart, ending an era of senseless and cruel separation between people, and reuniting families. Almost the entire Berlin Wall was eventually chipped away, into smaller pieces to be kept as mementos of a world no longer real. The fall of the wall paved the way for re-unification of Germany on October 3rd, 1990.

Forces of history operating in different countries and continents often work in conjunction with each other, unknown to the players whose destinies they shape. It was perhaps no coincidence that in the summer of 1989, a hunger strike by 3,000 students in Beijing metamorphosed into a mammoth protest of more than a million people crying for freedom and democracy in Tiananmen Square in Beijing, daring the might of the Communist empire that ruled with an iron grip and went by the name of the People's Republic. The People's Republic dispatched hundreds of soldiers of the People's Liberation Army to silence the voice of the people. On June 4th, 1989, their tanks surrounded the square occupied by the students who had camped there and fired volley after volley upon the unarmed students, killing hundreds, maybe thousands, and silencing their voice of protest. But as the tanks were rolling back, an unknown protester stood defiant before the formidable line of tanks, a 'lone Everyman' standing up to the might of the Middle Empire of more than one billion people, showing that hope was not lost from the world. And today scenes are playing around in Hong Kong that remind us of this anonymous man, whose image is indelibly etched into our collective consciousness.

It was also no coincidence that less than 2 years later, in March 1991, India, a country that was suffocating under the License Permit Raj of a state controlled, centrally-planned economy, would resolutely dismantle that command-control structure, ushering in a new era of liberalisation, privatisation and globalisation of its economy, letting in the fresh air of freedom and unleashing the immense entrepreneurial talent of its people, boosting growth and lifting a quarter of a billion population out of poverty within the next two decades.

The fall of the Berlin Wall not only marked the end of the Cold War, but held before the world the dream of a society based on economic and political liberalisation, consensual democracy and human rights; it also paved the way for a new multipolar world and ushered in a new worldview. It ended the debate about communism which some said made everyone ‘equally poor’ and capitalism which they said made people ‘unequally rich’, and gave unfettered rein to free market capitalism the world over. The market was recognised as the ultimate God. It also connected the world by ways other than the market. Just one and a half years later, in room no. 31 of the Centre of European Nuclear Research (CERN) at Geneva, Tim Berners-Lee would invent the World Wide Web that would connect the world as never before. Within 5 years, there would be 40 million internet users, before the concept of web-browsing would be used for the first time in August, 1995 by a small start-up company called Netscape Navigator whose browser would be embedded in Windows 95, changing the face of the world for all times to come.

As the world celebrates 25 years of the fall of Berlin Wall, it reminds us of the defining chant of that historic night: “We are one people.” The lesson from that momentous epoch in history is to tear down all borders–physical as well as mental, and transcend all artificial barriers–religious, linguistic and cultural–that divide people from people, in a world that is increasingly becoming vulnerable to strife.

5. THE SOUTH CHINA SEA DISPUTE[54]

(The South China Sea has now become a hotspot for Chinese muscle flexing.)

After the landmark ruling by the Permanent Court of Arbitration (PCA) in The Hague against China's claims over the South China Sea, Beijing predictably rejected the ruling with characteristic fierceness, questioning the court's jurisdiction over the dispute. It has aggressively declared to protect its territorial sovereignty and maritime rights and interests, while its state media had called the court a 'puppet of external forces'. India, still smarting from China's blocking of its NSG entry, advised all nations (read China) to resolve the dispute peacefully without resorting to threatening the use of force. The US, which has signed but not yet ratified the 1982 UN Convention on the Law of the Sea (UNCLOS) on which the ruling was based, urged the disputant parties to comply with the 'final and legally binding' ruling and to avoid provocations.

India probably has a right to assume the high moral ground in the case. It has already abided by a ruling by the same Court in 2014 that awarded to Bangladesh nearly 80 percent of an area sprawling over 25,000 sq. km disputed between the 2 countries for over a decade for economic exploitation for oil-exploration and fishing. But the big powers behaved no differently from China whenever any decision by an international tribunal went against their interests, with an identical refrain about the jurisdiction of such a tribunal. Britain did the same in its dispute with Mauritius last year, and in the 1980s, when the International Court of Justice (ICJ) at The Hague ruled against the United States for violating international law by supporting the Nicaraguan right-wing rebels, the Contras, and by mining Nicaraguan waters during that country's civil conflict, the US reaction was no different. The PCA, established in 1899 by the first Hague Peace Conference, is one of the oldest institutions for international dispute resolutions. It predates the ICJ, also located at the Peace Palace in The Hague, which was established as a judicial organ of the UN in 1945 by the UN Charter. Even though the rulings of the PCA or ICJ are supposed to be legally binding, there is no power of enforcement though military action like

[54] Originally published on www.academia.edu, 20th July, 2016.

a multinational Peace Keeping Force or otherwise. It is therefore no wonder that international justice works more to the advantage of the biggies and less for those having lesser global clout. But in the present case the ruling throws up the possibility of escalation of fresh tension and confrontation in the region.

To go to the root of the problem, China has always claimed a huge swath of the South China Sea (SCS) as its own territory. With $5 trillion or one-third of global trade flowing through the area every year and fishing equivalent to 12 percent of the global catch, besides the potential for huge reserves of undersea oil and gas, the SCS is one of the most important strategic and commercial hotspots in the world. Understandably, the area is among the most fiercely disputed in the world, with rival claims by Brunei, Malaysia, Vietnam and Taiwan, apart from China and the Philippines. China claims sovereignty over almost all the islands, reefs and rocks in the SCS—including those located hundreds of miles away from its shores. To legitimise its territorial claims and assert its 'indisputable sovereignty' over the area, China has feverishly embarked on a massive island-building spree since 2014, by piling sand on the submerged reefs and rocks and transforming uninhabitable specks on the sea into military bases equipped with proper infrastructure. There are 2 main island chains–the Paracels and the Spratlys disputed between rival nations–besides dozens of rocky outcrops, atolls, sandbanks and reefs. China has laid claim to a number of islands in the SCS, turned at least 7 reefs and rocks into nascent military outposts, and built airbases on them while installing powerful radar and missile launchers.

International law, or the UNCLOS to which China and the Philippines are both signatories, allows a nation to exercise sovereignty over waters up to 12 nautical miles from its coast, and grants it exclusive economic rights within 200 nautical miles. But the convention says that only natural islands that can sustain human habitation may qualify for such maritime rights, reefs that are entirely submerged at high tide and artificial islands cannot be used for asserting and justifying these rights.

The Philippines took China to the PCA in January 2013 after the Chinese navy had wrested control of Scarborough Shoal, a submerged chain of reefs and rocks in the rich fishing waters off the Philippine island of Luzon, more than 400 nautical miles from the Chinese island province of Hainan and just 120 nautical miles from the Philippine coast. The PCA has now ruled that none of these reef and rock features are islands within the scope of UNCLOS, in effect telling China to stop its activities in the waters surrounding its island bases in the SCS. It virtually rejected Chinese claims over the South China Sea on the basis of what China considers its historical rights, something that follows from a map drawn by it after the defeat of Japan in the Second World War, with an ambiguous '9-dash-line' that stretches south from China's Hainan island, encircling almost 90 percent area of the SCS. Though China has so far desisted from drawing any continuous line clearly marking its claim, it asserts control over the area that it says the Chinese fishermen have been using for centuries. The PCA has now ruled that there was no evidence that China had historic rights to the waters or resources that fell within its 'nine-dash line', and that it was violating the Philippines' sovereign rights with its operations in the SCS.

The area has always been a potential flashpoint. Recent decades have seen military flare-ups between Vietnam and China, besides stand-offs between the Philippines and China since 2012. In 1974, China seized the Paracels from Vietnam, killing more than 40 people. Again in 1988, China and Vietnam clashed over the Spratlys, with Vietnam losing over 60 men. In taking the dispute to the PCA in 2013, in which China refused to participate saying it was a 'law-abusing tribunal' and terming its proceedings a 'farce', the Philippines was only trying to avoid a similar military confrontation with China.

While signing the UNCLOS in 1996, China was certainly aware that the act would entail giving up its 'historical' territorial claims over the SCS, but that was the period when it was seeking global acceptance and respectability. Now it probably feels powerful enough and that it has enough global clout to ignore the treaty, which it even might renounce after the present ruling. Its efforts at garnering international diplomatic support in this dispute have so far met with limited success–except for partial support from Russia, the support has so far remained confined to a few African and small island nations that are heavily dependent on Chinese economic support, e.g. like Angola, Madagascar and Papua New Guinea. This may not be convincing enough for it to claim that 'justice and righteousness always have popular support'. While the European Union and other countries have advised it to accept the verdict, the ruling clearly weakens the Chinese position in the ASEAN, in whose meetings China has repeatedly blocked all discussions over its claims on the South China Sea. After all, refusal to abide by the ruling also undermines China's own position and commitment to a rule-based global order that befits a superpower status that China claims for itself.

After the ruling, there are now 2 alternative courses open before China. Eager to reinforce its superpower status, it may turn more aggressive and further militarise the islands it claims as its sovereign territory in the SCS, risking confrontation with its neighbours and also with the United States. Such confrontation may even escalate into a conflict. China has repeatedly blamed the United States, which is engaged in military ties with the Philippines, for stirring up trouble in the sea. The US Navy has already conducted several 'freedom of navigation' exercises there, sending warships within 12 nautical miles of islands, reefs and rocks controlled by China. China may now deploy more military might and upgrade its construction on islands; it may even impose restrictions on air traffic movement over the sea. If it does that, it will obviously force the US to deploy its aircraft carriers which it already has in the vicinity. It will definitely push China's Asian neighbours into the US axis, something China would abhor to see. The other, and the only pragmatic alternative, is therefore for China to work towards a reduction in the existing tensions.

The Philippines will probably use the ruling to exact economic and other prices from China in the form of Chinese investment rather than getting into direct confrontation with its powerful neighbour, especially after the election of its new president, Rodrigo Duterte. China may try, and even win over the other rival claimants in the sea in making them acknowledge its sovereignty over the disputed islands in return for a promise for their continued equitable access to the rich fishing grounds, besides joint development and harnessing of the natural resources like oil and gas and other material rewards. The world may be prepared to expect some heat and smoke, but hopefully no fire.

6. DRIFT IN BANGLADESH[55]

(Recent events in Bangladesh are indicating an almost irreversible slide towards medieval times where a secular state is proving itself to be incapable of containing the strident rise of religious fundamentalism in the country.)

Last month, invoking a rare colonial law that made insulting any religion a crime, a Bangladeshi court jailed two teachers of Hijla High School in the Bagerhat district. Their crime was to deny the existence of a heaven above earth where mortals go after death, apart from asserting that the Holy Quran is not the word of an Allah one cannot see or hear. The students along with others from a nearby Islamic Madrassa became incensed when the high school's head teacher backed up his colleagues. A mob including students, their parents and villagers thrashed the teachers with sticks, who were then sentenced to 6-month prison terms each by a magistrate on the spot under the rarely-used colonial-era law aimed at preventing or inciting communal violence. The sentencing was done on the evidence of statements from seven Muslim students of the tenth grade, who were minors. The Magistrate claimed to have done a favour to the accused by reducing their prison term from one year allowed by the law to only six months in consideration of the fact that they were respected teachers and not ordinary criminals.

Secularism was one of the 4 fundamental principles enshrined in the 1972 Constitution of Bangladesh, but it was removed from the Constitution by the Fifth Amendment in 1977 by President Zia-ur-Rahman, and replaced by a statement of "absolute trust and faith in Almighty Allah". Islam was declared the state religion in 1988 by President Hussain Muhammad Ershad. In 2010, the Bangladesh Supreme Court restored secularism in the Constitution but Islam remains the state religion. I had the opportunity to live in that country for some time, and I can testify that the people of Bangladesh are thoroughly secular in their thinking, outlook and behaviour and are no different from the average Indian on that count. But the politics of Bangladesh is deeply polarised between the secularists and those wanting Islamic *Sharia* rule–the chief proponent of which is the Jamaat-e-Islami supported by the opposition Bangladesh Nationalist Party (BNP) formed by

---

[55]Originally published in *The Statesman*, 26th May, 2016.

Mr Zia-ur Rahman, of which his wife, the ex-PM Begum Khaleda Zia, is the President and under whose rule during 2001-06, militant outfits such as Harkat-ul-Jihad-al-Islami Bangladesh and Jamat-ul-Mujahideen Bangladesh had thrived, being patronised by the state. Jamaat today is beleaguered and is fighting for survival due to the ongoing trial against war crimes and genocides committed during the liberation war of Bangladesh, in which many of their leaders have been convicted and some have already been executed. The death-sentence on its Chief, Motiur Rahaman Nizami, has just been upheld by the Bangladesh Supreme Court.

During the last 2 years, the country has been reeling from a relentless wave of brutal attacks and murders of secular writers, atheist bloggers, religious minorities and civil society activists and the horrific spate of such murders continues unabated. In the latest of such killings, a Rajshahi University professor, editor of a gay magazine and a theatre artiste were hacked to death in two separate incidents, with the Islamic State and al-Qaida respectively claiming responsibility for the brutal murders. Unable to control the spate of killings, Prime Minister Sheikh Hasina continued to be in denial, exhorting secular writers and bloggers to refrain from hurting the religious sentiments of people.

Religious intolerance and Islamic fundamentalism, like Hindu fundamentalism being seen in our country today, is nothing new in Bangladesh, long before the recent killings of bloggers like Abhijit Roy in 2015, Islamic fanatics had driven away poet Daud Haider in the 1970s and Taslima Nasreen in the 1990s into permanent exile. As writer, K. Anis Ahmed pointed out in a recently published article, in a highly ruralised country like Bangladesh with low literacy rates, 'there is little comprehension or sympathy for anything intellectually as rarefied as atheism'. But by targeting liberals and freethinkers, the Islamists are posing as defenders of religion. Worse, the void created by the decimation of Jamaat is now being attempted to be occupied by other Islamic terror groups, whether home-grown or from outside, which can then spread their sinister terror designs into Indian territory as well. It is undeniable that religious fundamentalism is growing in the country and the government is showing little firmness to control it. It is in this context that the jailing of two innocent teachers should be examined, because it indicates a new low in Bangladesh's fractious politico-religious history. It also bears an uncanny resemblance to another trial that took place in USA during the 1920s and was immortalized in the 1960 movie "Inherit the Wind".

In 1925, a high school biology teacher named John Thomas Scopes in Dayton, a small town in Tennessee, was arrested for teaching that humans had evolved from lower forms of life, according to Darwin's Theory of Evolution, after the Tennessee state legislature had enacted a law forbidding teachers in publicly funded schools to 'teach any theory that denies the Story of the Divine Creation of man as taught in the Bible, and to teach instead that man has descended from a lower order of animals'. Many other states in the USA were soon to follow suit. In the famous trial, the prosecution represented by the noted lawyer Mr William Jennings Bryan noted that in biology textbooks, humanity was clubbed together with 3,499 other species of mammals and argued that it was unfair not to distinguish between man and lower forms of life, doubting the intelligence of those who "put a man with an immortal soul in the same circle with the wolf, the hyena and the skunk". "What must be the impression made upon children by such a degradation of man?" he asked.

Despite being defended by one of the best lawyers of his time, Mr Clarence Darrow, Scope was convicted and fined a hundred dollars by a prejudiced court that refused to accept any evidence from outside the Bible, in spite of the fact that Darwin's *Origin of Species* was published in 1859, and by the 1920s, the Theory of Evolution was well established and accepted almost universally. But then the Bible says, God created man in his own image, to have dominion over the fish of the sea, fowl of the air and over all the earth and 'over every creeping thing that creepeth upon the earth'. Similarly, the Holy Quran teaches that merciful Allah is the creator of everything including heaven and everything on earth. Each religion has its own explanation for the creation of the world, which is not necessarily a scientific description established through hypothesis, observation, theory and direct or indirect validation through experiment. Faith and science are never to be mixed together–the mixture then becomes a dangerous cocktail that only creates confusion and conflict. The only sensible thing is to leave them alone in their respective spheres. The world has already seen too many Galileos and Brunos.

Till the 1960s, and even during the 1970s, the teaching of creation by an almighty God and biological evolution had to be given equal time in most publicly funded schools in the US. But from the second half of the last century, the US Supreme Court was becoming more sensitive to the requirements of the First Amendment to the US Constitution which had built a 'wall of separation between the state and religion' by forbidding the passage of any law 'respecting an establishment of religion'. In a landmark judgment in 1987 against the so-called balanced treatment of creationism and evolution in public schools, the Court firmly struck down a Louisiana law, ruling that its purported aim of promoting academic freedom was a sham, hiding behind its real intention of advancing the religious viewpoint that a supernatural being had created humankind. Thus, since its primary aim was to endorse a particular religious doctrine, it went against the First Amendment. But even though anti-evolution laws have been declared unconstitutional, opinion polls show that 45-50 percent of the US population still believe otherwise.

'The forces of darkness and ignorance are never permanently defeated', the celebrated scientist and science-writer Isaac Asimov noted. Since the 1990s, such forces have been trying to reassert themselves in the form of the Intelligent Design movement in the US, in order to sneak back into the classroom through the backdoor. These forces should never be appeased. As Thomas Dixon points out, the debate about evolution and ID is not between science and religion but really about who should control education, the state or religion. The jailing of 2 teachers has demonstrated who is in control today in Bangladesh. If Bangladesh fails to take the lesson from history, it might irrevocably slip into medieval conservatism, from which it will be difficult to remerge into a society defined by rational objectivity and scientific inquiry.

Bangladesh was born with the ideal of secularism which has reinforced itself after a tumultuous period in its history. As Mr Anis Ahmed asserted, it could serve as a model of a Muslim-majority nation with the progressive ideals of tolerance and pluralism. As he said, "The less we do to challenge the inhuman arrogance of violent extremists, the more we are in danger of allowing the normalisation of intolerance. To reach our most profound ideals, we Bangladeshis, and our government, must avoid appeasement, and muster the courage once displayed by those who died for our language, and for our independence."

7. CHINA'S MARKET CRASH[56]

(The Chinese economy is in a critical phase now, with China being caught in the middle-income trap.)

The recent market crash in China has sent shockwaves throughout the stock and commodity markets across the globe, raising existentialist doubts over the future of the communist nation ruled with an iron hand for 67 years by the Communist Party of China (CPC). So far, a story of unprecedented success, China registered unhindered double-digit growth for more than a decade to transform itself from a low-income to an upper-middle income country, becoming almost an economic superpower. The success of the Chinese model within the short time-span that it took to transform the country's economic landscape has been nothing short of a miracle. Through sustained double-digit growth, China has created world class infrastructure. Prosperity had spread rapidly, creating a sizeable and supportive middle class which today constitutes about 25 percent of the population.

China's growth rate averaged 10 percent between 1980-2010, and then fell to 7-8 percent between 2012-2014, after which it has been slowing further. Pundits have identified many factors behind it: the diminishing returns on capital investments, high levels of state control and corruption, environmental factors, demographic challenges arising from China's one-child policy, rise in wages after continued high growth, and also the absence of democracy. As Jeffrey Frankel, a Harvard professor, pointed out, China is caught in the 'middle income trap', and the transition to high income will be a great challenge. China has just rescinded its one-child policy to correct the demographic distortions that has burdened it with an aging population, but needs to do much more. As Frankel points out, China's competitive advantage in labour-intensive manufacturing has weakened and its economy has shifted from manufacturing towards services, where there is less scope for productivity growth. The risk for the global economy is that the excess unutilised capacity may lead to a financial crisis, leading to plummeting growth and dragging the rest of the world along with it, a world in which economies are more integrated and interconnected than ever before.

---

[56] Originally published in *The Statesman*, 31st March, 2016.

The stock market crash may be just an offshoot of this slowdown process. The People's Bank of China have started cutting the interest rates since November 2014 to stimulate growth, and in June, 2015, the Shanghai index peaked, after which the fall was only to be expected. The Shanghai Stock Exchange Composite Index has declined by more than 40 percent since then and trading was suspended twice in January 2016. The Chinese currency, renminbi or yuan, already an international reserve currency on a par with major global currencies and one in the basket of currencies that determines the value of the Special Drawing Right, the unit used by the IMF in dealing with its 188 members, has also lost much of its value and sheen since then.

Obviously, Chinese leaders have not been sitting still while the growth has been slipping by. In 2013, the 370-member Central Committee adopted far-reaching reforms in areas ranging from health-care, social-security and taxation to environmental regulation in what the *People's Daily* called "China Model 2.0 Edition", reforms that involved structural changes in the economy rather than massive state-led investment. Most of these reforms are being implemented with the seriousness characteristic of Chinese governance. These reforms seek to accelerate the shift from an export-oriented, environmentally damaging growth model based on heavy manufacturing to one based on domestic household consumption and services to support growth.

Riding piggyback on global demand and helped by a cheap currency, as well as cheap rural labour ever willing to migrate to urban areas for better prospects, China has vastly expanded its manufacturing capacities during the last decade. But once the recession had set in in the West following the 2008 crisis, Chinese companies were finding it difficult to sell their products abroad in profitable quantities. As growth slogged, unemployment soared, credit became distressed and banks became loaded with toxic assets. The quick-fixes like devaluing the renminbi to boost exports and import substitution to boost domestic growth were no longer working. The renminbi has been devalued several times now since August 2015, each devaluation sending fresh shockwaves throughout the world, amplifying the anticipation of global financial instability in the event of failure of the world's second-largest economy.

China's growth model so far has been based more on investment and external demand rather than on domestic consumption, but since 2008, China has been trying to correct it. Negotiating such a huge structural transition in a country as large and complex as China, against the backdrop of sluggish global growth, is always difficult. Some turbulence was therefore, not unexpected, and leaders were not unaware of this. What has taken them by surprise is the extent of the shock.

The challenge the Chinese economy faces today is about striking a balance between the market forces and control by the all-powerful Communist Party of China (CPC), as well as between its domestic and international economic obligations. It has no option but to gradually internationalise its financial system rather than aggravate the global financial instability any further, even if that means adjusting to the new normal of lower growth.

But the real problem lies elsewhere. Renminbi still lacks full convertibility, which cannot come without transparent financial systems in an open economy, which in turn cannot come without democracy, an idea that is still an anathema to the CPC. They fear that it will lead to civil war and the disintegration of China. The Middle Kingdom in fact has always been one of the bloodiest of places on Earth, and even after takeover by the CPC in 1949, not a small quantity of blood was spilled by its policies dictated by Mao. The CPC is not yet ready to let loose its iron-grip on the economy and surrender itself to the vagaries of the market, even though it cautiously opened its markets. But as Joseph Stiglitz pointed out, once markets are freed, they acquire a life of their own, and the journey to a domestic consumption-based economy hence may be bumpier than anticipated. Markets certainly are more powerful than the CPC's diktats as the recent market crash has shown. The only way they can be controlled is through setting the rules of the game in a transparent manner. That means more democracy, where China faces the real challenge.

Rising social conflicts between urban and rural populations, tension between the private and state sectors, rising levels of mass protests and civil unrest against corruption in its powerful bureaucracy and party-elites require an overhauling of its governance system and allowing a lot more democratic rights to its citizens than the Chinese leadership is prepared to yield today without triggering excessive social instability. From China's past history, they fear this might lead to widespread unrest and a possible meltdown of the party, dilution of its powers and ultimately, disintegration of China as we know it today. The unrest in Tibet and Xinxiang are pointers to that possibility. How much openness to allow is the challenge they face, but this is possibly the only way to circumvent the middle-income trap.

Francis Fukuyama, who predicted the End of History at the collapse of the Berlin Wall and the subsequent disintegration of the USSR, perceives in the declining growth of the Chinese economy the forebodings of a historic contest over competing development models followed so far by China and the West, the outcome of which in his opinion will determine the fate of much of Eurasia for decades to come. According to him, China's development model based on massive state-led investments in infrastructure–roads, ports, electricity, railways and airports–is fundamentally different from the Western model of large investments in public health, education, women's empowerment and anti-corruption measures. The comparison is a no-brainer, as the realities of the developed world are quite different from those of low or middle-income countries. It is not really a contest between China and the West as Fukuyama would have us believe, but between China's own shifting priorities and ground realities.

For one thing, the Chinese economy is nowhere near collapse. It is resilient and strong enough to withstand quite a few more shocks. True, it has seen an exodus of foreign capital since the stock market crash–about $100 billion has left the country every month during the last 8 months, and both government and private debt has soared to 240 percent of its GDP to $25 trillion. But despite falling demand, China's exports in 2015 declined by only 2.5 percent over 2014. In 2015, it had a record trade surplus of $595 billion. It still has $3.3 trillion forex reserves, enough to cover more than 4 times its short-term external debt, providing sufficient cushion against any crisis of currency or liquidity. A sizeable chunk of the currency reserves of many countries has been shifting towards the yuan. The government expects the growth to be maintained at 6.5 percent for the rest of the decade, but even if it becomes lesser, for an economy the size of China's, it will still be huge.

In the past, China has demonstrated its capacity and resolve to implement radical reforms, like in the late 1980s, when falling GDP growth and rising volumes of non-performing loans of its public sector companies were threatening a meltdown. China arrested the slide by introducing far-reaching reforms, including large-scale privatisation of industry and elimination of price controls, protectionist policies and regulations. Even in the face of growth deceleration, China in 2014 had created 11 million jobs, against the target of 10 million, most of these in the services sector, which constitutes half the country's GDP. This sector grew by 8.3 percent last year against a 6 percent growth in the combined construction and manufacturing sectors. China must and certainly will take bolder steps to reduce state control, unleash the dynamism of the private sector and boost household demand. Aligning its policies to the market will surely cause some pain, and China may have entered a critical phase in its economic transition. But it does not spell any imminent crisis for either its economy or its polity.

8. THE DEATH OF A PRISONER[57]

(Liu Xiaobo's death has not shaken China's conscience even by the tiniest bit. The Chinese state, in its all-out efforts to erase all memory from the public domain, remains as arrogant and despotic as ever.)

After Nelson Mandela, the most famous prisoner of conscience of our time, Liu Xiaobo, died on 13th July. Sentenced to 11 years in jail for "inciting subversion of state power" in 2009 and treated as a common criminal, Liu's end came after a long ordeal in the Chinese dungeons with no one, not even his wife who was also under house arrest from 2010, being allowed to stand by him during his lonely fight with liver cancer until the very end. Fittingly describing him as "one of the global giants of moral dissent", *The Economist* compared his release from prison with that of Carl von Ossietzky, the only other Nobel Laureate to have been released from prison only to die. Ossietzky was awarded the prize in 1935 while in a Nazi concentration camp, and succumbed to consumption upon release. The gruesomeness of the parallels cannot be missed, because both regimes believed in silencing the voices of their people and stifling dissent by applying the most ruthless repression. It was not known how late Liu's cancer was diagnosed or why he could not be sent to the hospital for treatment until a week before his death. The state never allowed him to go abroad for treatment; instead it deployed a platoon of guards around his hospital bed and an army of internet censors to wipe out any reference to him, doing everything in its power to erase his existence out of public memory.

Liu's case became a *cause celebre*–a symbol of a struggle–because of his stature, but there are thousands of prisoners rotting in the hell of Chinese jails just because they hold a view their rulers disapprove of, demanding the freedom to speak against the merciless oppression by state machinery, the endemic corruption at higher echelons, and the inhuman suppression of people of different ethnicities in Tibet or Xinxiang, who, according to the Chinese government, are all counter revolutionaries. There numbers are anybody's guess, as hard information rarely slips through the solidity of the iron curtains erected by the Chinese censors. But the scale of their surveillance can be measured from the fact that not a single message of

[57] Originally published in *The Statesman* as "China's Conscience", 25th July, 2017.

condolence slipped into the public domain from any of more than 700 million users of Chinese social media. Not one dared to express any sign of sympathy for what Liu stood for–or if anyone did, it was not allowed to escape the ever so watchful eyes of the censors. The state ensured that his death remained a non-event, and no memorial would ever come up to stand as a symbol of eternal defiance against tyranny and dictatorship. Even the responses of the Western democracies, otherwise loud in protestations against the suppression of human rights elsewhere, were unusually muted. A Chinese foreign-ministry spokesman warned that no country had the right to interfere in what he claimed was China's internal affair. Not one voice was heard loud enough to shake China's conscience. The censors may raise a toast to their success–July 13th, 2017, in all likelihood, would remain as anonymous as June 4th, 1989, except in the hearts of worshippers of freedom and democracy, hidden from the Dictator's prying eyes.

Yet Liu did not rise in armed revolt against the might of the state, or for that matter plan any upheaval to challenge its unbridled power over people's lives. He even criticised the Chinese dissidents who migrated to the West, incurring their wrath. During the Tiananmen Square rebellion, he had returned from a fellowship at Columbia to take part in the historic movement. He sat on hunger strike along with three other dissidents and persuaded many of the occupying students to withdraw, who otherwise would probably have been killed, and suffered incarceration for 19 months, emerging from it ever stronger in faith and hope for an oppression-free, democratic China.

In 2008, the last time he was incarcerated, he had merely petitioned people to sign for democracy. When he was awarded the Nobel Peace Prize in 2010, still in prison, for being the "foremost symbol" of the struggle for human rights in China, it was only expected that he would not be allowed to go to Norway to receive the prize. Rather, as would befit the rulers of a totalitarian regime, pulling its economic might and flexing its military muscle, China forced as many as 19 timid countries to boycott the Prize award ceremony, and downgraded its diplomatic relations with Norway. An empty chair received Liu's Nobel Prize. A speech he had prepared to deliver during his trial in 2009 which was disallowed by the judge, was translated and delivered on that occasion. In that speech he said, "Merely for publishing different political views and taking part in a peaceful democracy movement, a teacher lost his lectern, a writer lost his right to publish, and a public intellectual lost the opportunity to give talks publicly…Freedom of expression is the foundation of human rights, the source of humanity, and the mother of truth. To strangle freedom of speech is to trample on human rights, stifle humanity, and suppress truth."

"No one can bar the road to truth, and to advance its cause, I am prepared to accept even death",–another dissident Nobel Laureate, Alexander Solzhenitsyn, wrote in the preface to his autobiographical novel *Cancer Ward* that symbolised the malignancy that would end in the demise of the Soviet Union. Both cancer and concentration camp condemn the victim. Whereas cancer only destroyed his body, the camp dehumanised him, before decimating and destroying his soul. Liu did not allow his soul to be destroyed, and his humanity to be substituted by hatred and fear. "I have no enemies and no hatred," he said during his trial in 2009. In *Cancer Ward*, Solzhenitsyn wrote, "Sometimes I feel quite distinctly that what is inside me is not all of me. There is something else, sublime, quite indestructible, some tiny fragment of the Universal spirit." Liu's faith and love, against the face of repression, were indestructible.

Truth of Chinese repression cannot indeed be hidden away or overlooked, and there have been and will be many more like Liu to die "unwept, unhonoured and unsung". He spent 13 of his last 28 years in prison, moving in and out of it. In 2008, he was imprisoned just 2 days before the release of the so-called "Charter of 08", which replicated Charter 77, the appeal issued by dissidents in Soviet-era Czechoslovakia in 1977, demanding an end to one-party rule, democracy and human rights. Charter 08 was signed by hundreds of people. That was some time after he had urged the Chinese government to talk to the Dalai Lama in the wake of severe unrest in Tibet, angering the communist leadership beyond measure. "We stand today as the only country among the major nations that remains mired in authoritarian politics. This must change… The democratisation of Chinese politics can be put off no longer", he demanded in the Manifesto of Charter 08.

In his Nobel speech, Liu had said, "I hope I will be the last victim of China's long record of treating words as crimes." Though it seems extremely unlikely, the hope may not be altogether ill-placed. The night is darkest before the dawn, and as Minxin Pei, author of *China's Crony Capitalism*, has pointed out, China's economic miracle over the last 3 decades seems to have almost run its course and when economic growth starts faltering, an authoritarian state turns to ruthless repression and appeals to nationalism to hold onto power. The regime's mistreatment of Liu was actually a sign of its weakness, insecurity, and fear, not of strength.

It was heartrending to watch his wife, Liu Xia receiving Liu's ashes after his cremation in the presence of state officials. Liu's Nobel speech was equally touching in love for his wife he could not spend enough time with, "I am serving my sentence in a tangible prison, while you wait in the intangible prison of the heart. Your love is the sunlight that leaps over high walls and penetrates the iron bars of my prison window, stroking every inch of my skin, warming every cell of my body, allowing me to always keep peace, openness, and brightness in my heart, and filling every minute of my time in prison with meaning…I am an insensate stone in the wilderness, whipped by fierce wind and torrential rain, so cold that no one dares touch me… Even if I were crushed into powder, I would still use my ashes to embrace you." Xia has to live her life now even without those ashes which have since been immersed into the sea by the government.

9. THE FUTURE OF ARTIFICIAL INTELLIGENCE[58]

(Given the speed and exponential nature of technological progress, artificial intelligence will soon cease to be artificial. Man and machine will also become a unified hybrid entity in future.)

The recent spat between Elon Musk, the Chief Executive of SpaceX and Tesla and Facebook's Mark Zuckerberg has added fresh fuel to the ongoing public debate about the future of artificial intelligence (AI). AI is at the heart of Facebook, it thrives on data which AI knows how to handle and analyse best. Privacy is no concern for it. But Musk believes that AI can take us nearer to the apocalypse, by running amok. The debate is decades old, but the future of AI may defy our wildest imagination.

When Garry Kasparov, a world chess champion, lost his famous match against the supercomputer Deep Blue in 1997 after beating it the previous year, *Time* magazine commented, "Luddites everywhere were on notice: here was a machine better than humankind's best at a game that depended as much on gut instinct as sheer calculation." A distraught Kasparov sighed and rubbed his face in disbelief before abruptly walking away. That was the first time that a machine had beaten an expert at an intelligent game. Since then milestones have been breached at regular intervals. In February 2011, history was again made, when IBM's supercomputer Watson beat two contestants on a TV serial called Jeopardy, answering questions that they failed to answer and processing data at an astonishing speed of 500 GB per second, with a RAM of 16 terra bytes. It had access to 200 million pages of material in its memory, which it could analyse on live TV within seconds. Watson won the $1 million prize money.

We are living in the era of artificial intelligence in which machines have been taught to think like humans and act. They still lack self-awareness, an essential attribute of human consciousness and cognition. Robots do not yet know that they are robots. But given the exponential growth of technology, it is only a matter of time before they will acquire self-awareness that rivals human intelligence. The logical conclusion of this process will be the

[58] Originally published in *The Statesman*, 6th August, 2017.

development of machines whose artificial intelligence will surpass human intelligence itself, imbibing super-intelligent machines to whom no problem will be hard enough to solve.

Of course, the advent of such super-intelligent machines will take some years yet to happen. Human intelligence is essential for reasoning, planning, learning, communication (using the rules of natural language), perception, decision making, and the ability to manipulate objects and perform complex tasks. AI today can handle only some of these tasks, such as visual perception, speech recognition, decision-making, and translation between languages, writing reports based on data analytics, etc., though the AI wave-front is being expanded to include new areas of cognition almost on a daily basis.

Today's computers have super memories; they can easily perform millions of calculations every second and perform consistently at peak levels combining peak skills for an almost indefinite length of time. Using these calculations, they can break up an object into its tiniest elements, pixels, lines, circles, triangles, and squares. This is the way a machine tries to recognise patterns and identify objects. It can possibly identify a rose, but will have no idea about the 'rosiness' of roses. It cannot yet attribute any qualia to an object, something the human mind does effortlessly. Machines also do not understand the simplest of things about our physical world, let alone the subtle nuances of the working of the human mind with all its complex web of emotions. Robots are just machines that can be programmed to perform some cognitive tasks, but unlike humans, they cannot anticipate and plan for the future either, at least not yet.

But as human knowledge migrates to the Web, their horizon will expand exponentially. Then they will be able to read, synthesise and intelligently apply all human-machine information, and their non-biological intelligence will someday probably be able to match and then surpass 'the subtlety and range of human intelligence' in almost each area, as the futurist Ray Kurzweil visualises in his book *Singularity is Near*. But intelligence also needs emotion; without emotions, we would often find ourselves constrained to make judgments and decisions. The problem is, how do you create a robot with emotions and a value system? Emotions often defy logic and AI is dependent on logic and logic alone.

The Turing Test is recognised universally as being the touchstone on which the intelligence of a machine is to be measured and determined. Turing said, "A computer would deserve to be called intelligent if it could deceive a human into believing that it was human." This simply means that the responses of the machine to a given situation would be no different from that of a human being. At Meiji University, Tokyo, scientists have taken the first step to create a robot with self-awareness by creating two robots, the first of which was programmed to execute certain motions, and the second to watch and mimic it. The next step was achieved in 2012 when a robot was created at Yale University that passed the mirror test–the ability to recognise oneself in a mirror, which is considered a proof of having a concept of self.

Whether it would be intelligent design or Darwinian evolution of robotic intelligence is a question which is still open-ended. Just as our intelligence was not designed by an omnipotent creator but had evolved gradually, it is not necessary that we have to design the intelligence of machines we create and teach them how to think; in all probability they may not think like us, but 'think' nevertheless. As Quentin Hardy of the University of California at Berkeley says in his essay "The Beasts of AI Island", intelligence is merely a toolbox we use to reach a given goal, which doesn't entail motives and goals by itself. The new "Age of Thinking Machines" may even force us to fundamentally rethink and redesign our institutions of governance, allocation, and production which today are far from being perfect.

Never before in the history of humanity have we experienced technology changing the entire landscape of the man-machine paradigm so swiftly and so profoundly. Revolutionary breakthroughs have been achieved in image recognition, data analysis, autonomous learning, and the construction of scalable systems. These have spawned applications that were unthinkable only a decade ago, giving birth to systems that display significant language skills, skills for manipulating objects, leaning and problem-solving abilities, factual and procedural knowledge and even some rudimentary imagination. AI is increasingly replacing human decision making in many areas of cognisance–routine administration, engineering and construction, design, data analytics, and even robotics and AI programming itself. Of course, there is still a long way to replicate human intelligence, but it may not lead to any humanlike intelligence. It may usher in an era in which there will probably be no such thing as 'pure' human intelligence, because all humans will be a combination of biological and non-biological systems which will constitute integral parts of our physical bodies, vastly expanding and extending their capabilities. Humans and machines will merge together to create a human-machine civilisation. The initial impact will be highly disruptive and there will be ethical, socio-economical and other unsettling issues that will have to be addressed requiring a level of maturity humanity has not yet perfected. As Quentin says, "We're building new intelligent beings, but we're building them within ourselves. It's only artificial now because it's new. As it becomes dominant, it will simply become intelligence. The machines of AI Island are also what we fear may be ourselves within a few generations. And we hope those machine-driven people feel kinship with us, even down to our loneliness and distance from the world, which is also our wellspring of human creativity."

Man and machine will then become one unified, hybrid entity. These entities will learn to think, emote and empathise in their own ways which might be different from our human thought processes, emotions and expressions of empathy. As the author Clifford Pickover says, "We'll share our thoughts and memories with them. We will become one. Our organs may fail and turn to dust, but our Elysian essences will survive. Computers, or computer/human hybrids, will surpass humans in every area, from art to mathematics to music to sheer intellect. In the future, when our minds merge with artificial agents and also integrate various electronic prostheses, for each of our own real lives we will create multiple simulated lives."

10. IMMORTALITY IS MY NAME[59]

(Sanskrit has a great and immeasurably rich heritage. But the current efforts to rehabilitate Sanskrit lack sincerity and honesty of purpose.)

I am your root, *vija*, your past glory and present embarrassment. I defined and united your world and your time. I myself am beyond time. I convey who you are, something you yourself have forgotten. I am your marker to history, but not only that. I am also a living testimony to your shared origins, your inheritance of this earth. I am Sanskrit, refined and perfect.

I am the repository of all scientific and philosophical truths your ancestors discovered through their insight and bequeathed to you. The word for truth is *rita*, cognate with Greek *arête*, from which the English word 'truth' derives. The connection runs much deeper than mere similarity in the pronunciation of these words. I share many roots with many other languages. Our common and shared origins are rooted in the distant and dim past at the cradle of humankind where we all dwelt together. We carry our linguistic genes from the days of our early evolution even though we may not have any memory of that. I ushered in a different meaning unto the world, like the Greeks, through *yukti*, which actually means 'junction'. It is cognate with the Latin verb *iugare*–'to join'–which gave the derivatives: joint, junction and yoga. Like all languages, I joined the minds of people.

I am the DNA that has transmitted the code of the living through words since the ancient dawn of civilisation. I am your genetic code. The world is affected by the words you use; they surround you, condition you, define you and constitute your choice. You cannot disentangle your language from your roots. When the character of a people changes, their language also changes. It is an immutable law. As wave after waves of invasion unsettled life in medieval India, I too had to change. When people lost their vitality and physical strength, I degenerated. When they were not courageous enough to embrace other cultures and religions and sought relief and complacence in obscurantism, I became a symbol of all your escape and defeat, your withdrawal into casteism and lifeless rituals, the mandalisation of your politics and the politicisation of your *dharma*, which derives from

[59] Originally published on www.ourstories.org, 22nd November, 2015.

my root *dhri* meaning 'to hold'. As you failed to hold together, things fell apart and disorder and chaos reigned supreme. A language carries the signature of the soul of its speakers; it represents their way of dealing with life. A nation that loses its language loses its soul and its history. Language moulds the organic unity of a culture. Rediscovering a language is rediscovering your lost soul.

I carry within myself the ritualistic hymns of your *Vedas* and the philosophical richness of your *Upanishads*. I not only united ancient India that did not have a political boundary, but I gave it a cultural boundary which was much more potent than any political boundary. In the fourth century BC, my fluidity was frozen by Panini in his *Astadhyaya*, and the rigid rules of phonology and morphology framed through his 4000 aphorisms gave me a structure almost like mathematics. No wonder the first concepts of zero and infinity were expressed through me. Even the later unorthodox transformations of *Prakrits* and *Pali* could not alter my dynamic structure which absorbed and assimilated all currents of contemporary thought. It also gave me the strength to survive the silence of the next few centuries, allowing me the space to transform myself seamlessly into other Indian languages you speak today.

I united Sankara, Ramanuja, Madhva from the south of India with Kalidasa, Rajasekhara and Bhavabhuti from the north. By the 8th century AD, with the expansion of Indian commerce, I had spread outside, and found new niches in Central Asia, Tibet, Indo-China, Indonesia and China–binding India with the rest of Asia. Yes, I was the language of ridiculous *Brahmanical* rituals, but I was also the language of the elites in royal courts and of higher education. Through two millennia, I provided linguistic and cultural unity to India and moulded life according to the *Dharma-Sastra* texts and that outrageous code of conduct called *Manu Samhita*. I did propagate *Varnashrama* as a social hierarchy and discipline, but even in my wildest dreams could not have imagined what the Brahmins would make of it. Today, of course, it is the political Brahmins of your country who are making the most of it for their own gains. You made me synonymous with liturgy. You identified and equated me with the Sanskrit teachers at your schools who are universal objects of derision and ridicule, and with everything that is archaic, anti-modern and irrelevant. It amuses me to see that today you are campaigning for my revival and rehabilitation.

You have branded me as the carrier of obscurantist ideas and meaningless rituals. You have forgotten that my efflorescence from the 4th to the 7th century AD saw not only a flourishing of secular literature of the *kavyas* and *natakas* of Kalidasa, Dandina, Magha and Bharavi, but a great surge in scientific ideas too: in geometry, algebra, astronomy, medicine, chemistry and architecture that reached the highest levels of excellence. Today when you are losing the distinction between science and mythology and cannot tell evidence-based reasoning from the mindless acceptance of authority or speculation, may I remind you that at a time when European scholars were invoking God to explain the world, I gave you the infinite series and theorems that today form the basis of calculus? Through *Sankhya* philosophy, I taught people to believe in *yukti* (logic) and not in the sacred scriptures, propagated *Nirisvaravada* (atheism) saying that there was no *pramana* (proof) for the existence of *Isvara* (God) and rejected creationism by saying that nature experiences evolution due solely to its internal dynamics. Unlike now, then there was a great deal more inquiry and openness in society.

I have no memory of where and how I came into being–whether from the nomads roaming the plains of Central Asia or from the pastoralists in the steppes north of the Black Sea, or from myths. I only know that I flourished here in all my grandeur some 5000 years ago as one of the Indo-European groups of languages that are today spoken by half the world. Today though most proclaim me dead, from what they call my lack of adaptability to the scientific-technological civilisation ushered in by the British. Phew!

Dead I am not, nor shall I ever be. Through the shared origins of languages and of all life, I transcend death. I am deathless. I am born again and again. The word 'cognate' means 'born together', from Latin *gnatus* meaning 'to be born'. It is akin to the Sanskrit root *jan* from where the word *janma*, 'to come into existence', derives. Jan is also cognate with the Latin *genus* meaning 'origin', from which the words genetics, generate, generation and even genocide are derived. I have survived through scores of indifferent generations and many genocides. I am timeless. Time in *kaala*, from *kal*, meaning 'to count' which is cognate to Latin *calculare*, from which derive the words 'calculate' and 'calendar'. *Kaala* is also death, but my death will come only at the end of time, or when there will be none left to measure time. I have survived the silence of umpteen centuries and shall continue to live in the heart and soul of the country whose thoughts, culture and life I have shaped.

I symbolise *vidya* meaning knowledge which is derived from *vid*, meaning 'to perceive, observe', akin to *Veda* which is cognate with Latin *videre*, 'to see'. The words video, vista, vision, divide and dividend are derived from this. I have the wisdom to 'see' with my *manas* or 'mind'. It is again cognate with Latin *mentis*–'to think'–which gave the word *mental*. My world was mental; I showed the way to unity, while you only divided the country into narrow domestic walls of castes and sub-castes, religious vote-banks, social elites and caste-pariahs. I symbolised and perfected an almost mathematical language of which complexity and diversity are but natural offshoots. Like the combinatorial operations of digital circuits, I also devised an iterative procedure to yield an infinite array of hierarchically structured expressions. Is it my fault if society copied my hierarchy within hierarchies and produced an unbelievably complex, elaborately interwoven and ruthlessly unjust class structure?

I embodied and symbolised a spirit of inquiry which, alas, no longer exists here. No wonder, people do not study me anymore in the country of my birth, where openness and analysis are now discouraged. No wonder, the serious-minded ones now migrate to the universities of Oxford, Chicago and Heidelburg to study me. No wonder today in India, you don't find scholars like Surendranath, Hiriyanna or Radhakrishnan who flourished even during the oppressive colonial rule. It is not really about the difficulty of making a living with a language others perceive dead. It is actually about the ability to think, argue and analyse. It is about the excellence, openness and inquiry I always personified: *Vichara paramam gnanam*–inquiry is the highest wisdom. Today, you only champion mediocrity.

Death is *mrityu*, from *mri*, 'to die'. It is cognate with Latin *mori*, from which the words 'mortality' and 'mortgage' derive. I do not mortgage my soul to petty minded politicians who want to profess their love for me by negating everything I stood for. Their patronage is the last thing I want: *"Yachna mogha varamadhigune nadhame labdhakama!"–Far better is that my entreaties should fail with the great than prevail with the unworthy.*